Evolutionary Medicine

Evolutionary Medicine

Rethinking the Origins of Disease

by Marc Lappé, PhD

Sierra Club Books San Francisco

The Sierra Club, founded in 1892 by John Muir, has devoted itself to the study and protection of the earth's scenic and ecological resources—mountains, wetlands, woodlands, wild shores and rivers, deserts and plains. The publishing program of the Sierra Club offers books to the public as a nonprofit educational service in the hope that they may enlarge the public's understanding of the Club's basic concerns. The point of view expressed in each book, however, does not necessarily represent that of the Club. The Sierra Club has some sixty chapters coast to coast, in Canada, Hawaii, and Alaska. For information about how you may participate in its programs to preserve wilderness and the quality of life, please address inquiries to Sierra Club, 730 Polk Street, San Francisco, CA 94109.

Library of Congress Cataloging-in-Publication Data
Lappé, Marc.
Evolutionary medicine : rethinking the origins of disease / by Marc Lappé.
p. cm.
Includes bibliographical references and index.
ISBN 0-87156-519-6
1. Diseases—Causes and theories of causation. 2. Environmentally induced diseases. 3. Environmental health. 4. Human evolution. I. Title.
[DNLM: 1. Disease—etiology. 2. Epidemiologic Factors. 3. Evolution. 4. Environment. 5. Hominidae. QZ 40 L316e 1994]
RB152.L37 1994
616.07'1'01—dc20
DNLM/DLC
for Library of Congress 94-5892
CIP

Production by Robin Rockey
Jacket design by Laurie Dolphin
Book design by Abigail Johnston
Illustrations by James Lovera

Printed in the United States of America on acid-free paper containing a minimum of 50% recovered waste paper, of which at least 10% of the fiber content is post-consumer waste
10 9 8 7 6 5 4 3 2 1

Dedicated to Richmond T. Prehn, M.D.,
whose ideas about evolution
and medicine are seminal

Contents

Preface

"Why," you may ask, "does anyone need to read a book that tries to bring evolution and medicine together?" From the outside looking in, it would appear that medicine has done very well without being saddled with the baggage of evolutionary theory or natural selection. Those theories, you might argue, are the stuff of ecologists and wild animal parks, certainly not doctors and human beings. But consider just a moment the possibilities.

What if the constantly recurring ear infection that bedevils your child (and your own well-being as a parent) were the result of some kind of microevolution among the bacteria in her body as her system is flooded with antibiotics? What if the reason AIDS is such a fatal disease were related to the evolutionary changes that occur at lightning speed within the viral culprit that causes it? What if your grandmother's cancer proved fatal because oncologists could not keep up with the evolutionary race between new chemotherapeutic agents and resistant tumor cells? And what if asthma could be traced to an age-old evolutionary function of the immune system that is now defunct? What if the "autoimmune" diseases were the result of a predictable failure in the immune system? And what if the spreading epidemics of AIDS, malaria, dengue, and Lyme disease were the result of ecological disruptions that propelled these diseases into the human population?

I have written this book in the hopes that a fresh evolutionary perspective on each of these queries would provide illumination if not insight. I am not a doctor. But I am a trained experimental pathologist who has followed the course of human disease and disability with the special perspective that can come with distance from the patient. I trace the impetus for writing this book to my earliest impressions about the neglected role of evolution in medical education.

A definitive moment in this process occurred on a fall afternoon in 1966 on my very first day as a doctoral student at the University of Pennsylvania, the oldest medical school in the country. While walking up the steps toward the imposing facade of the medical school, I met a medical student I had known in high school. Dr. Bruce Furie, now a prominent hematologist at Tufts University, was just coming from his first bacteriology class. After some small talk, I asked him whether one of the subjects in his syllabus was the then burgeoning concern about the evolution of antibiotic resistance among bacteria.

His answer set me on the path that led to this book: "No," he said. "Come to think of it, I haven't heard the word *evolution* since I got here. But why should I have?" This book is an answer, belated to be sure, to that question asked almost 30 years ago.

Today, I am convinced that evolutionary theory is as essential for understanding how the body works and responds to disease as it is for understanding how ecosystems work together. This perspective was powerfully influenced by my mentor and advisor, Dr. Richmond T. Prehn, who was among the first to apply evolutionary theory to the process of carcinogenesis and to the role of the immune system in shaping tumor development. I gratefully dedicate this book to him.

Acknowledgments

While I stand on the shoulders of many others who have thought about evolutionary theory and the human condition, the ideas and views in this book are mine. Many of its themes in this book incubated in a course entitled "Ecosystem Disruption and Disease" that I taught at Berkeley, California, between 1968 and 1970. I thank the students who established the Free University there and who encouraged the free expression of ideas.

Robert Bayudan and Pam Brookstein, M.P.H., helped me assemble the many literature searches and original documents on which much of this book is based. I also thank Bernice Coleman who helped ably with correspondence. Many of the ideas presented in this book could not have been formed or articulated without the sharp mind and insights from Nichol Lovera, ardent critic and soul mate. All of the figures in the book were composed and drawn by James Lovera, an artist who translated ideas into beautiful forms. Betty Berenson poured over the original manuscript and provided excellent copyediting. Finally, I am grateful to my editor, Jim Cohee, for the vision to see the value of an evolutionary perspective in understanding human disease.

1 Introduction

Medicine needs a new infusion of vitality and a fresh outlook on what it can achieve. Even as medical scholars and the media herald new advances in treating deadly diseases, old therapies lose their effectiveness and new ones provide only Pyrrhic victories over still fatal illnesses such as cancer, tuberculosis, and AIDS. Our health is said to be better than ever, and longevity is on the rise. Not so. In fact, the prevalence of illness and early deaths are increasing sharply for some subgroups in our country, and recent improvements in life expectancy and infant mortality are now at a virtual standstill.[1] In 1992–1993 alone, six major outbreaks of infectious diseases took the medical community by surprise—these included a widespread outbreak of intestinal illness in Milwaukee; a lethal viral disease that began in the Four Corners area; severe antibiotic-resistant intestinal infections at New York City hospitals; a major flu epidemic; multidrug-resistant infections at several urban day-care centers; and a large outbreak of meat-borne food poisoning in the West.

The present disturbing trends of increasing death rates and disability are largely due to the burgeoning incidence of diseases such as AIDS, tuberculosis, asthma, and some types of cancer, such as melanoma and breast cancer. All are reaching epidemic proportions even among those who are not impoverished or lack access to medical care. Other diseases, such as diabetes, skin cancer, senile dementia, and autoimmunity, are on the rise among the well-to-do in developed countries, while malaria, dengue, AIDS, cholera, and such parasitic diseases as leishmaniasis and schistosomiasis remain scourges of the poor in the Third World. But the old addage that poverty and ill health go hand in glove does not begin to explain either the pattern of these diseases or their spread.

For infectious diseases, the present pattern of worldwide dissemination of intractable forms of malaria, dengue, tuberculosis, and cholera reflects a major increase in the spread of parasitic and infectious diseases that come "fully armed" to resist therapeutic drugs. This pattern of multidrug resistance is among the most serious problems facing modern medicine.

For more complex disorders, such as diabetes, autoimmune diseases, and asthma, the current upswing in their prevalence may reveal fundamental weaknesses in our metabolic and immune systems, exaggerated by environmental insults and opportunistic infections. Certainly the present approaches to detection and treatment of these disorders are wanting–diabetes runs rampant among the elderly and obese; autoimmune disorders affect increasing numbers of young women; and asthma-related deaths in the very young in our inner cities have increased dramatically over the last few decades. At best, medicine has provided only incomplete therapies for patients with these disorders. At worst, as in the case of asthma, there is a sickening suspicion that some treatments may have made the disease worse. And autoimmune diseases such as systemic lupus erythematosus, scleroderma, and a whole new class of atypical disorders associated with silicone breast implants remain progressive and intractable challenges to medical therapeutics.

Other diseases, such as AIDS and Burkitt's lymphoma (which may be our legacy from ancient environmental destruction of rain forests), kill their victims inexorably. Many common bacterial diseases, such as staphylococcus infections, pneumonia, and enterococcal disease, which were once eradicated by a single antibiotic "shot," have now become resistant to multiple antibiotics. Hospitals that were once the safest places to be are now the most dangerous, especially if you are immunologically depressed.

These disturbing realities point to a failure of medicine on an entirely different level–its conceptual base. These trends point to an incomplete understanding of the interplay of disease, human and microbial co-evolution, and modern therapeutics.

This book is a modest attempt to fill in the gaps—to identify the "missing links" in our knowledge by exploring the origins of these new patterns of disease and the forces that shape their evolution and, sometimes, to suggest new therapeutic options. To gain better control over nature requires understanding the dynamic forces that shape its interaction with us and the roots of its resilience. (Sometimes a "cure" may mean yielding control altogether and strengthening age-old, innate resistance.) Where do exotic diseases come from in the first place and why do they show up here? How do so many bacteria and viruses come to be so resistant to antibiotics? Why are some diseases more virulent and intractable than others?

Other fundamental issues in medicine involve understanding the role of aging and cell growth in the genesis of diseases such as cancer and atherosclerosis. How do we explain the paradox that immortality among our cells leads to cancerous transformation and death for us? Or that our genetics and diet routinely conspire to generate new growths of atherosclerotic plaques in our arteries? Why does our immune system so often fail to protect us against cancer? And, why does it "turn" on us to produce autoimmune diseases so often and at such young ages?

To answer these queries, I have turned to ideas that were first incubated among anthropologists, evolutionary biologists, and population geneticists. These ideas are the basis for a new field, that of *evolutionary medicine.*

Origins of Therapeutic Nihilism

When I started writing this book, I worked and taught in a medical school in Chicago that serves patients suffering from the broad range of diseases that afflict Americans. Asthma, AIDS, sickle-cell anemia, sepsis, heart disease, rheumatologic disorders, diabetes, cancer, and tuberculosis were all represented in the corridors of our university hospital. On my rounds I found an extraordinary level of pessimism. Interns and medical students alike were more often frustrated and angry about their duties than satisfied from their ministrations. It didn't take long to discover the reason for this pessimism—medicine at the end of the twentieth century is a medicine of curative nihilism.

No longer do "simple" infections like TB, staph, or pneumonia give way like ships before a storm to antibiotics. In our hospital, AIDS, chronic diabetic, and demented geriatric patients rarely get up and walk out. Many die from hospital-acquired infections, including the fungal infections in AIDS patients that were once so rare that medical textbooks dismissed them with only a paragraph. Many aged patients simply languish, becoming chronically hospitalized. Multidrug-resistant strains of tuberculosis show up with disturbing frequency. Patients suffering the pain of sickle-cell anemia turn to addicting drugs and acquire blood-borne bacterial infections that defy eradication. And metastatic cancers, with few exceptions, are as intractable as they ever had been.

Today, many clinicians attribute their therapeutic failures to the patient. Unremitting blood poisoning and accompanying septic shock or tuberculosis are the alleged result of the patient not taking his medicine, or at worst, to the inappropriate choice of the drug or treatment regimen. Rarely does a clinician question the *fundamental* wisdom of a particular therapeutic choice or the basis for a drug's long-term efficacy. In 1992–1993, the entire biotechnology industry was badly shaken and three firms were driven to near bankruptcy when "logical" therapies for septic shock proved ineffective or unsafe.

It is true that at hospitals throughout the metropolitan regions of the United States, patients with sickle-cell anemia and bacterial and TB infections sometimes refuse to follow a doctor's instructions or ask to be discharged AMA (against medical advice) before completing a protracted course of pain medication or antibiotics. In my experience, this non-compliance is as often because the patient believes (often correctly) that the medicine is not working as out of obstinance. Quietly and in private, many third-year medical students confided to me their own anxieties—that drug addicts with blood poisoning, sickle-cell anemics, AIDS patients, and cancer victims often just would not respond at all to some of their medicines.

The problem clearly goes deeper than simple noncompliance. In the last few years, more and more students would approach me and ask, "Is medicine really helping these people?" And there is reason for their concern. Many of the most intractable diseases are today more prevalent than they were 40 years ago: asthma, tuberculosis, and septicemia to name but three. All dramatically reduce the quality of life of their victims. AIDS in particular has had a numbing effect on medical optimism:

it produces chronic secondary infections; it is transmitted to children in the womb; it causes premature—and often horrendous—deaths.

Today's young medical resident more often battles diseases that defy resolution than did the resident of 20 years ago. AIDS is the scourge of a whole generation of young, sexually active people. Today, in my home town of Newark, New Jersey, AIDS is the major cause of death among young African American women aged 22 to 45. It has been the major killer of young white males in San Francisco. Vaccines to activate a besieged immune system are still a decade or more away. And the therapeutic strategies that rely on antiviral drugs have come up against the same patterns of resistance in the human immunodeficiency virus (HIV) that have plagued antibiotic therapy for more traditional organisms.

Historical Perspectives of Chemotherapy

In this environment of rampant parasitic diseases and newly incurable infections, it is hard to remember that 40 years ago, physicians were heralding our apparent dominion over the microbial world. Antibiotics, those "miracle drugs," were our salvation. By the late 1950s, medicine was fortified with semisynthetic antibiotics and scientifically derived pharmaceutical agents such as insulin and anti-inflammatory steroids. Hormones that controlled the "flight or fight" response were identified, and stress-related diseases appeared to be on the cusp of control. Psychiatric illnesses were newly medicated with powerful if blunt psychotropic medications such as imipramine and Thorazine, and the discovery of apparent biochemical "causes" of mental illness appeared to herald biochemical cures.

Twenty years ago, a new generation of nonsteroidal anti-inflammatory drugs promised to spell relief for painful, chronic conditions such as arthritis and rheumatism. Cancer was to give way in a "war" in which chemotherapeutic agents would conquer any aberrant cells. But this apotheosis of Hippocratic medicine never happened.

Many drugs, like the powerful corticosteroids (for example, prednisone) and nonsteroidal anti-inflammatories (ibuprofen and its congeners) were found to have powerful side effects of their own. And a scant 2 to 3 years after their first widespread use in 1944 antibiotics began to encounter resistant strains of bacteria. And even as we began to regain some control of infectious diseases in the late 1970s, a new disease, which was to defy all of our therapeutic interventions, was incubating.

When it emerged in the 1980s, AIDS was only belatedly seen as a population-wide threat. And in the 1990s, it has become clear that the "rational" antiviral drugs such as AZT, ddl, and ddC (discussed in Chapter 7) do not work to control the disease or even delay its onset. Even Dr. James Curran, a pioneering advocate who heads part of the AIDS effort at the U.S. Centers for Disease Control and Prevention, expressed dire pessimism about using our pharmaceutical armamentarium alone to conquer this devastating disease. Dispirited at the lack of real progress reported from the summer 1993 Ninth International AIDS Conference in Berlin, he declared that prevention is "all we have left to fight with."[2]

Tuberculosis, too, is reaching epidemic proportions again, after being almost eradicated just 25 years ago. Genetic diseases, for which few therapies and even fewer cures exist, are more prevalent today than a decade ago because of the success in eradicating other sources of childhood morbidity and mortality. And heart disease and cancer still strike the young even as they remain (with stroke) the major killers of the old and infirm. For many of the burgeoning over-80 set, the meaningfulness of their extended lives is undercut by Alzheimer's disease and other incapacitating chronic illnesses.

Evolutionary Responses to Disease

My response to these plights has been to urge my students to take the broadest possible view of the context of each patient's disease and the reasons for the failure of the treatment. Barton Childs, a geneticist who teaches at Johns Hopkins University, expresses a similar view when he writes that students are best able to understand illness if they pay attention to "not only the qualities and functions of the molecules that constitute a human being, but no less to the forces that have determined which molecules are around for them to study, and which molecules . . . account for the diseases that they will meet."[3] This evolutionary perspective, while particularly apt for genetic diseases, is the essence of this book.

Understanding how sickle-cell anemia and related genetic disorders have come about and what mechanisms have evolved to cope with them provides an invaluable asset to the clinician who wishes to devise the best strategy for treating this genetic disease. This perspective is also invaluable when regarding infectious disease. Understanding the factors that select for disease resistance and also shape the evolution of the causative organism helps the student appreciate that *both* the pathogen and the host undergo concomitant evolution. Bacteria that provoke arthritis and viruses that seem to produce autoimmune diseases may each be working on similar features of the immune system. How did these features evolve? Why would it be advantageous for a bacterium or virus to provoke an autoimmune disease? These issues will be addressed in Chapter 8.

These questions may also be profitably asked for other conditions, such as allergy and its related disorder, asthma. What factors selected for the apparently overesponsive immune system in asthma? Why? What function did the now maladaptive system once serve? Possible answers in part involve recognizing how evolutionary mechanisms have shaped the recrudescence of some of the old killers and are responsible for much of the bedevilment caused by new ones.

First, we should recognize that human resistance to disease has been a major factor in our emergence as a successful species *before* we had medicine. Hence, understanding the interplay between the natural world and human adaptations is an intrinsic part of medical education–or so it should be. By now it should be a truism that the basic properties of disease are best understood in terms of their evolution.

The Consequences of the Neglect of Evolution

Medical neglect of evolutionary approaches to disease has undermined the long-term success of some of the major advances of modern medicine. As a result of failing to factor evolutionary forces into disease control strategies, much valuable ground has been lost, particularly in the battle against microbial disease. Multidrug resistance to the vast majority of antibiotics in use is the legacy of the failure of those designing therapeutic strategies to incorporate evolutionary thinking. And virtually all modern-day epidemics have deep evolutionary roots. Focusing solely on the microscopic causes of these diseases misses the bigger picture.

A veritable host of microorganisms lives in and on us. They and the pathogens that have enjoyed the most intimate contact with us have evolved the longest with us. What we do by way of enlightened or brutish attempts to limit their persistence will in turn shape their future evolution and spread.

As the two pioneers of evolutionary medicine, George C. Williams and Randolph M. Neese from the State University of New York at Stony Brook and the University of Michigan Medical School point out, medical advances to limit the occurrence of disease would be "more rapid if medical professionals were as attuned to Darwin as they have been to Pasteur."[4] This viewpoint suggests that a disease perspective that incorporated the evolutionary potential of the microscopic world might have produced a more sanguine outcome than relying on the identification of causative organisms and developing chemicals to kill them.

At the root of the resurgence of old infectious diseases is an evolutionary paradox: the more vigorously we have assailed the world of microorganisms, the more varied the repertoire of bacterial and viral strains thrown up against us. Resistance to antibiotics and related drugs has compromised our treatment of TB, pneumonia, staphylococcal infections, and sepsis just to name four common infections. I wrote about this emerging problem some 13 years ago.[5] Today, multidrug resistance has made TB a new killer.[6] And pneumonia, staph infections, and blood poisoning have become increasingly refractory to antibiotic treatment over the last decade. The crux of this problem lies in the ubiquity of antibiotic-resistant genes that can be spread from one organism to another.

As a result of the overuse of antibiotics, the commensal (literally, "living at the same table") organisms that reside in our own bodies now carry the genetic information needed to confer resistance to antibiotics to any new invader.[7] And more and more data suggest that the aberrant reactions to bacterial substances activate the immune system to attack the body's own tissues, a topic discussed in Chapter 6.

Approaches to Understanding Disease

I suggest that part of the answer to these medical dilemmas lies in our learning to incorporate evolutionary thinking into our anticipation and treatment of disease. All too often I have observed that medical education consists of snapshots of disease–glimpses of illnesses frozen in time and space. This is particularly true in my early discipline, pathology, which relies largely on "fixed" tissues to record the consequences of illnesses and disease processes. This unfortunate tendency to abstract dynamic, evolving processes into discrete moments, generates an understandable lack of appreciation of what came before and what will come after.

In spite of years of verbiage about "green" politics and "living with nature," medical practitioners still comport themselves as if they were apart from nature. And the idea that we are somehow apart from the forces of evolution is part of our contemporary hubris. We have failed to recognize that disease is a part of life. Diseases do not arise fully armed to strike unsuspecting hosts. Patterns of disease and illness have millennial roots. Egyptian mummies have been found with the characteristic muscular and bony disfigurations that signal systemic tuberculosis (Pott's disease) and Paleolithic Chilean Indian remains carry the hallmarks of rheumatoid arthritis.

Diseases and patients alike evolve toward contact, struggle, and resolution. The ecology movement taught us that our belief in human sovereignty cut us off from understanding our interdependency with the environment. It taught us that ignoring how our massive disruption of the natural order is ultimately inimical to our own well-being. Global disturbances in climate, destruction of the ozone layer, and permeation of the ecosphere with bioaccumulating chemicals that resist degradation have contributed to this new state of dis-ease.

This book is written in the hope that by presenting diseases as dynamic, evolutionary processes in intimate linkage with environmental and ecological forces, I may generate a new perspective on illness. My premise is simple: most medical problems are problems of evolution. How a disease evolves and how our treatments reshape that evolution may be as critical to "right" thinking about how to treat cancer as it is for the treatment of infectious diseases.

The two axioms of this premise are that (1) we need to understand the evolutionary origins of diseases in order to fully comprehend their prevention, and (2) we need to incorporate evolutionary models of disease in order to treat them effectively. To perform this analysis means exploring the implications for human evolution of the occurrence and severity of disease. What are the mechanisms underlying susceptibility to certain diseases? How have the vectors that carry disease to human hosts (such as the ubiquitous arthropods we know as lice, fleas, and ticks) evolved? Why are *we* now part of *their* evolution? Why do some disease-causing organisms evolve toward a wider host range while others appear to limit their objects of contagion? Why do some diseases become more virulent and others less so with time? How do we explain diseases that strike and kill infants and young adults?

The thesis of this book is that evolutionary concepts provide a wonderfully rich perspective from which to understand these and other examples of our present medical dilemmas. If successful, this book will show how such seemingly unrelated events as the proliferation of HIV, the emergence of antibiotic-resistant bacteria, and some autoimmune diseases have common roots. It is written in the belief that medicine cannot be limited to blind ministrations to the ever-changing panoply of human ills and disorders but must understand the evolutionary consequences of such acts.

This thesis differs from that of contemporary critics who place all of the blame of modern ills on mechanisms by which medicine itself causes illness. While I have always been a great admirer of Ivan Illich, author of *Medical Nemesis,*[8] it is not my belief that our present medical woes are self-induced. Rather, they are the result of a special blindness to the natural forces that have shaped human disease and the consequences of adding powerful medical forces to the very organisms they are intended to control. The evidence before us resonates with the reality that all of human disease has evolutionary origins. Understanding those origins is my purpose in writing this book.

2 Ecosystem Disruption and Disease

All human illnesses have their roots in the forces that shaped evolution. Understanding the evolutionary potential of pathogens provides a perspective into the process by which new diseases become established. The emergence of new infectious diseases is a function of the extent to which pathogens can cross species lines to infect new hosts and the evolutionary resistance of those hosts to infection. The evolutionary biologist is thus concerned with how the prior history of each organism–how host and parasite, microbe and man, virus and woman–allowed them to find each other, respond to each other, and permitted or denied successful transmission and growth.

Initially, no organism "wants" to cause disease. Provoking illness and death is generally an unfavorable way for a pathogen to remain alive. Hosts have evolved highly coordinated defenses against disease-causing organisms that make it difficult if not impossible for even the most wiley invader to simply "set up shop" in a new body. The immune system in particular is geared to recognizing novelty and can usually mount an effective response to an invading organism within days to weeks of colonization. When the organism has a long-standing relationship with the host population, immunity is often set up in childhood, making adult reinfection difficult. But some parasites, viruses, and bacteria, such as the malarial or influenza organisms and the TB bacillus, have "learned" through aeons of coexistence with humans how to slip past these defenses and survive, sometimes within the cells of the immune system themselves.

Paradoxically, other organisms have been successful precisely *because* they evoke immunological defences. Many produce an immune response that turns on the host, creating conditions that lead to autoimmune diseases (discussed in Chapter 8). And some organisms are pathogenic (literally, "suffering producers") because the by-products of an aroused immune system include mediators of inflammation and fever that generally make a person feel crummy. Parasites generally produce disease when their metabolic needs deprive their human hosts of needed resources. (A malarial infection "costs" the body more than 5,000 calories a day, some two to three times the normal intake in tropical climes.) Finally, there are the rare microorganisms that use up their own valuable genetic resources to make noxious chemicals (toxins) that poison their host. Why do they do so? Finding out the evolutionary whys and wherefores, the raison d'être of these and related microbial characteristics, is part of the task of this book.

Breakout: Emergence of a New Disease

When pathogens enter human populations for the first time, they often produce transient, highly fatal illnesses that may or may not take hold. Only infrequently does a "new" pathogen last long enough in a human population and become transmitted well enough to become endemic, or to become a chronically recurring disease. It is an evolutionary maxim that to be successful (that is, survive a long time), a disease-causing organism must somehow become integrated into the ecosystem from which it initially emerged. Even when it has become fully integrated, disturbances of that ecosystem can spring a pathogen loose, placing any at-risk interloper in harm's way. In recent history, many of the human incursions into new ecosystems have been the precursors to the emergence of new diseases.

Inadvertent exposure to new pathogens can result from close contacts with previously unencountered species. Often, these species harbor their own parasites or pathogens. Rarely, these parasites or pathogens can cross species lines.[1]

A case in point is the first occurrence of a disease known as oropouche in Belém, Brazil. This disease, which causes a flu-like illness with severe muscle pain and high fever, ultimately affected more than 11,000 residents. The first reported cases occurred in 1961, just a few years after the completion of the highway through the Amazon that connected Belém with Brasilia. Indeed, just a year earlier, in 1960, the viral agent that eventually was found to be associated with oropouche was isolated from the corpse of a sloth found dead along the new highway. It took 19 more years to put together the ecological puzzle that linked this forest virus with human activity: When settlers cleared the forest for cacao plantations, they disturbed the habitat of a resident species of midge that harbored the suspect virus in its gut. Discarded cacao shells provided a new breeding ground for more of these insects. The resulting population explosion of these flies and their proximity to human habitation created the opportunity for the spread of the virus from midge bites.[2]

The Tropics as Incubators of Disease

Why tropical areas have served as the epicenters for so many diseases is in part a result of their unique evolutionary history. The density and richness of species' interactions is hundreds of times greater in the tropics than in temperate zones. A single hectare of tropical rain forest may have more insect species than does the entire New England region of the United States or all of Great Britain. When new habitats are abruptly opened through extensive forest-clearing activities (beyond the small-scale slash-and-burn agricultural practices of indigenous peoples), extinction of some narrowly confined species and invasion by many others may occur. In particular, as we saw with the Brazilian midges, "opportunistic" species, including many insects and pathogens, may exploit the new environment. Sudden population expansions also afford expanded evolutionary opportunities.

In Papua New Guinea, newly planned logging operations that will clear virgin timber near inhabited areas have been proposed as a testing ground for this idea. Native populations in the nearby villages will provide the test subjects for the prospect of new viral and other pathogens entering the human ecosystem.[3] While the ethics of this grand "experiment of nature" are certainly suspect (for instance, if the exposure may put unsuspecting people at risk, can it be ethically allowed to take place?), the potential findings are of substantial importance. If "new" diseases do in fact come about by bringing together previously isolated populations of pathogens and humans, greater care and attention might be given to the conditions created by the environmental disruptions caused by the expansion of the human population. We might also ask if such belated confirmation of the theory of ecosystem disruption and disease is really necessary.

Dissemination of Disease

We already recognize the joint roles of human ecological disturbance and population movement in the emergence of new diseases. In 1992, a subcommittee of the prestigious Institute of Medicine of the National Academy of Science concluded that human-made environmental disturbances were likely to account for most of the newly emergent diseases seen in contemporary human populations.[4] And population movements often provide new routes for "microbial traffic."[5]

We know such traffic has had devastating consequences in the past. The plague of the Black Death of the Middle Ages followed caravan trade routes from Asia to Europe. The major, near-genocidal destruction of indigenous peoples in the New World, the Hawaiian Islands, and Polynesia can be traced to the introduction of novel pathogens (intentionally or inadvertently) by conquering peoples. Clearly, policies that consider the potential of microorganisms to colonize and depopulate new hosts following ecological or political disturbances and new contacts are desperately needed in an era of global movement and rapid ecological dislocations.

The Evolutionary Perspective

To understand how disruption and new contacts can lead to the introduction of new diseases and why those diseases are so often virulent, we must first understand how species evolve and achieve stability. Secondly, we have to understand the basis for the precarious balance between hosts and their pathogens. Organisms do not evolve so much as they coevolve with their natural surroundings, including other living things. Because living matter already concentrates the key substances that are necessary for life in conveniently "prepackaged" forms, parasites and opportunistic organisms that can invade and capitalize on these resources automatically have an advantage over those that have to synthesize or gather their own foodstuffs and energy source. The proglottids that every first-year biology student learns are the basic unit of life for the infamous tape worm are not so remarkable for their number as for the fact that they require no digestive system of their own!

Opportunism in Nature

Among those most adept at surviving environmental disturbances are those species that are able to capitalize rapidly on new circumstances. Often these are species of rodents or arthropods, which, like the ixodid tick involved with Lyme disease, can serve as vectors of human disease. Humans may simply displace the previous "alpha" carnivore or kingpin species in an area or now actively exploit the local species for food. When they do so, the human form may become a new host for a parasitic or infectious disease that previously, for example, had been limited to monkeys or other primates in the area. This process of displacement and acquisition of new parasites has undoubtedly happened more than once in human history, with malaria and possibly AIDS being the most likely candidates for contemporary legacies of primate-centered environmental disruption.

New parasitic infections and mass epidemics accompanied the large-scale disruptions caused by the practice of agriculture in both the New and the Old World. The ecological disruption caused by the irrigation, dam building, and deforestation of the increasingly large-scale agricultural practices in the Yucatán Peninsula and central valley of Mexico may have contributed to the abrupt decline of Mayan civilization after A.D. 1000. Certainly this proved true in the Fertile Crescent and possibly in northern Africa, where agricultural practices brought together previously separated hosts and parasites and increased the likelihood of major new diseases such as leishmaniasis, river blindness, and schistosomiasis taking hold in the human population.

Indeed, the earliest forays into virgin forest at the dawn of the agrarian revolution may have been responsible for the most significant new disease of all—malaria. (The story of this event and its evolutionary consequences are described in Chapter 10.)

In fact, many of the most important diseases that have afflicted humankind had their origins in protected enclaves, tiny pockets of ecosystems, where they originally had little or no impact on the life forms around them. A classic example is tick-borne Bitterroot fever, which was once confined to the specialized ticks and their rodent hosts in a tiny valley in Wyoming. It only became a human disease with the in-migration of the first human settlers. Then it spread with the ebb and flow of migrants elsewhere in the U.S. West.

Tristes Tropiques

A more contemporary example is the emergence of Argentine hemorrhagic fever, a devastating disease associated with fever, muscle pains, rashes, internal bleeding, and central nervous system involvement leading to tremors or convulsions. Up to 20 percent of affected persons die. The cause of the disease is an organism known as the Junin virus. Prior to the expansion of corn farming in northern Argentina, this virus was a simple commensal in the wild mouse population. With the cultivation and storage of corn in the 1930s and 1940s, people came into contact with these and other rodents, leading to the appearance of this new and expanding disease entity. Argentine hemorrhagic fever now strikes some four to six hundred people each year.

The African cousin to the Argentine form of this disease, African hemorrhagic fever, is a much more lethal (50 percent mortality) and prevalent (several thousand affected) viral disease. Like AIDS, it is suspected that the causative organism (the Ebola virus) probably arose first in monkeys and then was transmitted to the humans who invaded their habitat. The first victim was a trader who arrived at a mission hospital in northern Zaire in August 1976, bleeding internally, vomiting, and raging with fever. He died a few days later, but not before infecting half the nurses at the hospital and a large number of patients who carried the virus back with them to their native villages. By the time this short-lived epidemic waned, five hundred people had died. Fortunately, as would be predicted from an evolutionary perspective, this new agent was too virulent to establish a focus of further infectivity. Without the ability to survive outside its victim, any parasite that kills its host quickly diminishes its own chances of propagation.

Even though the first Ebola epidemic quickly subsided, it does not mean that the virus is gone. A related virus was inadvertently imported with a group of Philippine monkeys brought to a Reston, Virginia, research laboratory in 1989, leading to belated but urgent curbs on the importation of monkeys (a story told in detail in Chapter 9).

Less well known is the so-called Kyasanur Forest disease, a classic example of human disruption of a wildlife environment causing an outbreak of epidemic disease. The illness first appeared in 1957 in Karnataka, India, caused by a virus that previously had reproduced in game animals and in the ixodid tick. Human incursions into the wildlife refuges and the destruction of habitat led to contact between the tick and people, with the outbreak of a severe epizootic infection.[6]

Even these few examples illustrate why it is so often true that we cannot disrupt natural relationships without imperiling our own welfare. This axiom is as old as human disease. The environmental disruptions caused by farming, logging, and, of course, war, have had more profound effects on the occurrence of disease than previously acknowledged. Major epidemics of pestilence and illness have been documented following every major human migration, war, or revolution. Coupled with new waves of exploration and commerce, local epidemics became pandemics, sweeping the globe in the thirteenth and fourteenth centuries as the Black Death, and today in the form of epidemics of influenza and cholera.

Disturbing Ecological Stability

New England as a Model

One of the truisms of evolutionary theory is that most organisms that have evolved together exist in a state of dynamic equilibrium. When this equilibrium is disturbed, one or more of the involved species may undergo a dramatic shift in population.

Much of the farmland of New England, once forests, has been allowed to lie fallow, to return to the previous wooded state. In fact, more of New England is now forested than it has been since the colonial era. But the new forest lacks its previous checks and balances. And, most importantly of all, many more humans now live in close proximity to the new woodlands.

In the transitional stages between cleared farmland and forest, a number of species have expanded and contracted as their habitats changed. Rapidly expanding areas of weedy grasses and shrubs provide new habitats for rodent species in particular. Without the predator species such as wolves, bears, or mountain lions to control deer populations, these populations also expand. (Wolves also predate rodents.) And with that expansion, the arthropod parasites carried by deer and related hosts grow. Populations of ticks, in turn, carry an abundance of diseases. With a plethora of intermediate hosts in the form of various rodent species, including mice that carry nymph and larval forms as well as adult ticks, potentially infectious ticks can come in contact with humans or their pets, carrying previously rare diseases to nearby inhabitants. In some of these disturbed habitats, the *Borrelia* organism (one of the classic pathogens that contaminate tick salivary glands) has found new species of ticks to infect. Many of the ticks have also expanded their range by infecting new rodent intermediate hosts. This circumstance is so reminiscent of the conditions that preceded the outbreak of other major disease (such as sylvan plague, discussed below) that we might well have expected epidemiologists to have sounded a warning about the need for environmental monitoring for pathogens that might transmit tick-borne diseases to humans. The unfortunate result of the lack of surveillance is the current epidemic of Lyme disease.

Historically, a pattern of disruption followed by novel contact between ecologically distant species has often provided the conditions necessary for the spread of disease. Once in the human population, further evolution of the causative microorganisms often occurs. For these events to happen, three circumstances typically coincide: (1) a focus of infection must preexist in the ecosystem (that is, some form of the disease must already be present, or endemic); (2) social disruption or unusual population density leads to increased contact with the organism or its vector(s); and (3) the opportunity for secondary spread must exist. For a new disease to become particularly virulent, the infectious organism must be one that is highly transmissible under the new conditions.

Plague as a Model

The social disruption that preceded the Black Death that began in Europe in 1347 had all the hallmarks of the type of upheaval necessary to spread a major human disease. In the preceding decades, population growth in Europe had led to the decimation of woodlands by extensive farming and the need for lumber in building major urban centers. In 1216, King Henry III was forced by land barons to allow them to cut the major forests of England, including Sherwood Forest of Robin Hood fame. With the freeing of the serfs, mass migration to urban centers occurred, creating a new underclass of the very poor. Unhygienic conditions in the inner cities coupled with the newly abandoned farms, were a deadly combination as plague-carrying woodland rats invaded the cities. There they encountered and spread fleas to roof and sewer rats which in turn brought fleas in contact to the crowded urban populace.

With hindsight, we can see that the Black Death was a composite result of bringing a new intermediate host into contact with a disease-causing organism and the creation of conditions ripe for the expansion of the organism in the human population. When these conditions occur, a "new" disease can arise.

The hand of evolution is especially evident in the circumstances surrounding the reemergence of plague in England. Long before the concept of natural selection and the origin of species was accepted, prescient observers such as Samuel Pepys (1633–1703) recognized a process much akin to evolution in the dramatic changes wrought on society by disease. The agent for change in Pepys' time was the Great Plague of London, which began in 1665. Pepys' powerful observations on the social history of the plague, catalogued in his diary through the years 1660–1669, revealed both how social disruption and poverty contributed to the origins of the epidemic and how the epidemic contributed to further social decay. In writing his observations of the waxing and waning of the London plague, which took the lives of about one-quarter of all those who lived within its ambit, Pepys charted the evolution of a disease.

Pepys noted the crowding, poverty, and lice- and flea-ridden environments in which plague broke out again in seventeenth century England. What he did not note was how extensively the population centers of London and Edinburgh had expanded in recent years and how deforestation had encouraged the spread of rodent populations. Rats and squirrels could now serve equally as intermediate hosts for the fleas that carried the plague.

These events set the stage for the expansion of the plague bacillus.

Following the original deforestation, woodland rats came into contact with urban ones, and the exchange of fleas that followed led to the introduction of sylvan plague into London. Ironically, parallel conditions of our own doing were the antecedent to the most widespread outbreak of plague in modern times–Vietnam.

Plague in Vietnam: A Case Study

Wars are a graphic example of massive ecological disruption. Like other major conflagrations, the Vietnam War compounded the misery of the citizenry by increasing the spread of deadly diseases such as cholera and dysentary. But ecosystem disruption in Vietnam occurred on a exceptionally large scale, creating the very conditions we hypothesized would lead to the emergence of new diseases. During the Vietnam War, some 30 million tons of herbicides were broadcast over the countryside to deny cover to enemy troops and, less publicized, to destroy civilian food crops. Coupled with napalm attacks, these herbicides (including the notorious Agent Orange, but also highly toxic Agents Purple and White) denuded the countryside and devastated previously forested regions, particularly along mangrove swamps in the south and hardwood forests in the highland areas of the west.

As in the Middle Ages and seventeenth century England, this large-scale disruption forced different rodent species into contact with the plague bacillus.[7] The creation of large "dead zones" drove indigenous and Norway rats into new habitats and expanded their territories. Fleas went with them, moving the plague bacillus from rat species to bandicoots and other rodentlike species that had previously been free of plague. One of the first clues that plague had become integrated into the ecosystem in these areas was the discovery of plague in scout and tracker dogs that picked up ticks and fleas during their forays into the countryside near Pleiku and other outposts in the hill region of Vietnam.[8]

While all eyes were on the dramatic physical events of the war in Vietnam, a more insidious horror was occurring within the environment. A search of the literature reveals that studies had charted new outbreaks of plague in the disturbed areas as early as 1962–1963. Although certain areas of Vietnam, notably the highlands in the western region, were historic endemic areas for plague,[9] virtually no cases of plague had been reported since the French occupation in the early part of the century. Then, in 1964, the first major outbreaks occurred in isolated areas inhabited by the Montagnard peoples. The outbreak spread in 1965 through 1966.[10] But only in 1968 was the U.S. medical community alerted to the problem.[11] By 1970, a major epidemic of plague was raging throughout South Vietnam. Military censorship prevented public dissemination of the extent of this outbreak until 2 more years had elapsed.[12] By the end of the war, plague had spread widely through the provinces of South Vietnam.[13]

Cultural traditions (for example, biting the flea to kill it) inadvertently spread the plague bacillus (*Yersinia pestis*) in its pneumonic or airborne form by allowing the germs to get into the respiratory passages. As in the classic Black Death of the Middle Ages, pneumonic plague was often more virulent than the bubonic form,[14] particularly among Vietnamese children. In Quang Ngai Province, plague was a major source of death and morbidity for children under the age of 16.[15] Often, only heroic treatment by U.S. medics saved infected children from being killed by this secondary effect of the war.[16]

Before the war was over, plague had spread to new rodent species and had spread to other Southeast Asia regions. More critically, the bacillus itself had evolved to a form that could be carried in the pharyngeal tissues of the throat without causing symptoms, thereby bypassing the intermediate host (the flea) and permitting human-to-human transfer.[17] By the end of the war, a new, atypical plague bacillus was being isolated from rodents, fleas, and humans in Vietnam.[18] The disruption of the war thus expanded the plague bacillus' host range and habitat in Southeast Asia,[19] and selection pressures led to the emergence of a new plague variant.

This example highlights the role of ecosystem disruption on encouraging the emergence of new variants of old diseases and forcing the evolution of new bacterial forms. Had this lesson been better learned by the Centers for Disease Control, it might have prevented the emergence or spread of Lyme disease 30 years later in the United States. Lyme disease provides an evolutionary window into how ecological disturbances and increased opportunities for human contact shape an emerging disease.

Lyme Disease as a Model

A disease much like Lyme disease, characterized by a migrating rash and arthritic symptoms, was reported sporadically in Europe throughout the last century, but was virtually unknown 20 years ago in the United

States. Then in 1975, two housewives in Old Lyme and East Haddam, Connecticut, reported to a Yale physician that their children had a strange malady that produced symptoms of malaise, bony aches and pains, and neurological symptoms, including poor concentration and memory. The physician took their complaints seriously and subsequently collected more than a dozen cases. The rest is history.

Since then, Lyme disease has swept the New England area, especially along the coast, and has spread to the Midwest (primarily Wisconsin and Minnesota) and the West Coast, where it has become established in California, southern Oregon, and the Puget Sound area. As shown in Figure 1, all states except Montana have reported at least one Lyme disease case.

Many observers express surprise and alarm about this spread. But it was hardly unforeseeable. In the Americas, Pavlovskyella ticks have been reported over the years to serve as reservoirs and vectors of the group of spirochetes in the genus *Borrelia* now known to cause Lyme disease. The more than nineteen different species of these spirochetes are small, slender, helically coiled bacteria measuring some 300 to 500 micrometers in length. The *Borrelia* genus is assumed to have evolved as a symbiont of ticks, which serve as the primary host. Birds, mammals, and now humans serve to "amplify" the spread and growth of these infectious spirochetes by serving as opportunistic hosts, but they are not essential for the spirochetes' propagation in nature.

Four separate tick species carry and spread *Borrelia* to humans in their salivary secretions, causing a condition known as relapsing fever, a disease characterized by recurring episodes of high, unexplained fevers. In Africa, *Borrelia duttoni* causes African relapsing fever. Relapsing-fever-bearing ticks commonly parasitize burrowing rodents, including some of the same species only recently "discovered" to spread the agent of Lyme disease—the wood rat, deer mouse, and white-footed mouse.[20]

Evolution appears to have prepared ticks to be especially suitable hosts for various bacteria and other pathogens. Unlike other insects that carry potentially disease-causing organisms, which disrupt their internal metabolism extensively during molting, the tick undergoes only limited changes during molting (for example, replacing only the salivary glands), thereby providing uniquely well-adapted conditions for the intercellular survival of infectious agents.[21]

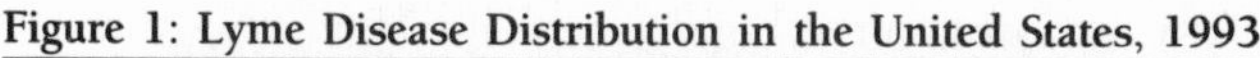

Figure 1: Lyme Disease Distribution in the United States, 1993

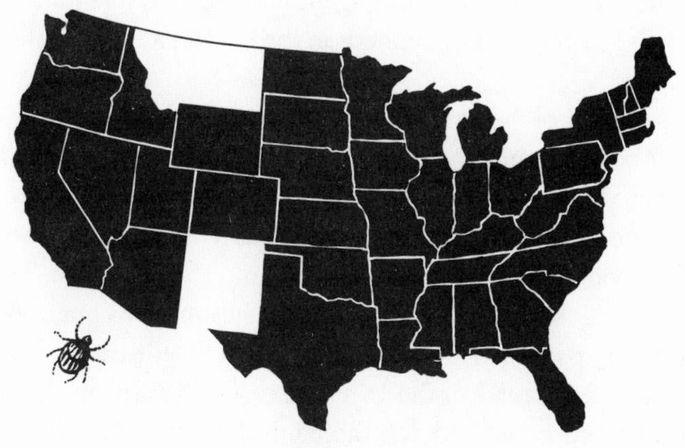

Borrelia organisms are especially well adapted to survive in ticks. (Note that the concept that vertebrates are the source of *Borrelia* is mistaken—*Borrelia* originated in ticks.[22]) *Borrelia* organisms are transmitted from generation to generation of ticks in the tick's eggs. Thus, the common conception that deer are the carriers in the life cycle of *Borrelia* is a myth. Rather, it is the rodent population that maintains large numbers of the early developmental stages (the larvae and nymphs) of the ixodid tick (a fact known since the early 1970s[23]). As the principal reservoir of the forms that give rise to new, sexually mature adult ticks, such rodents serve as the epicenter of Lyme disease. (In California, it appears that the dusky-footed woodrat carries the infecting tick.) Some of the early stages of tick development, such as the nymphs, can also feed on humans and transmit Lyme disease. Such transmission usually requires feeding of 48 hours or more.

When humans enter a previously undisturbed ecosystem, the ticks have an opportunity to parasitize a new host. A key observation is that when such opportunistic feeding by ticks occurs, the tick's blood meal may prove unsuitable for supporting its life cycle, and may even be toxic or lethal to the tick.[24] Nonetheless, transmission of a disease-causing organism that had a commensal relationship with the tick can occur under circumstances of prolonged feeding. When a tick-borne agent infects humans for the first time, it is often highly virulent. This is because the new host has had little or no opportunity to evolve defenses against the invader and because the causative agent may be as virulent as its biology dictates since it does not depend on the human as an obligate intermediary host.

The "greening" of the United States has led to suburban living where a deer may be as common as a squirrel.[25] Unfortunately, deer are one of the intermediate hosts for adult ixodid ticks that also carry the Lyme organism. The proximity of human populations to areas infested with ticks has provided an inadvertent opportunity for infection.

In spite of its recent origins and severe health consequences, I believe that we are paying insufficient attention to this disease's evolutionary potential. The spread of the Lyme disease organism in the human population should be considered the equivalent of the colonization of a new island in which evolutionary opportunity abounds. Because of the rapid expansion of the intermediate hosts for the *Borrelia* organism, a dramatic population expansion of the spirochete itself can be expected. Left to itself, this expansion alone would provide new opportunities for genetic change. But the Lyme disease organism is also being subjected to selective pressures in what may become a new intermediate host, humans. While insufficient numbers of people are probably now infected with the *Borrelia* organism to return many spirochetes back to the gene pool via subsequent tick bites of sick hosts, it is not too soon to consider the consequences of microevolution of the Lyme disease organism within antibiotic-treated patients.

In my current environs in California, local physicians routinely prescribe antibiotics for everyone with a real or imagined tick bite. Often, patients demand such treatment, even though public health authorities have discouraged prophylactic treatment with antibiotics for tick bites without the characteristic rash that signals the spread of the *B. burgdorferi* organism or confirmation of the tick as a known vector of Lyme disease. This behavior is likely to encourage the emergence of antibiotic-resistant Lyme disease organisms, especially if the protocol for prophylaxis is not followed, since suboptimal treatment will select for resistant organisms. It remains to be seen if any antibiotic-resistant spirochetes return to the pool of *Borrelia* carried by ticks through subsequent bites, or if antibiotic resistance will remain a host-specific problem.

Irrespective of the movement of antibiotic-resistant genes, the rapid spread and transmission of this parasite are likely to encourage evolutionary changes that will permit the *Borrelia* species that carry Lyme disease to humans to remain virulent or become more so. Vector-borne diseases such as Lyme disease are under little pressure to become less virulent. Unlike diseases that must be transmitted directly from host to host, such as AIDS and tuberculosis, a vector-transmitted disease can kill or incapacitate its host quickly and still be transmitted. In the case of host-to-host transfer of disease, the affected victim must remain viable long enough to transmit the organism in an infective dose. In the case of Lyme disease, humans are not part of the essential intermediate hosts required for *Borrelia* to complete its life cycle. As Paul Ewald of Amherst College has observed, an insect vector such as a tick or mosquito does not care what happens to the host it infects, thereby permitting it to transmit the most lethal of organisms.[26]

I think it is plausible that the Lyme disease organism will slip its present evolutionary constraints that have confined its life cycle to such nonhuman vertebrates as rodents and such insect vectors as the ixodid tick species. As it increases the number and variety of nonobligate intermediates such as humans and deer, the *Borrelia* species may evolve toward a strain that will circulate primarily in humans and ticks. This possibility is suggested by the fact that *B. duttoni*, the relapsing fever organism previously carried by ticks and several rodent vectors, now exists *only* in humans and ticks.[27]

In the instance of Lyme disease, the chance coming together of humans and ticks has presented an opportunistic source for feeding. This opportunity is especially ripe for exploitation for the pervasive and nearly invisible nymph stages of the *Ixodes* ticks that commonly carry *B. burgdorferi* to humans. And, what had been a relatively benign agent when in its natural host (the deer mouse or other rodent species) has become a major source of human illness. In the expanding suburban population newly living in proximity to a burgeoning deer population, the *Borrelia* spirochete found a evolutionarily unprepared host in which it could proliferate with little or no innate resistance. In fact, rather than generating an effective immunity that limits its spread, the Lyme disease organism provokes an immune reaction that contributes to the arthritis and other complications associated with Lyme disease. (The mechanisms for such provocation are discussed in Chapter 8.) Hence, the organism's control and eradication are all the more urgent.

Solutions

When Lyme disease entered the Americas, an initial presumption was that control of the disease could be accomplished with antibiotics such as tetracycline. This after-the-fact approach leaves much to be desired since, as I have argued, it encourages the emergence of resistant *Borrelia* strains and provides no buttress against the continued spread of the tick nor the enhanced pathogenicity of the *Borrelia* organism itself. Attempts to control the spread of the tick by using pesticides or spreading pyrethrin-treated cotton in or near mouse burrows has proven ineffectual since many different rodent species are now recognized to spread the tick. Solutions developed for pets have paradoxically been more readily approved by the Food and Drug Administration (FDA) than similar approaches suggested for humans. A Lyme disease vaccine is now available for cats and dogs. This vaccine protects against the *Borrelia* organism's spread in the pet's body by encouraging the elaboration of antibodies against it. Human vaccine trials began in 1994.

A promising approach that to my knowledge has not been recognized by the medical establishment would be to ensure the death of the tick known to transmit the disease, thus breaking the cycle of contagion. Yet, while this can be done readily in pets by flea collars treated with pesticides, it is not likely to be a feasible method in the wild. I believe the most effective approach to achieve this end is to immunize the intermediate host against the *tick* and not the germ. Such an approach has been used effectively to reduce or prevent the transmission of disease-causing agents to intermediate hosts (humans in this case). For instance, if the deer and/or rodents were immunized against ticks, they might actually kill any tick that bit them. A similar approach has been effectively used to control rabies by adding a vaccine to bait for foxes and skunks. This idea is plausible because blood meals from immunized hosts can kill ixodid ticks (whose larvae feed for a long time on their hosts) but not ticks of other families.[28]

Dengue Fever as a Model

A disease much like Lyme disease in terms of the rapidity of its spread and dispersion is commonly known as dengue fever, a mosquito-borne viral disease with deep historic roots in the subtropical areas of the world. Dengue exemplifies how ecological disruption can create novel opportunities for the rapid spread and dispersion of a disease vector. Also known as hemorrhagic fever because of the bleeding it produces in its victims, dengue was a long-standing disease in tropical Asia, but it was believed to be quiescent in the early part of this century. However, since the 1950s, dengue hemorrhagic fever has undergone a resurgence, becoming a major cause of death and hospitalization among Southeast Asian children.

Epidemics were first seen in Manila and Bangkok in 1954, largely as a result of flooding and resultant expansion of the mosquito population. Its victims are characteristically young children. Today, in the Philippines, Thailand, Burma, Cambodia, and Vietnam, dengue affects a broad cross section of the population and is responsible for some 600,000 victims per year in Southeast Asia. The rapid spread of dengue to North and South America beginning in the late 1970s is shown in Figure 2.

Such explosive spread was not always the case. Since the turn of the century, public health authorities had assumed that this ancient scourge had all but disappeared from the Asian subcontinent. When dengue reemerged in 1954, it staged what one National Institutes of Health writer has described as a "spectacular comeback."[29] In the first of three waves of epidemics in Southeast Asia, dengue struck the impoverished areas of this region with a vengeance, carrying a mortality rate of up to 40 percent. As a result of ecological disturbances and poor flood control that have produced expanded habitats for mosquitoes, we are now facing the prospect of its gaining a toehold in the United States.

Dengue's first foray to our continent occurred in 1981. In that year, dengue struck more than 300,000 Cubans, leading to 116,000 hospitalizations.[30] And in 1985, the Asian tiger mosquito *Aedes aegypti,* which carries the dengue virus, was imported into Florida in water carried in shipments of used tires from Southeast Asia. This insect carrier or vector is now widely distributed throughout the southernmost region of the country, threatening to carry dengue to a large population. That it has not yet done so is largely the result of Americans' penchant for avoiding mosquitos. In 1992, dengue's reach extended to the Australian continent, sending 616 people to the hospital.[31]

Duane Gabler, currently the acting director of the Centers for Disease Control's division of Vector-Borne Viral Diseases, is alarmed about

Figure 2: Epidemic Spread of Dengue

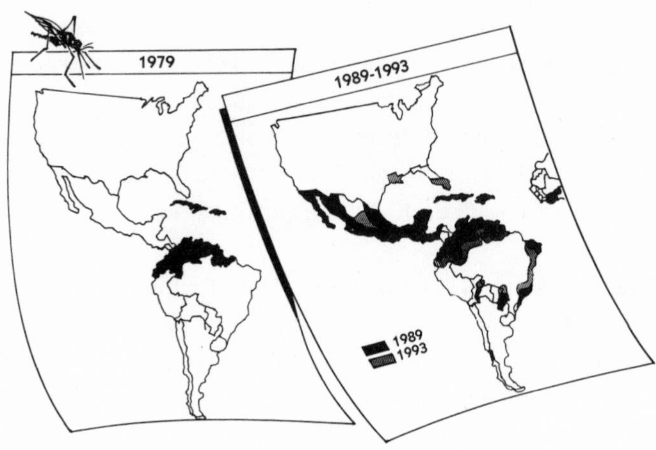

the prospect of dengue gaining a real foothold here. He has noted how readily dengue has made inroads in the Caribbean and South America. As shown in Figure 2, only Bermuda, the Cayman Islands, Costa Rica, Uruguay, and Chile have escaped colonization by the mosquito.

According to Dr. Gabler, "We have a very real crisis on our hands."[32] Pesticide spraying of *A. aegypti* mosquitos with malathion has had predictable effects–incomplete control (largely because of surviving indoor populations) and emergence of resistant strains. Until we recognize that the major source of the disease is the uncontrolled growth and dispersion of populations of this mosquito into new habitats, no feasible control is likely.

Past eradication efforts aimed at *A. aegypti* mosquitos were successful because their goal was restoring the ecological balance of natural predators and eliminating the standing water that is the mosquito's traditional breeding ground. In 1901, William Gorgas, then the sanitary engineer of Havana, successfully used such techniques to eradicate *Aedes* (also the carrier of yellow fever) in Cuba within 6 months. However, U.S. federal agencies see their only recourses as being the wholesale mobilization of citizens to take individual action to minimize contact with the mosquito and the development of a vaccine.[33] But these avenues of protection fall far short of the revolutionary steps taken by Gorgas to limit the vector's access to populations through conversion of mosquito-breeding habitats and the introduction of natural predators (recently, the mosquito fish). Unfortunately, as both Lyme disease and dengue show, once ecological disturbance has occurred, the spread of a dangerous pathogen through a burgeoning vector population is extremely difficult to constrain.

How well we succeed in controlling this disease will determine in part our success in future efforts. We will not lack for new threats. A case in point is another mosquito-borne illness that also lurks just offshore of Florida. Eastern equine encephalitis (EEE) virus, the cause of a neurologically disabling illness among horses, has recently been found in another aedes strain (*A. albopictus*) in Florida, expanding its previous territory from southern Texas and Hawaii. Previously limited to Asia, as is its dengue-carrying counterpart, this species was probably also brought to the United States from Southeast Asian countries.

The Centers for Disease Control has now isolated sixteen different strains of newly recognized viruses of the arbovirus group (arthropod-borne viruses) from this mosquito. The EEE virus was among this group. Although this is presently the rarest mosquito-borne disease among humans in the United States, it is a potentially fatal illness, killing up to 30 percent of its victims. To their consternation, even as inspectors first discovered the mosquito among used tire shipments, they found that the EEE virus was already establishing itself in some bird species.[34]

Patterns of Ecological Disruption and Disease

We lack an ecological master plan for the control of a disease, a plan that would take into account the particular characteristics of a disease-causing organism and how that organism has gone about adapting to the prevalence of human hosts as humans change its environment. Human forces are often the key shapers of disease, particularly during radical environmental disturbances and war.

Who gets sick is as much a phenomenon of what organisms are around to cause illness as it is of who is there to get sick. Humans, like ecosystems, can be radically disrupted by stressors, toxins, or pathogens. When this happens, new evolutionary patterns of disease are predictable. It has taken the tragedy of AIDS to show us just how "opportune" disease-causing germs really care—only because of the presence of multitudes of immunologically crippled hosts is it possible to find otherwise rare diseases like thrush (a fungal infection of the mucosal membranes of the mouth and throat) and Kaposi's sarcoma (a disfiguring, purplish growth of cells beneath the skin) flourishing. Germs colonize an AIDS patient much as we would expect to see a disturbed ecosystem colonized by the most opportunistic life forms.

Environmental disturbances are almost certainly at work today in shaping new patterns of disease and disability around the globe. Malaria has taken a startling upturn in Rwanda, a phenomenon linked to the global-warming-enhanced proliferation of its mosquito vectors.[35] Seals fall ill in unprecedented numbers in Lake Baikal; dolphins succumb to a new bacterial illness that causes their skin to become as thin and weak as cellophane and their immune systems to fail; coral reefs die; sea urchins succumb to a new, temperature-dependent disease organism; and riverine fish develop tumors in epidemic proportion. These apparently "new" illnesses and epizootic infections all have the imprimateur of human activities that have radically disrupted the global environment.[36] Inevitably, such massive die-offs are by their nature natural selective events. And whether their human counterparts in the form of our epidemics of AIDS, asthma, and tuberculosis will leave the next generation better prepared to resist these diseases than is the present one—or if we will need to depend solely on medical therapeutic interventions—remains to be seen.

To understand the impact of such diseases and how human attempts to master them have compounded the problem of their control, we must understand the engine of evolutionary change—natural selection.

3 Understanding Natural Selection

At the root of understanding evolution across the range of organisms it affects is comprehending how natural selection works at both the macroscopic and microscopic levels. The basic approach of this book is to show the linkages between evolutionary ideas on two fronts. One encompasses complex organisms (mosquitos, ticks, people, and so on) as a whole; the other focuses on the cells that comprise them—the cellular components of immune systems or the free-living single cell systems we have already explored (bacteria, viruses, and so on). The overarching theme that bridges these fronts is the role of cultural and medical invention in reshaping the human and microbial environment and thereby the selective forces that impinge on these evolving systems.

In examining this theme, it is also crucial to recognize that the microbial world has evolved concurrently with our own. All infectious diseases are encounters between at least two different living systems. Each system is subject to the laws of evolution. And each system obeys its own rules of selection and survival. To see disease as an evolutionary event for *both* parties is a marked departure from the old view of infection as an invasion of a static host by a resilient enemy. As we will see in the examples throughout this book, the immune system's capabilities have had to evolve in lockstep with the advances made by microorganisms and other invaders.

Natural Selection as a Unifying Theme

Natural selection in all of these applications is the single most important concept for anyone interested in evolution to master. It is at the core of Charles Darwin's (1809–1882) account of evolution, *The Origin of Species*,[1] first published in 1859, and all subsequent accounts of the causes of speciation. In spite of the extensive use of this term, much confusion exists regarding what Darwin originally meant by "natural selection."

Selection is the consequence of events acting directly and indirectly on the reproductive abilities of individuals in populations with appreciable genetic variation. The forces may be physical factors such as ultraviolet radiation, heat, cold, or humidity; or, natural ones such as pathogens, parasites, or predators. Or they involve diet or vulnerability to infection, cancer, or autoimmune diseases. But all have evolutionary impact to the extent that they affect otherwise random chance governing the coming together of gametes. That is, some individuals of a species will have the opportunity to reproduce, to have their genetic material carried in the next generation, while others will not.

The net effect of selection is to give the new holder of a genetic repository that confers a modest survival advantage greater representation in the next generation; that is, more offspring having this genetic makeup will survive to reproduce. Darwin himself envisioned a relatively constant production of variation in the descendants of sexually reproducing organisms on which selection could work. While he lacked the genetic insight to understand the assortment of genetic information that occurs during the process of meiosis and fertilization (he thought traits were somehow "blended"), he did understand the concept of genetic variability. According to Darwin, each new generation would have different proportions of novel variants or "sports." In this view, Darwin drew on his own experience as a pigeon fancier.

Darwin hypothesized that it was among such variants that selection could work to favor the survival of certain individuals whose heritable constitution conferred on them certain advantages. Because chance production of variants from generation to generation could not directly anticipate radical environmental change, Darwin was hard-pressed to explain why so many organisms seemed so well adapted to often extreme circumstances. Catastrophic or cataclysmic environmental events were well known even in Darwin's time to be inimical to survival of many species, leading to extinction. Yet, some organisms appeared particularly suited to survive, even when their past encounters were with much tamer circumstances. In part, the answer to this enigma lies in the degree of plasticity permitted by various adaptations to novel environments.

Adaptation

When the selected characteristics of an organism prove "beneficial" and are sufficiently tuned to the circumstances of life as to favor survival, they are termed *adaptations*. An adaptation is a solution to a survival problem. Darwin appreciated that for an adaptation to arise, it must be shaped by natural selection acting over long periods. Over time, adaptations eventually take the form of a trait, like the ability of vultures to smell carrion. Usually, traits are determined by highly integrated genetic systems, not just a simple single gene mutation.[2] A notable exception is the enhanced bill size in an African finch caused by a single gene.[3] The fact that such a major morphological feature can be shaped by a change in a single gene provides a clue to Darwin's own success in "seeing" evolution happen before his eyes. The unusual ability of a single genetic change to affect beak shape may be the secret of the rapid radiation of the one species that convinced Darwin of the role of natural selection in evolution–the Galápagos finches.

Darwin's Finches

Darwin's archetypes of an "evolving species" were found on the Galápagos Islands, located some 700 miles due west of Ecuador. These remote islands in the Pacific were visited by the *Beagle,* on the voyage that brought Darwin his greatest evolutionary insights. The most graphic illustration of natural selection was found among the bird life there, especially the finches. Progenitors of this widely divergent group of birds were probably among the first colonizers of the distant shores of the Galápagos. Survivors and descendants of those few colonizers successfully expanded their niches to utilize food resources that might otherwise have been usurped by other species had the finches been living on the mainland of South America. The geographic isolation of the Galápagos, and perhaps plumage or vocal signals that limited interbreeding, led to the emergence of 13 distinct species of finches, named after their discoverer, Charles Darwin.

Galápagos finches include birds with beaks adapted to cracking seeds, or to extracting nectar, or to plucking insects from tree branches or the ground. Darwin correctly intuited that these sometimes major differences in beak shape must have been present initially as subtle variations in beak conformation in the first flock of founding finches. Where a particular morphological difference in beak shape conferred a feeding advantage to some of the finches, it led to the differential survival of those with the nearest configuration of that form. By enabling these new variants to exploit previously untapped food sources, the finches were able to expand their range and population. On the mainland, many of these food sources would have been exploited by other avian or reptilian species; the rarity or nonexistence of members of those species on the Galápagos provided a much wider range of potential resources or niches for the finches to exploit.

Further deviation from the original beak shape coupled with behavioral adaptations allowed the finches to utilize still more distant and diverse food sources. Geographic spread to outlying islands further ensured the success of populations with potentially novel genetic makeups and also limited genetic exchange with the original flock members. These two features—geographic and reproductive isolation especially at the edges of the population's range—encouraged the interbreeding of the new genetic variants within their own kind, a process that eventually led to speciation: the effective genetic isolation of a novel, interbreeding population. After several hundred, perhaps thousands of generations, the joint processes of selection and isolation led to a number of unique adaptations, among them the Galápagos finch that utilizes a cactus spine to gather its food.

Once established as a freely interbreeeding subgroup, further behavioral and/or geographic isolation eventually prevents members of the founding population from interbreeding with their divergent descendants. In time, sufficient change occurs to block the reintroduction of the original genes back into the new population. When the new population can no longer mate successfully with the old, it is a new species.

Evolutionary biologist Ernst Mayr's view of this process is that species isolate themselves as a protective device to guard against any breakup of their well-adapted and tightly integrated genetic systems.[4] With this isolation and subsequent stabilization of their own genetic makeup, further genetic divergence assures that even hybrids between the original and new species are sterile, thereby "sealing" the genetic isolation of the new species. The endpoint is a group of individuals who freely share the same gene pool but exclude outside genetic comingling.

Origins of Species

The emergence of the diverse subspecies of Darwin's finches illustrates the three factors needed for evolution to occur: (1) a population sufficiently large enough to assure genetic diversity; (2) an event that selects individuals from this population who have particular, genetically inheritable traits; and (3) the differential survival and expansion of those genetically distinct individuals favored by natural selection. These factors recur as themes in the evolution of virtually all of the organisms of interest to medicine, from microbes to humans.

But the Galápagos were bare islands that were colonized rapidly, hardly the typical circumstances encountered by most life forms that coexist for long periods in relatively "filled" environments. The current thinking is that new species form sporadically, in fits and starts, as opportunities arise. For most of the time, species remain relatively constant in composition and size, existing in a state of stasis. This theory that species remain static and then branch into new forms in bursts of evolutionary change was first developed in 1972 by two evolutionists, Niles Eldredge and Stephen Jay Gould. They described the process of evolution as "punctuated equilibrium."[5] In this view, evolution does not occur at a constant rate, steadily generating new species. Rather, it occurs in bursts of speciation, punctuating long periods of stasis where species coexist without major disruption or change. During these periods of relative stability, however, local events can still disrupt genetic homogeneity and lead to the emergence of new strains or subspecies. A medical example would be the consequences discussed below of the rapid intrusion of antibiotics into the environment of intestinal bacteria.

Genetic Diversity

To survive and anticipate environmental novelty, most species maintain a high degree of what is called "genetic diversity." Genetic diversity occurs when the species carries many different variants of certain gene pairs and allows them to be carried in a heterozygous form by a high proportion of individuals. An example are the genes for hemoglobin, the red blood cell pigment. More than 160 variants of genes for the two homoglobin chains exist, and many individuals have combinations of variants that differ from normal hemoglobin A. For instance, about 12 percent of African Americans carry the gene for hemoglobin S (sickle-cell hemoglobin or HbS) in addition to hemoglobin A on their chromosomes. Coupled with rearrangements and mutations, this heterozygosity produces a pool of variability that serves as a kind of genetic insurance against environmental shifts.[6] Originally, the mutation for HbS was rare. But because it conferred advantages in malarial environments (see Chapter 10), carriers reproduced preferentially and increased their proportion in the population. Thus, when novel environmental changes such as a malarial epidemic occur, genetic diversity ensures that a proportion of the population will survive. Only rarely does a new disease or stressor require a completely novel genetic change to permit survival.

At some point, organisms come to "fit" a particular niche so that further genetic change is unnecessary to secure survival. Selective forces have favored certain genomes and maintain a high frequency of those genes in the population. In the integrated genetic systems represented by groups of species in an ecosystem, most of the members have arrived at a "balance" with one another. Their genetic makeup and patterns of resistance and vulnerability to disease are held relatively constant from generation to generation. This constancy takes place by virtue of the natural tendency of genetic systems to come into equilibrium, if they are not disrupted.

Genetic Disruption

Here's where human interference comes into play. By disrupting otherwise balanced ecosystems and their adapted genomes, human intervention disturbs this genetic harmony, dispersing species and breaking up genetic patterns by which groups of individuals have become adapted to their environments. Organisms that had previously been adapted to a limited range of hosts or environments, when disturbed by human intervention, are likely to die off. Those that maintained a high degree of genetic diversity and reproductive ability can become more widely dispersed and may invade new environments. This can happen within the microcosm of the body, as when otherwise rare bacteria such as certain *Clostridia* species (discussed in Chapter 5) are subjected to broad-spectrum antibiotics. *Clostridia's* subsequent outgrowth and invasion of the intestinal lining causes a serious human disease.

In the environment at large, human activities such as the use of pesticides and fertilizers, water contamination or purification, and livestock treated with antibiotics have selected for different compositions of organisms in the microscopic communities of soils; oceans, lakes, and aquifers; and stockyards and livestock water impoundments.

An analogous situation occurs in the body's microevolutionary environment when bacterial populations are subjected to massive die-offs when someone abruptly changes eating habits or his water intake that governs the mix of trace elements in the gut. In a country that has a high background level of toxin-producing intestinal bacteria, such as Mexico, this microenvironmental change may favor colonization of the intestinal tract with enterotoxigenic forms of *Escherichia coli* known as ETEC. Should someone also be taking an antibiotic to which ETEC strains are resistant, even a few colonizing strains can expand to fill the new niche created by the loss of the natural flora.

In addition to breaking up previously adapted genotypes, the disturbance created by the antibiotic intrusion permits the surviving organisms to acquire many new combinations and types of adaptations through exchange of raw genetic material. Similarly, new "colonists" can find antibiotic-depopulated regions in the vagina or small intestine, where they can take hold, creating other medical problems, an issue discussed in Chapter 5.

On a more macroscopic level, a disturbance in the number or variety of intermediate hosts may suddenly favor a parasitizing organism so that it increases the number and variety of hosts that it infects. This event may have happened in the case of the microorganism that causes Lyme disease. And, as we also saw in the example of dengue and related viral infections, other environmental disruptions or migrations may permit certain strains of a virus or bacteria to encounter and infect new hosts.

Population Disruption

Disturbance on the human scale can push survivors to breed outside what might previously have been a protected genetic enclave or reproductively isolated group. This expansion of a previously limited population can lead to the acquisition of new genetic combinations. "Bottlenecks," in which populations are suddenly reduced but then expand from certain surviving "founders," can also generate significant new genetic combinations. Each of these processes has likely occurred in human populations, and has had medical consequences.

Bottlenecks create evolutionary opportunities. Thus, the severe reduction of survivors that is hypothesized to have occurred during one or more of the Paleolithic traverses across the Bering Strait probably explains the unusual adaptations of many Inuit, Athabascan, and other Native American and South American Indian populations. Most Inuit populations (Eskimos) carry extra insulating fat, have thickened epicanthic folds on their eyes (to reduce glare and wind-driven snow), have thickly padded cheek bones for insulation, and have a hypothesized increase in disease resistance. A founder effect also helps to explain their reduced genetic variability and the fixation of certain genes, like those that predispose to autoimmune conditions such as ankylosing spondylitis (see Chapter 8).

Although a highly simplified version of reality, a bottleneck effect probably limited the amount of genetic variability that these Paleolithic colonists had available. If the original group included persons with genetic combinations that provided selective advantages during their migration, the net genetic contribution of those persons to the next generation would have been higher than usual. But those same adaptations may have traded resistance to other diseases, perhaps ones not part of the old or new environment. This pattern of inheritance helps to explain the unusually high incidence of diabetes in these populations, a topic addressed in Chapter 9.

Such possible trade-offs are critical to understanding the evolutionary basis for susceptibility to certain diseases. Adaptations that may have provided a certain advantage during a period of human prehistory may confer little or no adaptive advantage to holders today. As long as selection is "relaxed" in the sense of permitting reproduction and survival of these "compromised" individuals, possibly defective genotypes may persist into the modern era. Indeed, many of today's human ills can be seen as the result of interactions between bacteria or dietary factors with previously useful traits that retain little selective value in contemporary environments.

Negative Selection

Until now, we have been discussing evolution as if it proceeds only by *favoring* certain individuals. But *negative* selection is an equally important concept. In negative selection, individuals or cells with characteristics that are unsuited to a new environment are put at a disadvantage.

Negative selection explains the elimination of antibiotic-sensitive bacteria in the gut during antibiotic therapy. In practice, selective pressures exerted by the antibiotics must occur over protracted periods to provide a reproductive advantage to any genetically antibiotic-resistant cells. This is why the emergence of antibiotic-resistant bacteria usually occurs only after a course of drug therapy, especially if the dose is suboptimal to eradicate all of the infection. That is, a single application of an antibiotic may leave a rare resistant variant standing among a greatly decimated population of other bacteria, but that one treatment will be unlikely to kill all the competing "susceptible" forms. Many of them will grow back and once again swamp the "resistant" form. This is part of the current rationale for giving AIDS patients a single, high-powered dose of a new antibiotic as a preventive measure against infections.

Natural selection is a particularly powerful force in the case of microorganisms because constant selection pressures exerted generation after generation produce a cumulative effect. When even slight variations in the environment are continuously present over time, they may favor one type over another to a barely perceptible degree—say, at the rate of 1 to 2 percent per generation. Such an advantage equates to leaving behind 101 survivors for every 100 of a competitor after one generation. But as evolutionary biologists are wont to observe, even this slight advantage accrues rapidly. If a constant 1 to 2 percent advantage is compounded from generation to generation, a previously subordinate type may become the dominant form in only thirty generations!

In human terms, this is, of course, a long time, approximately 700 to 800 years assuming three to four generations per century. But in the lives of microorganisms or other short-lived creatures, the elapsed time can be catastrophically shorter since only 20 to 30 *minutes* may be needed to complete reproduction in some bacteria. For the fastest bacteria, thirty generations can elapse in less than a day. (At 20 minutes per generation, thirty generations takes place in 10 hours; at 30 minutes per generation, 15 hours.) At the end of thirty generations, 2 bacteria have increased to 2^{30}, producing approximately 1 billion descendants!

These numbers make it more understandable how a massive revolution can take place in the microorganisms that colonize the body after a protracted series of antibiotic treatments. When a patient is prescribed a broad-spectrum antibiotic to treat an infection, the natural flora and fauna of the body are subjected to a wave of killing or inhibition, followed by rapid recolonization. When the mayhem is over, new bacterial and fungal survivors—selected by the sparing effect of the antibiotic for resistant organisms—will replace antibiotic-susceptible ones, leading to an overgrowth of yeasts, fungi, and sometimes harmful bacteria. Often, the exotic strains were kept in place by natural competition with the other organisms that colonize the body. One group of organisms that commonly arises after even incidental antibiotic use is yeasts, especially candida species such as *Candida albicans.*

Antibiotic use is so prevalent, and such a common source of yeast infections, particularly vaginal yeast overgrowths, that it has created a whole secondary market for douches, over-the-counter antibiotics, and other female products for which virtually no demand existed prior to the antibiotic era. As I will show in Chapter 5, when such antibiotic use is repeated serially, patient after patient, a dramatic evolution of bacteria toward antibiotic resistance may jeopardize effective medical treatment for the community as a whole.

"Purposeful" Evolution

In spite of the appearance that a final "adapted" feature like antibiotic resistance is purposefully designed to resist the selective force applied to the population, it would be a mistake to see the emergence of better suited organisms as evidence of some kind of intentional activity. Organisms do not "try" to escape killing by acquiring resistant genes, any more than a toxic chemical intentionally selects susceptible cells. Only random, chance events that generate mutations in the population in advance provide the material for evolutionary change.

For example, the special characteristics of persons who carry the sickle-cell trait appear to be the result of purposeful activity. Yet, the sickle-cell trait arose randomly, as implied by the concurrent existence of many other but imperfect genetic adaptations to malaria. All of the adaptations are the result of random mutation and natural selection pressures. African peoples with sickle-cell trait look like they "fit" some cosmic plan only because of the constancy of the forces that operated within their particular environment–in this case, the pervasiveness of malaria.

While organisms that are better adapted to present conditions will survive and reproduce into the future, they are not necessarily an "improvement" over their past form. The same holds true for those persons with sickle-cell trait. Their adaptations will only be a benefit if the same conditions that existed in their past recur. In the absence of malaria, sickle-cell hemoglobin is hardly an "improvement."

As I will show, an evolutionary improvement can only occur if the circumstances that favored certain better adapted individuals living in an original environment persist relatively unchanged into future environments. That is, natural selection can only prepare offspring for the environment that favored their parents. In more technical terms, this concept is embodied in Fisher's theorem, a model of genetic change developed by the early twentieth century statistician, Ronald Fisher.[7] Fisher's theorem predicts that the natural selection made possible by genetic variation will always increase the average overall fitness of individuals in a population, but only to the conditions that existed immediately before the selection took place.[8]

Given the radical transformations of environments by humankind, we can expect that many human "adaptations" are not well suited to contemporary circumstances. In a more extreme sense, certain previously adaptive traits are now maladaptive and the basis for significant human disease. (This problem is discussed at length in Chapter 9.)

Opportunism

Rather than being progressive or purposeful, evolutionary change often results from the exploitation of a newly created niche or environment.[9] So-called opportunistic populations or species are most often those with generalized properties that allow them to move and expand quickly in new environments. Such species commonly reproduce rapidly, put little effort into protecting their offspring, and depend on sheer numbers to take advantage of new circumstances to populate a novel niche or environment.

Most disease-causing organisms are highly opportunistic by nature and can readily "fill" an open niche with billions of descendants. This dreaded circumstance occurs in the course of human disease only when the immune system is severely repressed or diminished (as in children with severe combined immune deficiency or in advanced AIDS patients) or when the metabolic conditions of the host favor rapid bacterial or fungal growth (as in diabetes).

Knowing that an organism is highly opportunistic may be turned to therapeutic advantage. By first creating a niche for the organism and then using its presence to achieve a medical objective, its opportunistic characteristics can be exploited. Some early attempts in this direction were made by bacteriologists who used biotherapy to encourage the overgrowth of healthy flora in the throat or gut thereby displacing more pathogenic organisms.[10] Similar approaches are used in bone marrow therapy where certain stem cells are encouraged to repopulate a radiation or chemically depleted host through the use of stimulating hormones. Therapeutic approaches in genetic engineering also depend on finding and encouraging the outgrowth of particularly "opportunistic" cell lines (such as so-called stem cells, primitive progenitors of many differentiated cell lines). Recognizing the opportunistic properties of cells or organisms can thus be used beneficially.

But opportunistic characteristics of microorganisms are often a reason for therapeutic failure. This is especially true among some viruses that have the capacity for both rapid expansion *and* high genetic mutability. As shown in the example below, the combination of these two traits makes for a highly adaptive adversary.

Viral Adaptability

The "Flu"

The influenza virus has proven to be one of the most evolutionarily adept organisms. As such it provides a model for appreciating how evolutionary factors compound the difficulty of medical control. The influenza virus has been responsible for recurrent epidemics throughout history. The most extensive one occurred during World War I and shortly thereafter and killed an estimated 40 million persons worldwide. Unlike infections by relatively stable viruses such as those that cause measles, mumps, or rubella, exposure to the flu does not always confer virus-specific immunity on its hosts. As a result, the highly mutable influenza strains do not have to wait for a whole new generation of uninfected children to find susceptible hosts but can reinfect adults who had a different flu variant earlier in life.

The most dramatic genetic changes of influenza strains have occurred in China, where avian strains of influenza in domesticated ducks have infected neighboring pigs and then the people in close contact with them. When such genetic reorganizations occur in the strain known as influenza type A, as they did in 1957, 1968, and 1977, and probably again in 1993, the resulting flu strain causes widespread illness throughout the world. In the late 1980s, a false alarm for such a massive genetic change led to the "swine flu" fiasco where thousands of persons were unnecessarily vaccinated against a strain that never emerged from China.

The reason for the success of these major genetic changes in influenza viruses turns on the ability of the variant flu strains to reinfect previously infected as well as previously uninfected hosts. The more radically altered influenza strains have a selective advantage over previous strains that left behind many thousands of immunized and resistant hosts.

Like the human immunodeficiency virus (HIV), influenza viruses rely on the form of genetic material known as RNA (ribonucleic acid). By forcing the cell to make a DNA copy of this RNA core, these viruses usurp the cell's own machinery to reproduce. But what makes the influenza and other RNA viruses so adaptable is their ability to change genetically and thereby immunologically from one epidemic to the next. Because the influenza virus changes its makeup so radically and so rapidly, the likelihood of any one person remaining immune to a new influenza pandemic wanes quickly.[11] In fact, if the changes in the virus are sufficiently great, the descendants of an influenza strain that caused an epidemic during a previous year might even successfully infect the same hosts who survived and developed immunity to its progenitor.[12] In this instance, the antiviral forces of the immune system are pitted against the rate of genetic change of the virus. When the virus's rate is high enough, the virus wins; when the immune system is sufficiently adept, the virus loses.

The evolutionary reality of rapid viral evolution and adaptability among the RNA viruses, is bleak for our side. For some viruses, the rate of evolution appears to almost always defeat the immune system. Populations of RNA viruses, such as those causing AIDS and influenza, actually have "maximally tolerable" rates of mutation.[13] That is, their rates of genetic change from generation to generation are so great that it is right at the cusp of survival. With multiple genetic changes the rule in each generation, the flu and AIDS viruses constantly risk compromising their ability to make new viable types. This extraordinarily high mutation rate nonetheless assures sufficient antigenic diversity that the immune system is often swamped in its ability to keep up. As we will see in Chapters 5 and 7, this radical rate of change means that even within a single human host, new "quasi-species" of an RNA virus may arise that baffle otherwise rational therapeutic efforts.[14]

Hepatitis D

Another example of viral adaptability is the evolution of the hepatitis delta virus. This virus causes a highly variable inflammation of the liver against which the patient develops antibodies. But as the disease progresses, so does the virus. A typical patient experiences swings in symptoms from extreme debilitation to partial recovery, while the viral invader undergoes a parallel set of changes. As many as three different forms of the virus can be produced in a single patient, each evolving at a different rate. As a patient's symptomology moves from serious to grave, the more virulent form of the virus is often isolated. Sometimes, the rate of change in the evolution of the virus can be correlated with rapid changes in the clinical outlook of the patient, showing the greatest flux when the patient's symptoms change the most rapidly.

The hepatitis D virus appears to pepper its host with a mixture of virus types that keep the virus ahead of any host defenses that might be mustered. Different RNA strains of the hepatitis virus evidently are selected by each imperfect host response, until a well-adapted form of the virus remains as the disease moves from its acute to its chronic stage. Such microevolutionary changes toward lowered pathogenicity help explain how hepatitis patients with this and other viral types commonly become chronic carriers of a virus that neither kills them nor succumbs to an effective immunologic defense.

Evolutionary Thinking for Viral Control

Recall that the genetic makeup of all organisms is constantly being honed and reshaped to "fit" the environments the organisms encounter. The adaptability of any organism is proportional to the rate with which its genetic system allows it to change in the face of new selective pressures (that is, its mutation rate) and to the ability it possesses to pass on any viable genetic alteration to subsequent generations.

In theory, the constant accumulation of mutations that characterize RNA-based viruses and related organisms should eventually diminish fitness. This is because most mutations are deleterious. Without sexual recombination to sort and "hide" deleterious alleles, asexually reproducing organisms such as the hepatitis, AIDS, and influenza viruses should become less fit over time. Thus, while a constant level of host resistance will winnow a mutated population and select for well-adapted and reproductively fit organisms, a *neutral* environment will not stop the constant accrual of deleterious mutations. Even when there are beneficial mutations that either back-mutate a gene to its original form or compensate for deleterious effects at other loci, the inexorable pull of entropy makes a high mutation rate intrinsically risky. In any asexually reproducing population, mutations accumulate inexorably and mutation-free individuals become successively rarer.[15]

These observations suggest that many RNA viral strains should self-destruct. But those of medical importance appear to be among our most formidable adversaries. How, then, do we account for the success of RNA viruses? The answer in part involves the intensity of selection exerted by the infected host. As long as the host's defense system selects out antigenically distinct viruses, it will also ferret out and destroy a certain portion of the most mutable and mutated viral strains. The immune system may thus be working against the best interests of the host as it refines the viral genome through selection against the less fit subtypes. In fact, immune selection pressure can explain the relatively sudden emergence of potent new viral subtypes from a previously stable population.[16] Paradoxically, if immunity were to be relaxed altogether, it is possible that the virus would accrue a sufficiently high load of mutations to be weakened. Reintroducing a clone of immunologically active cells could then eliminate the virus.

While this last scenario is unlikely because of the current difficulty in designing specific reactivity into the immune system and transplanting it to a given host, it may not be implausible in the future. The fact that RNA virus populations can be held in relatively stable states as long as their hosts exert little or no selective pressure against them[17] creates an opportunity to "set up" the virus for a single, concerted attack. A possible example can be found in mosquito-borne RNA viruses that remain relatively stable over time,[18] making them vulnerable to a single therapeutic agent or rapidly acquired immune state (for example, through vaccination). Similar strategies might be devised for controlling bacterial strains. By adopting a strategy of alternately intense and relaxed selection pressure by using antibiotics with different targets, it might be possible to avoid the emergence of antibiotic-resistant strains.

Another explanation for RNA viruses' success is the ability that some viral types possess to recombine characteristics of related viruses in a single genome. Theoretically, this remote possibility could occur in a host genome that has integrated two different viral types. As unusual as this likelihood appears, it seems to have occurred in the instance of the western equine encephalitis virus, which combines the brain-toxicity properties of its eastern variant with the antigenic makeup of a related virus.[19] This capacity for genetic complementation could be harnessed to link a highly antigenic virus to a genetically crippled version of a pathogen virus to make a vaccine. Such an approach has already been used with vaccinia (cowpox) and hepatitis virus antigens.

The Limitations of Selective Forces

Thus, it is clear that while natural selection exerts a powerful shaping force on all populations of living things, this force will lead to rapid evolutionary change only under relatively limited conditions. But some of these conditions are precisely those created by the chemotherapeutic regimens used against RNA viruses, bacterial strains, and cancer cells. We will examine representatives of each of these categories in the chapters to come. In each of these instances, the intensity of the selection pressures brought about by antibiotics and chemotherapeutic agents results in rapid evolutionary change, often compounding the difficulty of treating the original disease. And, as we have already seen in the section on ecosystem disturbance, broader selective forces that work on whole populations encourage the emergence of new diseases. These forces include agriculture, global commerce, and tourism, which bring old genomes into new environments and produce the conditions for change that encourage microbial evolution.[20]

Natural selection in humans also has profound implications for medical practice. The selective forces that shaped our own evolution toward resistance to disease have been dramatically relaxed during the last several hundred years. As one author observes, "This overall trend toward a diminishing selection for infection-resistance genes has obvious hazards. As we lower our genetic defenses against the old infections, we will almost certainly increase our susceptibility to new ones."[21]

Most critically, we need to understand just what is to blame for our current spate of seemingly untreatable infections. We must come to understand the major actors in this drama–the bacteria and viruses that we have subjected to selection with antibiotics. And understanding the weaknesses and strengths of those few microorganisms that have become pathogenic includes appreciating their coevolution with higher phyla, including ourselves.

The Universality of Life

The common origin and concomitant evolution of life on earth means that many of the genetic products with greatest medical significance can be found across different phyla. Early adaptive responses that emerged in bacteria include some reactions that have been retained in modified form throughout most living forms. Two of these common adaptations are the production of "heat shock proteins" as a protective response to various stressors or the conservation of one or more of the "oncogenes" that promote uncontrolled growth when present in mutated forms. (These will be discussed at length in Chapters 8 and 4 respectively.)

The universality of evolutionary forces in nature also means that we can use those forces in recognizing and potentially controlling microevolutionary events that occur within the body. The forces of evolution that work on people as a whole are at work on the cells within us. In our organ systems, evolutionary processes occur on a microscopic scale, removing unsuited cells and favoring other, more adaptive ones. In these processes, the *deletion* of cells is often as important for healthy growth and development as is cell division. Where such culling and pruning are not allowed to occur, birth defects may arise, memory and neuromuscular systems may be imperfect, and autoimmune diseases may flare. This is because the selective dying of cells is necessary for normal limb formation, brain development, and self-tolerance.

Thus, the common thread of natural selection can be seen in the properties of aging and cancer–our next topic–that can be found in the cells of all higher organisms.

4 Life, Death, and Cancer

Clonal Selection

To develop and function properly, the human body must constantly surveil and cull aberrant, dead, or dying cells from its ranks and encourage the growth and expansion of desirable cell populations. To accomplish this, the body exercises the internal equivalent of natural selection. The mechanism by which this process operates on cells in the human body is a composite of negative and positive selective actions. The target of these forces is usually a single cell, often one with only the slightest genetic difference from those in its surroundings or one that has just recently begun to die. Because even a single cell can potentially generate hundreds of identical descendants, all "cut" from the same genetic "cloth," such selective reinforcement or culling is often critical to the proper balance of the internal milieu. The genetically identical descendants of a particular cell are termed *clones.* When a clone escapes normal growth controls, cancer may result.

My personal realization of the critical importance of this elementary fact for understanding the dynamics of cancer dates back 30 years.

In 1963, I sat in on a lecture given by Dr. Richmond T. Prehn, a visiting scholar at the Weizmann Institute in Rehovoth, Israel. Prehn's topic that day was "A Clonal Selection Theory of Cancer." This arcane-sounding theme was, in fact, a revolutionary challenge to the current orthodoxy that held that all cancers were caused by mutations that allowed cells to escape the body's control systems. Prehn's revolutionary idea was to invoke evolutionary principles (then just beginning to influence thinking in immunology) to explain the cancerous process.[1] In Prehn's schema, cancerous cells emerged from fields of carcinogen-exposed tissue in much the same way as did new species: as a result of a slow and steady selective pressure that winnowed out less robust cells and left behind only those that could survive the noxious conditions created by the carcinogen. In support of this view, Prehn predicted that virtually all carcinogens would prove to be cytotoxic; that is, they would kill normal cells. Cancer cells would be shown to be universally carcinogen-resistant. Hence, Prehn's idea–precancerous cells would be those cells genetically equipped to survive a toxic environment. In time, these surviving cells would outstrip their flagging normal counterparts and we would label them cancer cells.

Prehn's theory was supported by the observation that protracted exposure to carcinogens is almost always necessary to induce chemical carcinogenesis. It was supported by the reality that the endpoint of constant selection pressure by carcinogens is predictably a cell that is resistant to toxic chemicals. Over time, secondary changes such as invasiveness and loss of growth-control receptors would allow the incipient tumor cells to escape from the growth-control mechanisms of the host and give rise to the descendants we know of as cancer.

This simple but profound theory not only challenged the orthodoxy (which I liked), but substituted a kind of Zen koan–in Prehn's vision, cancer was not caused at all! Cancer emerged from tumor cells that were *already* fully capable (in a genetic sense) to go on to independent growth. This powerful notion was buttressed by a spate of experimental data that showed that virtually all known chemical carcinogens were toxic to normal body cells. Cancer cells were, in fact, more resistant to chemical toxicity than were their normal counterparts. That is, the more robust precancerous cells flourished in toxic surroundings where their more fragile, growth-limited counterparts languished. In time, these cells took over the areas depleted of normal cells.

Many experiments have since tempered this picture by showing that carcinogens can directly induce cancer cells to form from any normal cell population. Evidence for alteration of specific "tumor suppressor" genes inside a cell (which predispose it to malignancy) has only recently been confirmed. But it remains true that carcinogens are toxic for normal cells, a characteristic that is still invoked by some contemporary scientists to explain carcinogenicity at high doses of chemicals. Scientists have also uncovered selective forces in other guises that operate on cancer cells during their escape from immunologic control and spread, affirming the centrality of Prehn's vision.

Aging

To understand the cancer process fully, it is first critical to understand aging—particularly at the cellular level—in light of evolutionary theory. In its simplest sense, aging (*senescence* in the vocabulary of the biologist) is the way one generation "clears the way" for the next.

But, at a deeper level, the question of why organisms age at all is tantalizing. It is thought that aging may not occur or is extremely protracted in some animals, notably certain species of tortoises and sharks. The evolutionist would say that the shark and tortoise are aberrations at the periphery of the norms of existence. From a geneticist's viewpoint, aging is simply a compromise between the need to reshuffle the genetic material each generation to provide for variation and the requirements of sustaining existence long enough to reproduce.

In an ideal world, the rate of aging of living things would be related to the rate of change in the environment around them. Where little change occurs externally, little need would exist for generating new genetic variants. Thus, the Galápagos tortoise and the open ocean shark may owe their extended existence to the fact that their environments remain largely unsullied by change and that they face no predators (other than humans). A deeper insight is that living systems do not simply hold their place in the stream of time, they battle against it in synchrony with the forces around them.

Living organisms are engaged in a constant battle to maintain themselves against the forces of entropy and decay. Repair enzymes designed to assure the integrity of our genetic material are a hallmark of this effort. More than forty-one different enzymes exist just to excise damaged sections of the DNA molecule and to allow replacement of damaged sectors. Surely this amount of biological effort points to the existence of compensatory mechanisms to some of the forces in nature that erode living things. Ultraviolet light, radiation, and mutagenic chemicals all conspire to reduce the fidelity of genetic exchange and reproduction. But DNA repair rates do not correlate precisely with longevity, nor do the rates of metabolism, growth, or size—although each has a rough correspondence to the rate of aging in respective organisms. Large animals, which mature slowly and have slow metabolic rates, live longer than small ones, for example.

What, then, is the best way to conceptualize the defenses against aging? Complex organisms such as humans clearly have vital organs with multiple "backup" systems. Forces acting during evolution have created elaborate intracellular defences against the damage wrecked by ultraviolet light, gamma radiation, heat, free radicals, excessive concentrations of harmful ions, and so on. In addition to the DNA excision and repair enzymes, cells have retained certain proteins and enzymes as defenses against oxidative stressors. Others have elaborate polymerase systems for reannealing damaged DNA. Each system works singly or together to minimize the wear and tear brought about by exposure to a constantly stressful environment.

The intrinsic redundancy in these systems is nonetheless subject to failure as multiple defects accumulate. As two leading Russian gerontologists posit, an organism eventually declines until it has no reserve repair apparatus left. Once depleted, the next insult is likely to be fatal to an individual cell, then an organ, and ultimately to the whole organism.[2] This model has some validity for most multicellular animals, but not for single-cell ones. Most single-cell animals have vital systems that lack redundancy but replicate sufficiently often and with sufficient precision that the animals appear never to age. Even complex single cell animals such as *Paramecia* can nonetheless be made mortal if they inherit particular genes.

Differential Aging

Unlocking clues to the aging mystery is complicated by the fact that cells in our body "age" at different rates. Different lineages of cells live for different periods (for example, neurons may last a virtual lifetime, while red blood cells have half-lives measured in days). If there is a genetic basis for aging, how do we explain this paradox: each of our cells has the same genetic complement as the next. But, with the possible exception of Dorian Gray, we die before all of the cells in our body die. Why does this happen?

The answer in part is that some organ systems age and deteriorate faster than others. With the exception of death from trauma, most people who escape atherosclerotic blood vessel disorders and stroke die because of the failure of one or more of the cellular lineages that make up our so-called vital organs–the kidney, heart, lungs, or liver. Yet, with the exception of the heart, each of these organs contains stem cell lines with virtual unlimited growth capacity. (The myoblasts of the heart are self-limiting, having little or no regenerative capacity. That is why once damaged, the heart loses functional capacity irretrievably.) The liver, for example, can regenerate virtual full capacity even if 85 to 90 percent of its mass is removed or damaged. And the capacity to do this repeatedly is retained by the liver over several cycles of loss and replenishment.

In as yet unknown ways, the rate at which we age is strongly determined by our inherited traits. But the rate at which our population has been extending its life span has been too rapid to be accounted for by single gene changes. Other data suggest that age-determining genes are present at multiple places throughout the genome and that gross chromosomal changes may play a role in limiting the life span. This possibility is underscored by the observation of accelerated aging in people with abnormal chromosomal numbers, like those with Down, Turner, and Kleinfelter syndromes–each involving the addition (Down and Kleinfelter) or deletion (Turner) of whole chromosomes.[3] Individuals with these chromosomal imbalances appear to age much faster than the rest of us, showing evidence of senility by their fifth or sixth decade. For persons with Down syndrome, it is now clear that accelerated aging may have a complex genetic basis.

Among some 162 candidate single gene abnormalities associated with changes in rate of aging, one condition stands out in particular. Progeria (from the Greek, "accelerated aging") is an affliction in which organ sites throughout the body grow old virtually before our eyes. Progeric children have extremely high basal metabolic rates. They lose their hair and teeth, develop characteristic skin changes of old age, and have failing immune systems before their tenth birthday.

Today, several different premature aging syndromes are recognized and the genetic control of cellular senescence is better understood.[4] The medical importance of understanding the genetic basis for accelerated aging at the cellular level and its whole body counterpart is self-evident. If we knew what makes some people age more rapidly than others, couldn't we cure their abnormality and ensure a normal life span? But what is a "normal" life span? With advances in medicine, some believe we have approached the outer limits of human longevity. Eighty-five years is now an expected lifetime for women living in Scandinavia. But what about the *quality* of life? Is the vast investment made in medical support care in the last 2 months of life (now averaging around 17 percent of all U.S. medical expenditures) worth the pain, agony, and plain discomfort for the recipient? What about the large percentage of the elderly who lose their independence and must be institutionalized?

Clearly, the goal of medicine is assuring a maximal period of mature well-being, not the prolongation of life at any cost. Indeed, researchers who have looked carefully at the contribution of medical care to the elevation in mortality rates associated with increasing age believe that modern medications have had little or no effect on stemming the rate at which people die as they get older.[5]

Aging and the Immune System

Some systems just seem to give way with age. One of the key systems to do so is the immune system, the biphasic system that protects the body against external enemies and internal threats from dying or aberrant cells. Most of the activity directed at internal threats (viruses, parasites, and abnormal cells) is mediated directly by cells within the immune system. Secretions of immune system cells, notably antibodies, deal with external agents like bacteria and toxins. In turn, as we will see, the immune system's failure opens the gate for the emergence of some types of tumor cells.

The immune system is among the first systems to wane with age, undergoing a profound loss of competence and strength to respond to new antigenic stimuli over time. (Interestingly, the capacity to respond to *previously* encountered antigens is retained much better, as immunological memory appears to be preserved well into old age.) As the immune system loses strength, it may be the pace setter for a host of other conditions of old age. Antibody production declines as does the ability to mount a cellular response. Susceptibility to infection and cancer also increase disproportionately as persons age, suggesting that the life span of certain critical cells within the immune system affects life processes generally.

A reasonable case in point is the thymus gland, which serves as the main "pass through" organ that provides activated T cell lymphocytes to assure that self-reactive cells are either inactivated or deleted. Early in life, the thymus is a light-bulb-sized organ that straddles the windpipe. Once into adulthood, the thymus shrinks dramatically and undergoes a progressive deterioration of function, until only a vestige remains in the 60s and 70s. Autoimmunity (discussed separately in Chapter 8) may be the consequence of the progressive failure of the aging thymus to "clear" self-reactive cells. A major philosophical and biological issue is whether such deterioration represents the "natural" decline of aging tissues generally or if it is a consequence of repeated environmental insults and stressors.

Evolution and Aging

In the absence of environmental insults, would we all live longer? Such an expectation is at variance with evolutionary theory. For one thing, as the late geneticist Theodosius Dobzhansky once observed, evolution only prepares us to reach sexual maturity.[6] "Dobzhansky's limit" predicts that optimal well-being persists through the reproductively active years—but not much longer. That is, our evolutionary heritage affords benefits in youth but leaves us wanting in old age. Evolution seems to only select for individuals to survive long enough to replicate their kind and then leaves them without a genetic safety net. In humans and certain higher mammals, scientists have posited that this genetic legacy creates an "evolutionary shadow." Theoretically, this is why most insects commonly go through an accelerated aging and death (in some butterflies it is almost immediate) just after mating.[7]

In humans, the penumbra or shadow cast by Dobzhansky's limit may confer genetic adaptations that extend life only long enough for adults to protect vulnerable newborns and participate in socializing infants, but then exact a high cost in postreproductive life by increasing susceptibility to certain diseases. If true, this theory would predict that the treatment of diseases of old age, such as cancer and adult-onset diabetes, might profitably involve *regenerating* normal protective systems—such as the immune system—which wane quickly after late middle age. The same theory would predict that the diseases of an extended life span would be legion and generally chronic and unremitting once under way.

The likelihood of dying or developing certain fatal illnesses of old age such as cancer appears to accelerate upward at a geometric pace once the reproductive life span is eclipsed.[8] This suggests that enhanced human survival has simply allowed the unmasking of latent susceptibilities to pathological conditions that increase dramatically with age.[9] This pattern also appears to hold true for conditions such as Alzheimer's disease, autoimmune diseases, and degenerative conditions of the joints and muscles, all of which show logarithmically increasing curves of incidence with age.

All of this is in keeping with evolutionary theory. Natural selection serves only to maximize our genetic contribution to the next generation, not to assure that a given genetic lineage is prepared for a distant futurity.[10]

A corollary of this theory is that every organism or cell has an upper age limit. Now, some remarkable experiments under the leadership of Professors J. R. Carey of the University of California at Davis and J. W. Curtsinger at the University of Minnesota have forced a reevaluation of these ideas. Carey and Curtsinger's team followed the survival patterns of some 1.2 million flies (including the perennial lab insect, the fruit fly, and its relatively recent compatriot, the medfly. Both generally complete their reproduction in the wild within a week or two of emergence). The Carey/Curtsinger team demonstrated that in the very old, mortality rates appeared to level off, and that a small number of fruit flies and medflies can live 100 or even 200 days. [11] This feat is equivalent to the survival of Methuselah, whose life span was reported to be 969 years!

These new data force us reexamine the beliefs propounded by researchers in the 1970s such as Leonard Hayflick of the Wistar Institute in Philadelphia who discovered what he believed to be evidence that cells have genetically determined, built-in clocks that trigger rapid cellular aging and death at preprogrammed times.[12] The new data suggest that past a certain limit, the rates of dying actually level off, and further long-term survival is a plausible outcome for those who reach a certain limit, say, 100 years for humans. If the Carey/Curtsinger fly data were applicable to humans, it would suggest that there may be new limits for human longevity.

Some gerontologists have challenged this interpretation. One group from the University of Chicago and the Argonne National Laboratory repudiates the idea that Methuselah-like survival is possible for those who pass the century limit on human longevity. While admitting that some rare survivors might well approach the outer limit of human survival (set at approximately 120 years), they believe that it will be a matter of chance, not genetics, which brings them there.[13] Given the realities of the prevalence and treatment costs of chronic diseases in old age, this group suggested that an unbridled assault on the human life span may be counterproductive.

Apoptosis

What happens to single cells is critical for the large, multicellular organisms they are part of. In large animals such as humans, cells that are components of various organs must sometimes give way to their counterparts in new organ systems or make space for newer, more specifically functioning cells. To do so, *individual* cells must have a way of dying without compromising the survival of their host.

The existence of so-called "suicide genes" is now well established.[14] Cells respond to the deprivation of growth factors or other external clues by self-destructing. They do so by breaking up their genetic material much the way a printer destroys his plates. Once broken, no further copies can be made. Cells that self-destruct undergo a genetically preprogrammed process of DNA fragmentation brought about by the activation of internal DNA-breaking enzymes (endonucleases). All of this makes sense from an evolutionary viewpoint, since cellular death and senescence is a prerequisite not only to ensure that "old" organisms give way to new ones but that cell lineages die off and not undergo the "immortalization" process that leads to cell transformation and cancer.[15]

The phenomenon by which cells accelerate and cause their own demise is known as *apoptosis*. This property appears central to all higher living things and may be one of the most important evolutionarily determined features of cellular life. Apoptosis is a form of genetically programmed cell death whereby the cell evokes certain sequences that ultimately cause the cell to differentiate, age, and die. Such cell death turns out to be a critical feature of normal organ development. During embryogenesis, for example, the early death of key cells in the embryo permits the full development of the adult features and the emergence of normal form and function in organs such as the eyes and the limbs. A line of cells along the future eyelids must die for the eyes to open; and cells in the web of the future fingers must die in the forelimb bud for the digits to form. Similarly, the immune system as a whole uses apoptosis during the process of "editing" in the thymus whereby it eliminates certain cell lines (clones) that would attack the body's own tissues (see Chapter 8).

This phenomenon of apoptosis brings us back to our discussion of cancer and evolution. Cells with normal amounts of certain "proto-oncogenes" will self-destruct following severe damage to their DNA, say, through toxic chemicals. From an evolutionary perspective, this adaptation ensures that genetically damaged cell descendants do not begin to overpopulate their host. Certain cancer fighting strategies intentionally employ genetically toxic chemotherapeutic agents that induce apoptosis.[16] These observations strongly suggest that a built-in ability for cells to die is essential to avoid the buildup of genetically damaged cell lines. In this sense, cell death is paradoxically necessary for life.

Putting Cancer in Check

Apoptosis in Cancer

Recent data suggest that understanding the molecular basis for apoptosis will provide a key to the control of cancer as well as avoidance of genetic misfits. The normal expression of certain genes, notably the one called p53, appears necessary to guarantee that cells have a normal life span, that they do not acquire the property of unlimited growth that characterizes most cancer cells. We now know that when released from their genetic constraints, defects in so-called tumor-suppressor genes such as p53 unleash the growth capacity of cells. (Other tumor-stimulating genes or "oncogenes" are lengths of DNA that code for special polypeptide gene products that cause or contribute to the neoplastic growth of cells.[17]) Many of these genes keep cells in check when in their normal form, only to lose this capacity when mutated.

It now appears that p53 is part of the "damage control" process that ensures that cells die after injury to their DNA. For example, DNA-damaged cells survive and readily become cancerous in mice lacking both copies of a p53 gene. In normal mice *with* p53, such dangerously damaged cells that can become cancerous are promptly expunged.[18] And families with Li-Fraumeni syndrome (who lack p53) are at high risk to develop multiple "spontaneous" tumors after only the mildest of environmental toxic exposures. Almost to a person, the at-risk members of such families lack *one* copy of the p53 allele. Those with the earliest and most fatal tumors lack good copies of *both* of their p53 alleles.[19] This gene, then, clearly plays a role in ensuring the selective elimination of DNA-damaged cell lines.

If the results of the studies with Li-Fraumeni families and related research can be extrapolated to cancer cells as a whole, it begins to explain why cancer treatments are so often ineffective. Where the targeted cancer cells of chemotherapy lack an apoptosis-conferring gene such as p53, the surrounding cells with the full complement of such genes will be more likely to respond "appropriately" to the DNA-damaging chemotherapy and accelerate their own dying. Paradoxically, lacking this "good" gene that ensures self-destruction gives the tumor cells a selective survival advantage as long as the gene-damaging chemotherapy continues.

In the case of ultraviolet exposure of the skin, the presence of p53 or related alleles is thought to accelerate the death of UV damaged skin cells. Should any spontaneous variants exist lacking one copy of the allele, such cells will likely proliferate at the expense of normal cells following the radiation damage. Should these multiplying survivors include a cell with another spontaneous mutation that deletes the remaining p53 allele, it will be on the way to becoming a full-blown cancer cell. And this realization brings us back to the centrality of Prehn's vision, since the p53-deficient cells will survive better after UV damage than will normal skin cells.

Controlling Cancer

We now know that most, if not all, cancer cells are cells that are genetically unstable and, if left alone, generally progress slowly to increasingly less well controlled cell types. Malignancy, the ability to invade and metastasize, is a property that is acquired sequentially by cells that have escaped initial growth-control mechanisms. Unlike normal cells, cancer cells are almost always immortal. Their unlimited growth is signaled by changes at the chromosomal or genetic level, including the movement of whole chromosomal sections (translocations); the loss of the normal "modal" number of chromosomes (aneuploidy); point mutations or deletions of genetic material; and duplications, deletions, or amplifications of localized areas of certain chromosomal regions that lead to altered gene expression.

As tumor cells grow older, they are prone to a form of genetic rearrangement where "amplification" of certain gene sequences occurs. Amplification entails the replication of gene sequences, leading to multiple copies of functional genes. When this happens, some of the amplifications give the cells a selective advantage over their normal compatriots.

Such experimental observations support Prehn's idea that malignancy is a consequence of selective forces operating on cells with genetic instabilities.[20] Those tumor cells that acquire the properties that give them the most increased growth advantages over their surrounding normal compatriots are usually those with the greatest extent of observed genetic alteration.

A Second Look at Oncogenes

Some researchers have hypothesized that the genes that cause cancer are relics of genes that were essential for the free-living condition of cells more than 300 million years ago. To explain how such relic genes persisted so long without being eliminated from disuse or acquisition of errors, researchers have evoked the idea that oncogenes include genetic code sequences that are immune to error by virtue of having multiple repeated units that cannot be damaged by mutations. As partial support for this theory, S. Ohno of the Beckman Research Institute of the City of Hope Hospital in Duarte, California, has found the predicted repeated sequences in at least one oncogene (c-*myc*).[21]

Related genetic alterations, notably those involving the *ras* gene locus, commonly accompany a wide variety of malignancies. As pretumorous cell populations evolve, especially in bone marrow, they commonly involve cells expressing more and more of mutations to *ras*. Evolution of cell lines with greater and greater malignant potential is marked by this increasing load of mutations. In the abnormal bone marrow state known as myelodysplastic syndrome that precedes many full-blown leukemias, as many as half of the patients have *ras* mutations in their blood.[22] While mutations to this gene do not explain the full picture of leukemia, they have helped researchers trace the evolution of malignant cell lines with unprecedented precision.

While some of these changes may occur randomly, most are manifestations of the cells' response to selective forces. Amplified genes are virtually specific for tumor cells since normal cells rarely if ever allow their genes to go into the overproduction mode typical of cancer cells.[23] Tumors that "overexpress" certain gene products make more copies of a given polypeptide than do normal cells. This overexpression appears to be one of the mechanisms by which at least three of the so-called proto-oncogenes encourage cells to undergo the unlimited growth and proliferation typical of tumor cells.[24] This property may be explained by noting that several proto-oncogenes contain gene sequences that bear a marked resemblance to growth factors that naturally stimulate cell growth.[25] Certain tumors, especially the leukemias, naturally secrete and respond to self-stimulating hormones in a process known as autocrine growth. In this process, instead of waiting for an external "push" from growth-promoting factors, the tumors make their own analogs of these factors and self-stimulate their own growth. Human leukemias generally evolve toward a state of independence where they no longer require growth factors to achieve independent, sustained growth.

To explain why the progressive decay of genetic integrity appears to lead inexorably to a malignant state, some researchers have pointed out that the reexpression of genetic programs suppressed during embryologic development could account for the reappearance of the embryonic properties of unlimited cell growth and migration.[26] The process of becoming malignant is probably considerably more complex than the simple unmasking of old genes would imply. For instance, in the stepwise acquisition of malignant potential in breast cancer, it is clear that cells sequentially acquire the ability to grow independently of hormonal stimulation, resist antiestrogen therapeutic agents, and increase their metastatic potential in an inexorable push away from dependency and normal growth control.

Each one of these attributes is likely to be controlled by a separate group of genetic loci. This can be demonstrated by growing breast cancer cell lines in animals that lack estrogen or immune resistance ("nude" mice) or by maintaining the cancer cells in animals subjected to antiestrogens. The resulting cell lines often include variants, each with specific properties and characteristics like those listed above.[27] These observations strongly suggest that evolution of clones of tumor cells occurs constantly in most if not all human breast cancer patients, since these are precisely the types of resistance problems encountered in treatment.

Since each of these properties contributes to the difficulty of treating human cancer, it behooves the clinician to understand evolutionary factors in tumors, or so it would seem. Unfortunately, it is the rare clinician who has either the skill or the time to trace tumor cell evolution. All too often, the oncologist is too busy loading the patient up on chemotherapeutic agents. Only rarely can he check for microevolutionary changes in the mixed constellation of tumor cells that characterize a full-blown malignancy.

Cancer and Chemotherapy

Unfortunately, when they are subjected to such chemical exposures, tumor cells characteristically acquire drug-resistant genes in patterns starkly reminiscent of those seen in bacteria. As tumor cells divide, advance, and spread through metastasis, genetic changes and rearrangements become more marked and help to shape their new forms and properties. Natural selection within the body culls slow growing or particularly immunogenic cells and favors the growth of ever more malignant cell types. In the words of one research team, "This tumor progression is a highly accelerated evolutionary process, which occurs not over billions of years but within a single human lifetime."[28]

Chemotherapy is also complicated by the continuation of the processes that initially allowed the cells to escape growth control early in their evolution. For instance, amplification of certain genes gives tumor cells a selective advantage in the presence of chemotherapeutic agents such as methotrexate, greatly complicating therapy in some patients. Part of the reason for this conundrum is the fact that amplification of gene sequences can occur throughout the tumor cell's genome, making it difficult if not impossible to localize the source of the chemoresistance.

This dispersed pattern of gene amplification also seems to support the further progression of tumor cells, allowing them to escape further host control mechanisms.[29] When a critical oncogene like c-*myc* is found to have undergone amplification in a tumor, it is often a signal that the patient is doomed to undergo a relapse. This is particularly true for breast cancer, where excess activity of this and one other gene is associated with tumor recurrence after initial treatment.[30] Amplification of related genetic loci also indicates a poor prognosis in patients with lung cancer,[31] and in the childhood brain cancer known as neuroblastoma.[32]

Controlling Tumor Growth

When cancer cells grow, their progressive divergence from normal is often a measure of their lethality. Tumor cells that have devolved to more primitive types often appear embryonic in origin and are called "blast" cells or anaplastic tumor cells–cells without form. Such cells obey few if any rules of normal differentiation and development and proceed to grow unchecked. Patients whose tumors arise as a result of exposure to chemical agents that damage genes (chemical mutagens such as benzene, for instance) have tumors that are often characterized by chromosomal breaks and rearrangements that drive them toward a more blast-like embryonic form. The resulting malignancies are often highly unstable and place their holders in peril. A case in point is the so-called myelodysplastic syndrome. When carcinogen-exposed patients develop this disease, it tends to progress rapidly and be resistant to therapy, properties that researchers relate to the degree and extent of the chromosomal changes that accompany the disease.[33] In patients with non-Hodgkin's lymphomas, a poor prognosis is associated with a greater number of chromosomal changes and additions than in patients with more minor genetic changes and chromosomal deletions.[34]

Often, tumor subtypes expand in a single patient like species on an evolutionary tree. When this occurs, the extraordinary genetic ability that accompanies tumor growth often permits the emergence of separate cell lines with extraordinary survival capacities. The presence of widely divergent clones of chromosomal types unfortunately often spells doom for the patient because of the different susceptibilities and patterns of drug resistance ensconced in each colony of tumor cells, dashing any prospect of success in destroying all of them with a single modality of treatment.[35]

Certain leukemias are examples of such chromosomally unstable tumors. Such instability permits the rapid emergence of divergent clones, making the leukemia prone to rapid evolution into subtypes. This finding is particularly common among patients with B-cell chronic lymphocytic leukemia, a malignant condition derived from cells that normally make diverse antibodies.[36] Because B cells are themselves genetically heterogeneous, it is tempting to think that these tumors arise from different cell types. However, it is more likely that the extreme microevolution that is observed traces its origins to a single cell origin that itself undergoes dramatic and rapid clonal evolution.

Clinical studies of chromosomal makeup rarely begin before a patient has full-blown cancer, making it difficult to study the evolutionary factors in the disease with great precision. However, such a study occurred with a patient with the myelodysplastic syndrome discussed above. In this condition, the patient has a chromosomal defect in one blood cell line that leads to a chronic anemia and the overgrowth of certain white blood cells. Seven years after first being diagnosed with this syndrome, a 42-year-old woman underwent a microevolutionary change in which one clone of the original cell line lost part of its number 7 chromosome. The woman subsequently died of leukemia as a result of the unbridled proliferation of this one clonal cell line.[37]

Emergence of Resistance

When resistance to chemotherapeutic drugs emerges in cancer cells, it is usually the consequence of a long process of inadvertent selection. In the life-and-death battle of the patient against cancer, the treating physicians pit chemicals against the tumor cells' survival. The resulting "resistance" of the tumor is often to multiple drugs, reflecting the common use of combination chemotherapy in the individual patient's case. Multidrug resistance occurs when simultaneous resistance to a variety of chemotherapeutic compounds, often including some that are structurally different from one another, arises in a tumor. One simple mechanism of multidrug resistance in tumor cells stems from a membrane change that lowers the likelihood of accumulating chemotherapeutic agents.[38]

Genetic lability in general makes tumors highly adaptive when subject to chemotherapeutic agents intended to suppress or stop their growth.

Sometimes, a secondary change in the chromosomal makeup in what was a controllable cancerous state can lead to the escape of a cell line.[39] When this occurs, it almost always is the result of intense selection by chemotherapeutic agents that winnow out susceptible cell lines and leave a new genetic variant room to proliferate and take over the host.

Evolutionary Strategies for Cancer Treatment

A few forward-looking researchers have concluded that a close study of the unique attributes of tumors under different stages of progression and in different species might provide innovative strategies for stopping or reversing the process of cancer progression.[40] Approaches that recognize the high evolutionary potential of tumor cells may have an important place in cancer therapeutic strategies. For instance, changing the selective forces rapidly and radically during therapy can create a kind of "evolutionary whiplash" that can catch tumor cell populations off guard in an evolutionary sense.

Strategies of this kind would be at marked variance from the traditional treatment modalities that put patients under a constant chemotherapeutic regimen for weeks or months at a time. The most recently developed strategies are often limited in their efficacy because they are based on a snapshot look at the tumor's genetic vulnerabilities. Others rely on finding unitary weaknesses in the tumor's growth regimen such as a hormone dependency. The newest antitumor agents for controlling breast cancer simultaneously block hormone receptors or cut hormone stimulation.[41]

Approaches to turn back the evolutionary forces that shaped the differentiated state of tumor cells are promising: these include such vitamins as beta carotene, which stimulates differentiation, or *anti*growth-factor hormones that impede or reverse the amplification of growth-factor-like proto-oncogenes. Theoretically, an ideal strategy would include agents that target different elements of the tumor process, combining hormones, chemotherapeutic agents, retinoids, cytokines (cellular hormones), and growth-factor antagonists with such traditional therapies as radiation.[42] Retinoids (derivatives of vitamin A) show particular promise because they appear able to reverse the blockade of normal differentiation that is the hallmark of the malignant state.

A compound that caused tumor cells to acquire more adultlike, functional characteristics would in theory provide a rational treatment strategy. Even more effective would be compounds that encouraged apoptosis, since, as we have seen, most if not all tumor cell populations will have escaped the programmed cell death typical of normal cells. Additionally, many chemical agents that bear a structural resemblance to vitamin A, such as the retinoids tretinoin and isotretinoin, have shown activity in preventing chemically induced carcinogenesis.[43]

Theoretically, such chemicals could be used early in the process of tumorigenesis, ideally at the premalignant stage. For instance, isotretinoin can cause the regression of premalignant changes in the mucosa of the cheek (leukoplakia), and in some initial studies it has proven effective in treating promyelocytic leukemia.[44] However, because the retinoids also encourage the differentiation of blast cells into basophils with a high histamine content and the subsequent release of toxic levels of histamine, their routine use in treating such leukemias is not without risk.[45] Another limitation of so-called differentiation therapy is the very high and often toxic concentrations of the active compound needed to bring about the desired result.[46] Nonetheless, such therapy is biologically "correct" and has great promise.

Once a tumor has been subjected to the intense selective forces of chemotherapy and survived, the success of subsequent therapy is severely compromised. But even here, an evolutionary approach may prove beneficial. For instance, recognizing that chemotherapy damages DNA means that surviving tumor cells are likely to have been selected for enhanced survival and DNA repair. Such enhancement suggests a mode of treatment targeted to those cells. The immunosuppresant drug called cyclosporin A appears capable of suppressing the induction of the genes needed to repair chemotherapy-induced DNA damage, thereby buying time for a second round of therapy.[47]

Some genetically determined conditions, notably Fanconi's anemia, are unique in conferring deficiencies in both DNA repair *and* immunological competence. Patients with this syndrome are uniquely at risk for leukemia and epithelial tumors, suggesting that a deficiency in immune strength may be as important as inability to repair DNA damage in permitting cancer to occur.[48]

Immune Surveillance

All of this points to the critical importance of recognizing that by virtue of their genetic instability and high replication rates, tumor cells have expanded capacities for adapting to changing environments. Often these adaptations provide the tumor cell with a selective advantage over its normal neighbors in terms of escaping from growth control or surviving in an otherwise toxic environment. But, most importantly, it is now clear that the body's primary system for spotting and eliminating tumor cells–known as the immune surveillance system–must also face the prospect of attacking a constantly shifting and evolving target.

My own work in this area began in 1966, shortly after the discovery that tumor cells could, in fact, be recognized by the body as "foreign." This research demonstrated that tumors induced by strong carcinogens such as 3-methylcholanthrene will usually be highly "antigenic" in the sense of provoking a strong immunologic attack. The effectiveness of this attack, however, appears limited to premalignant tumors. My work suggests that once a full-blown malignancy has developed, it has already successfully run the immunologic gauntlet and has evolved to escape immunologic control.[49]

The immune system's recognition of a tumor cell induced by chemicals, of course, does not ensure that a spontaneously arising tumor will be eliminated in a living organism. One of the difficulties in establishing that immune surveillance would work in nature was the apparent lack of antigenicity of spontaneous tumors. It is now clear that at least two different elements contribute to this problem. The first is that most spontaneous tumors are likely to have undergone a process of natural selection to include only those cell lineages that were best suited for escaping immune surveillance. The second is that tumors that are only weakly antigenic may be subjected to such an ineffectual immune attack that their growth is inadvertently stimulated, much as pruning a rose stimulates additional bud growth.

Some weakly antigenic tumors that arise spontaneously do, indeed, undergo some kind of immune stimulation, as postulated by Dr. Richmond T. Prehn. One rationale for the existence of immune stimulation in mammals is that it encourages the growth of any fetus that differs from its mother and gives more genetically different fetuses a slight selective advantage over those that differ only modestly from their mothers.[50] Some evidence for this effect can be found in the literature that demonstrates that the placenta grows larger and better when it differs antigenically from the mother by virtue of its genetic complement.[51] Such a process would ensure more genetic diversity in any mammalian species that acquired immune stimulation. But, at the same time, immune stimulation might also put the mother at risk for tumors that arise *from* the fetus, notably choriocarcinoma (a rare tumor that readily metastasizes), which derive from the fetal trophoblastic portion of the placenta. The existence of immune stimulation also helps to explain why some forms of neoplasia occur more often in organs subjected to weak immunologic attack during the early stages of autoimmune disease. The thyroid in Hashimoto's thyroiditis, for instance, appears to be vulnerable to neoplastic change.

These observations suggest that the initial optimism of using immunotherapy to control cancer may have to be tempered. The evolutionary reality is that tumor cells may indeed "need" to be antigenically distinct to escape from certain growth-controlling factors. But it is unlikely that most tumors can be controlled through reactivating the immune system of a cancer patient. This is so because natural selection via modest and incomplete immunologic assaults during the early stages of tumorigenesis will have selected for tumor types with the ability to evade immunologic assaults. Thus, with the notable exception of bladder tumors and melanomas, very little real progress has been made in controlling cancer via the immune system.

Hence, the evolutionary view of cancer suggests that powerful selective forces operate on a cellular level both to bring the cancer cell into existence and to reduce success in treating it. Future success will depend on combining expertise from evolutionary biologists, oncologists, immunologists, and pharmacologists because, like the insect survivors of millennia of evolution and decades of pesticide applications, the tumor cell is a cell that has evolved under tremendous selective forces.

The same selective forces that render a tumor cell unresponsive to further chemotherapy are at work in shaping the resistance of microorganisms to disease. In both circumstances, natural selection for genetically predisposed resistant cells operates. For this reason alone, understanding fully the nature and breadth of disease resistance must be a central topic for medicine in the twenty-first century.

ed, "The 1990s may come to be remembered as a decade in ctious diseases made a dramatic worldwide resurgence, largely f the appearance of antibiotic-resistant microbes."[1] This decla- n marked contrast with the pronouncements of bacterial con- re implied by virtually every statement or advertisement for s that has appeared since Sir Alexander Fleming's 1928 dis- f penicillin became a commercial reality after World War II. n the outset, antibiotics were heralded as a panacea for every- m fungus-infected pear orchards to the common cold. Penicillin were popular as were nostrums such as antibiotic mouthwashes at sprays. The unvarnished enthusiasm for using antibiotics was p in the ads of the day. Penicillin was touted as a cure-all for ath and body odor, and antibiotics were described as "the gold d" for killing virtually any kind of microbe. Penicillin-containing nouthwashes, and even drinks were available over the counter. ny wonder that when resistant strains emerged, they did so with ance?

ile supposedly under tight FDA control, modern ads still over- e antibiotics. A cross section of ads for antibiotics in a recent f the *New England Journal of Medicine* on my desk is representative.[2] nd recent products are heralded with such headings as "Over- ing Antifungal Success," "Power on Tract," and "The Only Anti- ve with Quinolone Power." The use of such words as *overwhelming* *wer* implies the great potency of antibacterials in vanquishing in- s agents even though true effectiveness is highly strain specific ose dependent. Unfortunately, only the fine print of the ads con- nformation about resistance, and the ad for the quinolone-like anti- neglects to mention that this "power" may be circumscribed by reported resistance to 4-quinolone antibiotics.

he continuing reliance of the medical profession on antibiotics as alls belies the reality that many of the targeted organisms have ac- d antibiotic resistance and continue to produce life-threatening dis- such as septic shock, bacteremia, and pneumonia even with massive iotic treatment. Some totally new infectious processes, such as pseu- embraneous colitis, are actually *caused* by the self-same broad- trum antibiotics originally designed to *prevent* infectious illnesses. In 1982 and again in 1986 I wrote about these problems, encouraging

5 Infectious D

While few physicians need be reminded th last several thousand years have been infect unaware that infections are still the number wide. And along with these deaths comes e the infecting organisms and their hosts. A pa an organism that causes disease symptoms) a selective effect on the population it infects. tailed as a result of the disabling consequence cholera in particular have undoubtedly exert sures on our genetic makeup: Malaria, by indu to sterilize its male victims; cholera, by select dren before they have had a chance to repro

It is less obvious that the converse is also erted powerful selective pressures on infectious force of selection in the microbial world is from we have applied. Antibiotic use has silently shape severity of many of the most important disease

The Antibiotic Connection

For infectious diseases generally, what was once a biotic controls prevailed has since deteriorated badly.

has decla which inf because c ration is trol that antibiotic covery o

Fro thing fro lozenges and thro picked bad bre standar soaps, Was it a veng

W promo issue o New a whelm infecti and p fectio and d tains biotic newl

cure quir ease anti dom spe

public health authorities to take heed of a pattern of antibiotic excess that was jeopardizing human welfare.[3] Neither my own nor others' protestations were taken very seriously, and by the late 1980s, medical problems associated with excessive antibiotic use were rampant.[4] The major source of these problems is simple–chronic overuse of antibiotics has selected bacteria and viruses with multiple resistance to antimicrobial agents.

In economic terms alone, such antibiotic resistance is costly. A recent estimate is that the extra expense of treating multiresistant infections is $100 to $200 million annually in the United States.[5] But economic impact reflects only part of the true costs of dealing with antibiotic-resistant infections. The most serious consequence of antibiotic use is that it has irrevocably changed the nature and makeup of infectious diseases themselves.

Antibiotic Resistance

As documented in my books, Sir Alexander Fleming predicted as early as 1942 that antibiotic resistance to his new drug would be a problem. In fact, the first patient to be treated with a crude penicillin extract, a London bobby who developed an infection after he cut himself shaving, died in 1940 after initially responding to his treatment. This unfortunate policeman was presumably the victim of the first clinical case of penicillin-resistant *Staphylococcus*. After a brief, halcyon period in the 1950s when virtually every major infection appeared to respond to penicillin and its newly discovered copartners, aureomycin and streptomycin, persistent infections with antibiotic-resistant bacteria became common. Even as novel antibiotics such as macrolides, tetracyclines, and aminoglycosides accelerated the antibiotic arms race among pharmaceutical companies in the 1960s, bacteria kept apace through the emergence of novel resistance patterns.

The gonococcal bacteria responsible for gonorrhea (*Neisseria gonorrhoeae*) are a case in point. First becoming resistant to penicillin in the 1970s and then to tetracycline in the 1980s,[6] strains of this organism have kept ahead of most of our traditional approaches for controlling this common sexually transmitted disease. Penicillinase-producing *Neisseria* gonococci (PPNG), which can destroy penicillin directly (and not just be resistant to it) appeared in South Vietnam in the early 1980s and soon spread worldwide. Today, even the substitute drug, spectinomycin, has met resistance, further compounding the problem of treating gonorrhea.

Drug companies unleashed a new generation of antibiotics in the 1960s and 1970s with the hopes of stemming the tide of resistance. Among the inventions were novel beta-lactam derivatives such as methicillin and isozaxylyl penicillins that were resistant to common penicillin-degrading enzymes.[7] But success proved elusive. By 1964, naturally occurring variants of methicillin-resistant staphylococci had emerged, and researchers sounded a clarion call for caution in using any antibiotic. Some even warned of the evolutionary potential of this ubiquitous pathogen.[8] But these early warnings went unheeded.

Beginning in the late 1970s, there were clinically significant episodes of resistance to methicillin and to other antibiotics constructed to be resistant to penicillinases and related antibiotic-destroying enzymes.[9] By 1982, methicillin resistance has spread worldwide from a small epicenter in South Africa, dooming the usefulness of this antibiotic for treating staph until more effective control measures could be instituted.[10]

This disastrous consequence was spurred on by overuse of presumably fail-safe antibiotics such as methicillin and oxacillin. It was compounded by poor laboratory compliance to guidelines designed to assure detection and control of the methicillin-resistant staphylococcus, a strain that now accounts for about 95 percent of all *S. aureus* isolates.[11] Today, clinicians must rely on more traditional and humbling means to control staphylococcal infections. When a staph outbreak threatens hospitalized patients, modern treatments count on a combination of measures. These protective steps include detection and strict isolation of all cases with resistant infections; environmental and employee cultures to determine all potential sources of reinfection; sanitization and eradication of staph colonies, especially in health personnel carriers; and a broad educational effort.[12]

Enterococci Resistance

Enterococci, bacteria that commonly inhabit the intestinal tract, are especially prone to escaping control because they are inherently resistant to many antibiotics and are readily transmitted through simple nursing errors. (In one antibiotic-resistant outbreak, the multipatient spread was tracked to a contaminated rectal thermometer!)[13] Resistance to these pervasive microorganisms has emerged precisely during the period in which the use of broad-spectrum cephalosporins has increased in hospitals. Enterococci are intrinsically resistant to such drugs, giving them a tremendous selective advantage anytime a hospitalized patient is treated with one of the most commonly used cephalosporin antibiotics such as cefotoxitin. Partly for this reason, enterococci are the third most common cause of hospital infection in the United States.[14] Although they are potentially treatable with synergistic combinations of a beta-lactam (penicillin-based) antibiotic coupled with an aminoglycoside, resistance to both types of antibiotics has recently been uncovered. As I will show, enterococci thus pose a double threat in the hospital setting: they make people very sick, and, once resistance to multiple antibiotics emerges, they can pass this resistance on to other germs.[15]

Researchers now hope that the newest generation of antibiotics, which includes cephamycins, monobactams, quinolones, and fourth-generation cephalosporins, will prove more successful than those used in the past. Part of the basis for this optimism is that many of these broad-spectrum antibiotics incorporate features intended to circumvent antibiotic-resistance genes. For instance, the quinolones are designed to be relatively "resistance proof" by virtue of their chemical structure and the likelihood of reduced spread of antibiotic resistance. The quinolones are *supposed* to be able to eliminate the plasmids that carry antibiotic resistance from one bacterium to another and to prevent the conjugation of bacteria necessary to assure the transfer of plasmids with antimicrobial resistance. They are also supposed to leave the intestinal microflora relatively undisturbed.[16]

But, if history is any test, we should not be so sanguine. One quinolone (ciprofloxacin) touted as an ideal antibiotic by virtue of this purported ability was found to be able to eliminate and inhibit the transfer of plasmids only at maximal doses. In fact, resistance to ciprofloxacin and a near neighbor, nalidixic acid, was reported shortly after their introduction.[17] In the mid-1990s we can expect resistance to the quinolones to become widespread. However, quinolones do retain one virtue: they do not disturb the intestinal microflora as extensively as do other antimicrobial agents.[18]

Resistance in Bacteroides

The pattern by which an organism acquires antibiotic resistance has recently been charted by two French teams working out of the pharmacy facility at the University of Lille.[19] By focusing on a single pathogenic bacterium, *Bacteroides fragilis,* the clinicians were able to plot the delays between introduction of antibiotics and the emergence of specific resistance in a portion of the targeted population.

Bacteroides commonly produce colon and skin infections. During the 1970s, virtually no strains of this bacterium showed resistance to clindamycin, a powerful antibiotic. By 1980, 10 percent of the treated strains were resistant, and up to 19 percent were resistant just 7 years later. In 1985, the previously effective antibiotic cefotoxitin began losing its effectiveness against bacteroides, as did piperacillin. Metronidazole, a potent antibiotic known in the United States by its trade name, Flagyl, remained effective during this period but required increasing doses to achieve inhibition of bacteroides. In 1990, the first evidence of resistant strains was reported by one of the two research teams. Up to 1987, a combination of clavulinic acid and amoxicillin, designed to overcome antibiotic resistance to penicillins, worked well against the target organism. Then, forms resistant to even this combination appeared, leaving only imipenem still active against all bacteroides types. A similar pattern of susceptibility and then resistance has also dogged the heels of the one antibiotic most commonly used to overcome other resistant forms of bacteria.

Vancomycin Resistance

The likelihood that antibiotic usage patterns can rapidly become compromised if physicians neglect to consider the power of selective forces is underscored by the history of the rapid emergence of resistance to vancomycin, a previous mainstay of antimicrobial activity.

Vancomycin used to be the major antibiotic used to treat the enterococci bacteria. In developed countries, these pervasive and intractable bacteria are typically responsible for 10 to 12 percent of all infections acquired in the hospital.[20] Patients who acquire antibiotic-resistant enterococci in the hospital are also likely to die. In one New York City hospital, 42 percent of a group of 100 enterococci-infected patients died.[21]

What is particularly disturbing about these statistics is how severely antibiotic resistance has hampered treatment of bacterial diseases generally and enterococcal disease especially. Resistance to vancomycin was first observed among intestinal bacteria in a French hospital in 1988,[22] and soon involved staphyloccal species as well.[23] Beginning in 1989, resistant forms of enterococci spread to the United States and Great Britain, where they disrupted the effectiveness of hospital infection control in major metropolitan centers such as New York and London. At about the same time, vancomycin resistance also developed in so-called Gram-positive bacteria such as staph and streptococci. This development is particularly disturbing because vancomycin is the often the last remaining drug for controlling methicillin-resistant infections caused by these organisms.[24]

The appearance of resistance after more than 35 years of clinical use of vancomycin can be attributed to both the chronic overreliance on this antibiotic and to the presence of a so-called mobile genetic element. Data from Great Britain show that extended and unmonitored vancomycin therapy has been the rule, rather than the exception, generating intense selective pressure for the emergence of resistant enterococci and related bacteria.[25] Most disturbingly, the ability to resist vancomycin's antibacterial action is carried on a transposon (a kind of genetic suitcase) that can pass resistant genes between species of bacteria, including *Staphylococcus aureus* and potentially the *Clostridium* species responsible for pseudomembranous colitis, thereby compromising their successful treatment.[26]

The Extent of Resistance

But vancomycin resistance is only part of the picture. To get a full view of the extent of antibiotic-resistance patterns, it is useful to look at a cross section of the major sources of infection that have acquired resistance in the last three decades. A partial listing of the bacteria that cause the most serious human infections and the drugs to which they are resistant is given in Table 1.

Mechanisms of Resistance

Different bacteria adopt different solutions to resist antibiotic killing. Some of these adaptations include changes in cell wall permeability that exclude

Table 1: The Most Serious Antibiotic-Resistant Microbes

Organism	Diseases	Drug Resistance
Enterobacteriaceae	bacteremia, pneumonia, urinary tract and surgical infections	aminoglycosides, beta-lactams, chloramphenicol, trimethoprim, vancomycin
Hemophilus influenzae	ear infections, pneumonia, sinusitis, epiglotitis, meningitis	beta-lactams, chloramphenicol, trimethoprim+sulfamethoxazole, ampicillin, tetracycline
Mycobacterium species	tuberculosis	aminoglycosides, isoniazid, ethambutol, rifampin, pyrazinamide
Neisseria gonorrhoeae	gonorrhea	beta-lactams, penicillins, spectinomycin, tetracycline
Plasmodium species	malaria	chloroquine, primaquine, mefloquine
Shigella dysenteriae	severe diarrhea	ampicillin, trimethoprim+ sulfamethoxazole, chloramphenicol, tetracycline
Pseudomonas aeruginosa	bacteremia, pneumonia, urinary tract infections	aminoglycosides, beta-lactams, chloramphenicol, cirpofloxacin, tetracycline, sulfonamides
Staphylococcus aureus	bacteremia, surgical wound infections, pneumonia	chloramphenicol, ciprofloxacin, clindamycin, erythromycin, beta-lactams, rifampin, tetracycline, trimethoprim
Streptococcus pneumoniae	meningitis, pneumonia	chloramphenicol, penicillins, erythromycin
Bacteroides	septicemia, anaerobic infections	penicillins, clindamycin
Enterococci	catheter infections, blood poisoning	penicillins, vancomycin, aminoglycosides, erythromycin, tetracycline

the antibiotic; alterations in the cell surface membrane, the binding site for the antibiotic; and inactivation of antibiotics by bacterial enzymes.

The genetic agents that transfer these forms of antibiotic resistance are called transposons and plasmids. Both provide a vehicle for moving genetic material within and between bacterial species and have proven eminently capable of accelerating bacterial evolution beyond what simple chromosomal mutations can permit. The reason: transposons in particular can carry "pre-evolved" gene segments coding for multiple antibiotic resistance across diverse bacterial species lines.[27] Dissemination of whole blocks of resistant genes via plasmids can also generate high levels of multiple resistance, as has proven to be the case for the aminoglycoside antibiotics.[28]

Some of the most prevalent threats to human well-being, notably the *Salmonella* species, commonly carry such plasmids, adding to their threat to populations with inadequately treated water supplies. One of these bacterial types, responsible for typhoid fever (*Salmonella typhii*), can transfer the antibiotic-resistance genes via plasmids to our native *Escherichia coli* strains.[29] By a quirk of evolution, our intestinal tracts contain enormous numbers of *E. coli* that can serve as reservoirs of these plasmids and their accompanying resistance genes. Such "Benedict Arnold" strains of bacteria greatly increase the likelihood of future infections being difficult to treat. The following selected case studies illustrate some of the real life dilemmas associated with antibiotic use.

Case Studies

Case 1: A Hospital Grapples with Antibiotic-Associated Colitis

In a fateful memo to her staff dated September 10, 1987, Dr. Agnes Lattimer, Chief of Infectious Disease, alerted her colleagues at the hoary Cook County Hospital in Chicago about a new outbreak of intestinal disease among some geriatric patients. Her memo indicated that this colitis "might" be caused by a potentially lethal organism known as *Clostridium dificile*. While couched in diplomatic terms (noting, for instance, that 10 percent of patients carry this microbe without experiencing difficulty), Dr. Lattimer only indirectly alluded to the "possible contribution" of staff misuse of the antibiotic clindamycin. With hindsight, this reluctance to attach blame to this antibiotic is mind-boggling since clindamycin is notorious for causing pseudomembraneous colitis. Instead of banning the almost certain culprit outright, Dr. Lattimer only urged clinical discretion in its use. From the date of the memo forward, this antibiotic could continue to be used as long as it was prescribed "with a risk benefit equation clearly in mind."

This ineffectual guideline allowed the epidemic to grow. Faced with increasing numbers of colitis patients, the medical staff rebelled. Under pressure from one key doctor of pharmacy intern, pharmacy services issued a bulletin 5 days later that tightened controls another notch. This time, clindamycin could only be prescribed with a signature from a department head, division chief, or the infectious disease service. (This is clinicalese for saying, "If you're willing to take responsibility, I'll use the antibiotic.")

Faced with compelling evidence that the cause of the continuing epidemic of pseudomembranous colitis was the growing reliance on clindamycin and other broad-spectrum antibiotics, the alert doctor of pharmacy finally called an end to the saga of iatrogenesis. One week after the original Lattimer memo–and aware that broad-spectrum antibiotics also known to produce colitis were being used–a pharmacist issued a directive that extended the antibiotic restriction requirement to cefotoxitin and the other major antibiotics being overused. Finally, as word of this spreading nosocomial (hospital acquired) infection reached the risk management division (a euphemism for the legal services department) clindamycin use was banned outright and an entire ward was closed and disinfection begun. After a month of cat-and-mouse antibiotic chasing, Cook County Hospital rode out the storm, but not before one and possibly three patients had died and almost two dozen sick and debilitated patients were transferred to other units.

Case 2: A Rescue That Failed

Another case study underscores the related problem of controlling infections *after* they have become antibiotic resistant. An 84-year-old woman was admitted to a hospital from a nursing home complaining of gastric bleeding. Her blood cultures showed the presence of a rare microorganism, *Serratia marcescens,* which at first appeared to be susceptible to any of a group of standard antibiotics. (This serratia strain was once considered so benign that it was sprayed in the air as a "tracer" in mock biological warfare exercises conducted by the navy offshore from San Francisco.) So far so good: she seemed to be a prime candidate for antibiotic control. Her clinicians chose two of the most powerful modern-day antibiotics for an initial knockout punch. She was started on ticarcillin and tobramycin. Surprisingly, this course of treatment produced no clinical benefit. After 3 days, the clinical team switched her to a cephalosporin antibiotic (cefazolin) combined with an aminoglycoside (gentamicin).

This time she appeared to respond. Gratifyingly, by the eighth day of treatment, no serratia could be isolated from her blood. But while things looked good on the surface, a revolt was brewing within. On the ninth day, she was tested again only to find that the serratia had returned, but in mutated form. Only now it was resistant to all antibiotics tried, with the exception of a sulfa-trimethoprim combination. But even this combination could not contain the infection. The authors' terse description of the days that followed veils what must have been a desperate but losing battle with a multiply resistant strain of bacteria: "The doses of antibiotics were constantly adjusted because of deteriorating renal [kidney] function. The patient died of multiple organ failure on the thirteenth hospital day."[30]

Case 3: An Outbreak of Salmonella on a Hopi Reservation

In 1983, a previously healthy group of youngsters in a community of Native Americans on a Hopi reservation in the Four Corners area of the Southwest took ill. First one, then dozens sickened with a bloody diarrheal disease. Antibiotic treatments proved especially vexing, as the causative organism–a salmonella species–proved remarkably resistant to antibiotics.

The source of this outbreak was ultimately traced to an adult patient who had been chronically treated with trimethoprim-sulfamethoxazole in the hope of reducing the risk of a recurrent urinary infection. With this chronic treatment, her own intestinal bacteria slowly adapted to the persistent presence of the antibiotics and acquired resistance to this drug and to others. At some point, probably as a result of poor sanitation, the two bacteria met: her indigenous bacteria (*Escherichia coli*) transferred the genetic basis for this increased survival to the salmonella.[31] The result: a mass epidemic on the Hopi reservation that proved intractable to standard antibiotic treatment.

Lessons of the Case Studies

These cases point up a harsh reality—many old and some new disease-causing viruses and bacteria have acquired resistance to a broader constellation of antibiotics than previously predicted. Many, like the elderly patient's serratia infection, have proven remarkably resistant to control. As with the Cook County Hospital patients afflicted with colitis, much of this evolution is occurring in individuals whose immune systems are compromised by old age, infirmity, or AIDS.

Could these outbreaks have been foreseen? The persistent reliance on massively disrupting, broad-spectrum antibiotics at the Cook County Hospital would seem to have been contraindicated by earlier reports that patients treated with cephalosporins such as cefotoxitin carry a ten- to seventyfold increased risk of colitis due to *C. dificile* when compared to patients who receive narrow-spectrum penicillins.[32] Ignorance of evolutionary potential is also the root cause of the continued reliance on dangerous and outdated antibiotics such as clindamycin. While the precise mechanisms by which the body allows this toxin-producing *Clostridium* to propagate in the intestinal tract remain obscure, it is abundantly clear that overuse of broad-spectrum antibiotics is an avoidable medical error.

The problem of antibiotic-resistant bacteria is intensified by the ability of one species of bacteria to transfer resistance factors to another. The danger of otherwise innocuous or subclinical infections picking up this "preformed" resistance is exemplified by the crisis on the Hopi reservation. Following acquisition of the *E. coli* genes for antibiotic resistance, the salmonella were primed to produce an explosive epidemic. The reason—treating a latent salmonella infection with an antibiotic to which it is *already* resistant can transform a smouldering disease that produces few symptoms into a florid one with bloody diarrhea and severe illness and fever. Most critically, the antibiotic treatment of a preresistant salmonella infection can increase the pathogenicity of the strain, thereby reducing the number of organisms needed to transfer the infection to others. Such an effect probably occurred on the Hopi reservation, fueling the fires of an epidemic that had already been raging.[33]

This dangerous situation arises in settings like the Hopi reservation where population densities are high, sanitation marginal, and preexisting resistant organisms abound because of the chronic overuse of antibiotics. Under such circumstances, any further antibiotic use creates an evolutionary nightmare—by depressing the populations of normal, otherwise nonpathogenic bacteria, the antibiotic confers a selective advantage to the resistant strains throughout the population. This advantage leads to a massive proliferation of drug-resistant bacteria that, in turn, leads to greater disease, longer persistence in the body, and more widespread dissemination of disease-causing organisms.[34] Finally, the greatly increased load of billions of resistance-carrying germs can create the risk of explosive, secondary antibiotic-resistant epidemics.

This pattern holds especially true for the tuberculosis bacterium, which also now has antibiotic-resistant strains. (The common misperception that resistant TB strains would prove less virulent than susceptible ones has been disproven by clinical experience—for some key organisms, including the TB bacterium, death is *more* likely following infection with a resistant form than with an antibiotic-susceptible one.[35])

When massive amounts of antibiotics are used in an environment, be it a reservation or a dairy farm, the indigenous bacteria both in and around the people who live there can become antibiotic resistant. Such a sequence is exactly what happens on farms that rely extensively on tetracyclines for suppressing real or imagined bacterial threats to their dairy herds or swine. It is now clear that tetracycline use commonly leads to widespread excretion by farm animals and personnel of multiple resistant bacteria, including the *Salmonella* species that cause human intestinal disease.

Toxic Intestinal Bacteria Outbreaks

Disruption of our normal and healthy intestinal flora accompanies even the use of narrow-spectrum antibiotics. One consequence of such disturbance can be the rapid expansion of antibiotic-resistant strains of pathogenic bacteria. Such an event has been tabulated at the Biomedical Institute of the Central University of Venezuela. Writing in 1989, researchers at this institution demonstrated that the virulent form of enterotoxigenic *Escherichia coli* (ETEC) acquired multiple antibiotic resistance quickly after widespread reliance on standard antibiotics such as ampicillin, kanamycin, and streptomycin for treating diarrhea. (Keep in mind that ETEC is implicated in about 70 percent of instances of traveler's diarrhea.) At the time of their study (about 1987 to 1988), fully 84 percent of the tested Venezuelan strains were multiply resistant to three or more antibiotics while continuing to carry the genes for virulence.[36] Of great concern was the observation that this resistance took no single form but rather relied on a group of plasmids that could carry virulence and antibiotic resistance from strain to strain.

Parallel studies on shigella diarrhea were conducted in Madagascar, with similarly disturbing results. Like the South American ETEC dysentery, the Madagascar *Shigella* strains were multiply resistant to the *seven* most commonly used antibiotics. This multiple resistance made it exceedingly difficult to treat the patients successfully, leading to increased morbidity and deaths.[37] Even more critical, routine use of antibiotics during a shigella infection, especially in the elderly, can lead to a serious and sometimes fatal condition known as hemolytic uremic syndrome.[38] At least one author has suggested that this "antibiotic risk" phenomenon is due to an alteration of intestinal microflora that then allows greater toxin production by the offending *Shigella* species.[39] Such an event could easily happen when the commonly antibiotic-resistant *Shigella* organisms encounter an intestinal dose of antibiotic that wipes out the resident flora, allowing the resistant strain to survive. This also explains in part the fatal outcome for three victims of the recent epidemics of hamburger-carried *E. coli* 0 157-type infections in the western United States. At least one variant of this strain (O 157: H7) has been known for at least 5 years to be resistant to erythromycin, vancomycin, and metronidazole.[40]

Controlling Diarrheal Diseases

All too often, the solution proposed for diarrheal diseases, especially when they occur in developed countries, is to throw more antibiotics at the imagined source of infection. But this only ensures that the most well-off citizens will receive adequate treatment. Citizens in countries like Mexico and Brazil, who rely on available over-the-counter antibacterial medications (including many prescription antibiotics) are unlikely to take adequate doses, further compounding the problem of antibiotic-resistant strains. And this problem is aggravated by well-intended practitioners in distant countries who advocate that tourists be routinely given antibiotics such as cotrimoxazole, norfloxin, trimethoprim, or neomycin to control diarrheal disease before the fact.

While it is true that such routine prophylactic use of antibiotics can reduce the attack rate of diarrheal disease, it is not without cost. One deleterious consequence of such use for local inhabitants–namely, the emergence of silent antibiotic-resistant strains in their intestinal tracts–is rarely considered.[41] To the extent that traveler-mediated antibiotic resistance occurs, it also raises a major ethical issue. While nonindigenous visitors may be protected from infection, they put the native population at serious risk of acquiring infectious organisms that harbor multiantibiotic-resistant genes acquired from antibiotic-using tourists.

A simpler solution, taking bismuth subsalicylate (Pepto-Bismol®, for example) as a prophylactic measure avoids the antibiotic-resistance problem altogether and affords reasonable (65 percent) protection against traveler's diarrhea. A still more radical but simple solution is to mimic the natural resistance of the native population to ETEC strains by giving a concentrated form of milk with natural immunoglobins as a prophylactic measure during travel in high-risk places.[42]

Evolutionary Endgames

How does an evolutionary perspective help us deal with such realities? For one thing, clinicians can recognize that each time antibiotics are used in therapy, they exert tremendous selective pressures against our natural flora as well as the targeted pathogens. Normally, the naturally occurring bacteria and yeasts exist in a balanced and relatively constant state and composition. The metabolic activities of these commensal organisms normally prevent the colonization of the mouth, throat, and intestinal tract by disease-causing bacteria. Our natural microflora and fauna exert this control of unwanted bacteria by competing with them for nutrients and attachment sites on the lining of the throat and intestinal tract and by producing natural antibacterial agents such as volatile fatty acids and bacteriocins.[43]

The adverse health effects caused by overreliance and indiscriminate use of antibiotics is not limited to the emergence of resistant forms of bacteria in the targeted population. When a treatment schedule with a broad-spectrum antibiotic such as erythromycin or tetracycline is completed, it is probable that large, susceptible populations of bacteria throughout the body are decimated. In their wake, new types of bacteria and yeasts can proliferate, along with intrinsically resistant forms of the native types. As mentioned in the Introduction, overgrowth of yeast infections following antibiotic therapy has spawned a whole new industry of over-the-counter antibiotics whose potency would have precluded such potentially unbridled use just a decade ago. Presumably, the widespread occurrence of yeast infections in U.S. women spurred the FDA to consider shortcutting the normal process of careful review of such potent drugs (whose benefits are created by the misuse of other antibiotics). Instead of focusing on the potential risks in terms of secondary overgrowth of resistant strains of yeast, the FDA yielded to the pharmaceutical companies' demonstrations of efficacy.

Ironically, one of the most yeast-inducing programs, an extensive antibiotic treatment known as "selective decontamination of the digestive tract," is still used as a last resort for serious gastrointestinal infections. If this procedure is uncritically applied in too many patient settings, the massive destruction of indigenous bacteria can lead to the overgrowth of other antibiotic-resistant disease-causing microorganisms,[44] especially staphylococcus and enterococcus strains, creating still greater threats.[45]

Clostridium Infections Reconsidered

Understanding the often fragile ecological relationships among bacteria will help us understand and anticipate these major undesirable side effects of antibiotic usage. The massive changes in intestinal microflora associated with pseudomembraneous colitis are now widely recognized as but one of the side effects of the use of antibiotics. As we saw in the Cook County case, when broad-spectrum antibiotics such as cefotoxitin are used, normally protective microflora die in a wave of near extinction, opening up new ecological niches for in-migration and colonization by nonindigenous bacterial species. The cumulative impact of the repeated use of such antibiotics over a period of days to weeks can so decimate the natural populations of microflora that dense plaques or colonies of pathogenic organisms can replace them.

Not surprisingly, one of these interlopers is, in fact, our old friend *Clostridium dificile* discussed in the first case study. Bacteriologists have long recognized the danger posed by such toxin-producing species. (*Clostridium dificile* is a close relative of the botulism-producing bacterium, *C. botulinum*.) Under the protective wave of antibiotic suppression, *C. dificile* hen those infections are so commonly caused by antibiotic-resistant a.[49] Hospitals continue to be the major epicenters of new antibiotic-nt strains of bacteria because of their continued reliance on broad-um antibiotics and incomplete treatment regimens, particularly in ive care units (ICUs). Even at the most prestigious hospitals, the s an evolutionary crucible for antibiotic-resistant bacteria.

n the ICU, bacterial infections are often life threatening. Sepsis or l poisoning in particular poses a challenge to the infectious disease alist. Often such conditions merit the urgent use of potent antibi-, often without the necessary microbial-sensitivity testing. The net lt can be the emergence of antibiotic-resistant bacteria from multi-species.[50]

Overall, the effect of intense selective forces in the hospital is to duce nosocomial (hospital acquired) infections that tend to be more ere and more recalcitrant to medication than their community ac-red counterparts. This is particularly true because the main mode ransmission in hospital settings tends to be nurses and other health e personnel who serve as vectors or carriers of the organism to im-nologically or otherwise impaired patients. Newborns, the very old, AIDS patients are all at risk of acquiring hospital infections that are ctor-borne via health care attendants. As more seriously ill patients mand more caring, they are put at proportionally increased risks.

The often-observed fact that the teaching hospitals associated with ajor university centers will have the highest rate and most serious osocomial infections at first appears paradoxical. Why should the very ospital that ostensibly uses the most up-to-date techniques for sterili-ation and antibiotic coverage be the epicenter of serious disease? The nswer, according to evolutionary biologist Paul Ewald of Amherst Col-ege, may be that the very intensity of the sanitation and disinfection practices of such hospitals selects for only the most robust and virulent organisms.

Chronic care settings where infections tend to be smouldering and long lasting serve as foci for the most intense selection of all, bringing forth the most resistant and infectious organisms. Under such circum-stances, infections can last for weeks to months, and the mortality rate can approach 10 percent of an affected patient population. While other explanations are possible (for example, infections begun by intrinsically

proliferates so vigorously that it can coat th
with toxin-producing bacteria. When this ov
intestinal cells flatten, inflammation ensues, a
duces a sheath of tissue, causing pseudomemb
inflammation is what gives rise to the colitis.
characterized by a florid diarrhea and often a
fatal consequences.

In the case of Cook County Hospital, the b
antibiotic cause of the epidemic did little to reo
The reaction to the epidemic was too little, too
ally has little place in a hospital like Cook Cou
patients are indigent and many are immunolog
AIDS or old age—and hence at increased risk o
and opportunistic infections. In some Scandinavian
is banned altogether because of its well-known sid
the involvement of cefotoxitin should have been sus
since all broad-spectrum antibiotics are linked to
colitis. For the same reasons, risks from the prophyla
for Cesarean sections make it a questionable choice
strated that 9 out of 162 women who received cefot
ine surgery (for Cesarean section or hysterectomy) d
diarrhea.[46] A similar postoperative infection rate oc
monides Medical Center in New York after the use of th

These latter patients were more fortunate than w
Minnesota Veterans Administration Medical Center in M
149 patients were charted with severe *C. dificile*—ass
and colitis in a 1-year period from 1982 to 1983. Ful
the cases were acquired while the patients were in th
of the patients had received multiple antimicrobial agen
frequencies greater than had diarrhea-free patients at th
tal.[48] Many of these patients became severely ill, and it is
colitis contributed to deaths in at least a few instances.

Nosocomial Infections: Getting Sick in the Hospit

The first two case studies point up the risks inherent in u
spectrum antibiotics to treat serious infections in hospital setti

larly w
bacter
resista
spectr
inten
ICU

I
bloo
spec
otics
resu
ple

pro
sev
qu
of
ca
m
or
ve
d

virulent microbes), Ewald interprets such patterns of increasingly serious infections in chronic care institutions as evidence of evolutionary phenomena at work. In his view, a particularly potent nidus for infection can be created by subjecting hospital flora to repeated encounters with antibiotics and disinfectants.[51]

Support for this hypothesis comes from the observation that the most dangerous, multiresistant organisms are more common in tertiary care centers than they are in acute care hospitals. This is true in part because long-term hospitalized patients at veterans' hospitals and homes for the elderly are often immunologically depressed and subjected to repeated bouts of infection. According to Doctor M. F. Parry of the Stamford Hospital in Connecticut, clinical factors that promote the appearance of resistant microorganisms are most often encountered in such tertiary care facilities. These factors include prolonged therapy; the presence of persistent foreign bodies such as shrapnel; sequestered objects (including metal or prostheses common to veterans); and inadequate surgical removal of necrotic tissue or abscesses, an especially severe problem where patients often have chronic bed sores.[52]

Since such nosocomial infections are particularly virulent and affect the most seriously ill, it is of some great concern that researchers have charted a dramatic increase in the prevalence rate of nosocomial infections. A research group at the University of Virginia documented almost a threefold increase in hospital-acquired urinary infections in the decade between 1974 and 1985, reporting an increase from 12.3 to 32.2 per 10,000 patient discharges (a 263-percent increase).[53] Overall, nosocomial infection rates are commonly between 1 to 2 percent, but teaching hospitals occasionally report a 10 percent occurrence rate!

Solving the Resistance Dilemma

The commonly expressed opinion that such infections can be charted and controlled by improving sanitation alone or by attempting to outwit antibiotic-resistant organisms with the blind use of broad-spectrum antibiotics is simply wrong-headed. The continuing occurrence of passive carriers among hospital personnel and the intensity of most hospital antibiotic use patterns, both continue the process of selection for virulence and resistance.[54] In many instances, the result of failing to control these factors is a continuing pattern of deadly infections.

An antibiotic-resistant infection is an especially vexing event when it occurs as the result of the unnecessary use of antibiotics. This circumstance frequently occurs when treatment is given in anticipation of postsurgical wound infections. While a limited list of approved procedures for prophylactic antibiotics has been developed by the Veterans Administration, few hard-and-fast rules exist that limit the discretionary, preemptive use of antibiotics. The temptation to use an antibiotic as a "surgical cover" for high-risk procedures not on this list remains strong, especially during abdominal surgery. A case in point is hysterectomy. Postoperative infections are relatively common following uterine surgery, affecting up to 12 to 15 percent of patients. As we saw in the discussion of *Clostridium* overgrowth in uterine surgery, some researchers still advocate using broad-spectrum antibiotics as part of the "prepping" for elective abdominal hysterectomy. But this is a questionable choice at best, since using valuable cephalosporin antibiotics to assure sterility of the operating field has dubious merit and reduces their overall usefulness for treating more serious infections. And, as we saw in the case study of Cook County Hospital, such use also encourages the life-threatening overgrowth of intrinsically resistant bacteria.

Noncompliance with Evolutionary Common Sense

Other patterns of antibiotic misuse may be contributing to the growing spread of antibiotic resistance. A case in point is the routine use of antibiotics such as amoxicillin to treat children with a fever because the children "appear" to have a bacterial infection. Following findings that antibiotic use did not reduce the severity of the illnesses experienced by such children any better than did a placebo (sugar pill), a research team from Northwestern University and the University of Pennsylvania concluded that routine use of amoxicillin in feverish, sick children without a specific diagnosis is contraindicated.[55] Yet, even this caution has been greeted with resistance and apparent resentment for dictating "rules" for medical practice.

Even if antibiotics were to be used more rationally, it remains to be seen if the medical profession would apply effective evolutionary principles to control the most lethal or virulent bacteria. A promising example is the way in which dangerous infections in cystic fibrosis children are being handled. Here, recognition of transmission-related increases in virulence and the necessity for strict hygienic controls *before* antibiotics are called in provides a model for infection control. The problem is real enough: children and young adults with cystic fibrosis are particularly vulnerable to lung infections because of a greatly reduced ability to remove pulmonary secretions.

A previously rare cause of human infection, the organism known as *Pseudomonas cepacia,* has somehow shifted from plants to human hosts. In cystic fibrosis patients, the chronic overreliance on antibiotics has apparently contributed to its emergence. To limit the spread of multiresistant *Pseudomonas* strains, special steps have been proposed to limit contacts between patients with cystic fibrosis, especially at summer camps. By proscribing gatherings where rapid transmission between affected and unaffected patients could increase virulence, clinicians have begun to deal effectively with this dangerous problem.[56]

Solutions

The cystic fibrosis story suggests that solutions for limiting the continuing emergence of antibiotic-resistant diseases can be found. Some of the basic principles–derived from evolutionary theory–are as simple as they are reasonable–reduce the selection pressure exerted by routine reliance on antibiotics and shift control over to the body's own defenses where practicable. These ends can be accomplished by implementing a simple series of recommendations:

1. Strictly limit the use of antimicrobials, especially when they are proposed for prophylaxis (that is, when they are used in anticipation of infection, say, in surgery not involving a joint, the heart, or the intestinal tract.[57]

2. If antibiotics are indicated, use appropriate doses to assure complete eradication of the infectious organism.

3. Avoid drugs to which resistance has been shown to emerge rapidly in a particular clinical setting.

4. Use susceptibility tests prior to using antibiotics.

5. Use antibiotics intermittently to break up constant selection forces.[58]

6. Increase reliance on vaccines (for example, the pneumococcal vaccine).[59]
7. Take some antibiotics out of commerce altogether, to permit the re-emergence of vulnerable strains.

In spite of the reasonableness of each of these proposals, they fly in the face of habits and attitudes that have typified medical practice over the last century. European countries and Russia in particular, have resisted the use of vaccines such as the pneumococcal vaccine.[60] And the U.S. reliance on chemical control rather than available vaccines results in the unnecessary use of millions of doses of antibiotics yearly.[61] Moreover, the insistence on physician autonomy in this country often means that antibiotics that might otherwise be limited by hospital infection control committees are, in fact, employed in questionable circumstances. When one of the recommendations listed above appears in print, it is often honored in the breach.

A case in point is the response to recommendations to reduce the use of prophylactic antimicrobial therapy during certain types of routine surgery. When a prominent clinician stressed the limited usefulness of antibiotics prior to some widely used surgical procedures such as prostatectomies, installation of cerebrospinal shunts, and elective abortions,[62] he was met with a flurry of objections.[63] A similarly cautious report that downplayed the usefulness of antibiotic treatment of febrile children with nonspecific illnesses was met with an editorial response that said in effect that if the physician wants to use an antibiotic he should go ahead and do it even if its effectiveness remains unproven.[64] This in spite of the fact that the author had documented a higher incidence of diarrhea in childen so treated!

Adding to the mistaken belief that the solution to antibiotic resistance is simply more antibiotics, clinicians have urged that nosocomial infections be met by the development of still more agents with "improved antimicrobial activity" and have downplayed the reduction of antibiotic use.[65]

Ethical Concerns

Retaining the "right and privilege" to prescribe what is deemed best for one's own patient is a lofty ideal. But it can compromise the overall effectiveness of antibiotics for the community as a whole. If repeated often enough, such individually justified decisions can reduce the ability of antibiotics to control infection in the population at large. Resolving this tension between medical ethics (put the patient first) and public health ethics (protect the common good) requires a balancing of autonomy and justice. In the case of antibiotic-resistant diseases, it is evident that we have gone too far in the direction of autonomy by permitting physician discretion in all cases. Limits like those propounded by the Veterans Administration for general and prophylactic use of antibiotics[66] are both necessary and prudent if we are to secure our future against infectious disease.

At a minimum, it is clear that shifting public health efforts toward preventing transmission of infectious diseases rather than the current emphasis on treatment after the fact is critical. Improvements in hygiene both in the hospital and in the community would be minimal first steps; and reducing reliance on prophylaxis and increasing dependence on vaccine use are both essential.

And while it would seem that your personal choices of infection control are severely limited because of your role as consumer and patient, you need not allow yourself or your children to be needlessly exposed to antibiotics that may create resistant strains or dependency. For instance, not every ear ache in a nonfebrile child is a candidate for a course of antibiotics. Nor is a yeast infection necessarily best treated with potent antifungal medications, even if they are now available over-the-counter. Some alternatives include the tried and true nostrums of bed rest, better attention to diet, immunizations, and conditions conducive to maintaining a strong immune system.[67] Certainly, insist on your right to fully informed consent before accepting antibiotic treatment for you or your family. Remember that you deserve to hear both the benefits and the risks of any prescription, including the risk that future health may be compromised or limited.

Conclusions

As we have seen, multiple antibiotic resistance is a dramatic example of evolutionary change brought about by human activities. Part of the reason this rapid emergence of a health-threatening phenomenon took us by surprise is that we had expected bacterial evolution to move in the snail's pace of traditional, Darwinian norms. We now know that antibiotic resistance can occur by the radical rearrangement of the genes that determine resistance and by the high mobility of the genetic elements (transposons, plasmids, and so on) that ensures their rapid propagation and dispersal.[68] As one commentator puts it, "microbes are not idle bystanders, waiting for new opportunities offered by human mobility, ignorance or neglect. Microbes possess remarkable genetic versatility that enables them to develop new pathogenic vigor, to escape population immunity by acquiring new antigens, and to develop antibiotic resistance."[69]

These facts have been known for more than 20 years. It is now clear that radical solutions are needed to bring infectious diseases back under control. A downscaling of reliance on chemical fixes to our problem and a return to an emphasis on vaccines is paramount. New studies, particularly those focused on infants, establish that antibiotics are *not* necessary for the safe care of febrile patients.[70] The recent resurgence of a host of infectious diseases in Russia in the face of relaxed immunization policy is a tragic reminder of the cost of curtailing vaccination efforts.

To bring the immune system into play, we must also avoid toxicants and other agents that reduce its power. Immunosuppressant medicines, chemicals, and hormones are just now being recognized in the new field of immunotoxicology. And, finally, reliance on tried-and-true methods of increasing host resistance by nutrition (for example, by adding more sources of beta carotene) are the simplest and most cost-efficient methods of skirting the ultimate travesty of having miracle drugs that do not work. To continue to squander antibiotics in often superfluous treatments or to jeopardize their continued effectiveness by inappropriate prescriptions is evolutionarily foolish—the germs that survive are often stronger than ever. Perhaps most seriously of all, we still do not know what makes such diseases virulent in the first place.

6 Lethal Germs

"Why do some diseases kill so quickly?" is a question in the back of the mind of every medical student who confronts his or her first patient with septic shock, a heart attack, or a stroke. For the last two, the answer is physiologically straightforward: lack of oxygen. For the first,[1] and for related bacterial and viral diseases, the answer is still a mystery.

There is a tale of a nurse from Yale University who was treating an African patient who had what appeared to be a rare tropical infection—raging fever, hemorrhages, and fulminant shock. She stopped work, went to her room, and was dead before the next shift. The disease was caused by an agent that came to be known as the Marburg virus, after the town in Germany in which it was eventually isolated. The story would end there were it not for the burgeoning international trade in monkeys, stimulated in part by research in human viruses.

The Monkey Connection

In 1967, animal traders sent a shipment of African green monkeys from Uganda to the United States. There, several of the technicians who were developing cell cultures from the monkeys were taken ill—very ill. They experienced facial swelling, bleeding, and shock, and were only rescued by medical heroics at the local hospital. A few days later, several additional technicians in the laboratory below the cell culture lab suddenly became ill. Only immediate supportive therapy saved their lives. The cause of their illness was trace numbers of Marburg virus that had seeped through the floor or had been carried by air ducts to the workers below. Once again a virus had infected across species' lines.

And were this the only case of a potentially fatal disease arising from some imported monkeys, the story would end there. But 22 years later, a repeat episode jarred the medical community awake. This time the culprit was a near relative of the Marburg virus known as the Ebola virus. In a primate holding facility in Reston, Virginia, a strain of the virus was isolated from cynomolgus macaques brought over from the Philippines. Again, three lab technicians were infected, but, mercifully, their symptomology was much less extreme than that of the earlier technicians.[2] A quick check by the Centers for Disease Control (CDC) turned up two other laboratories, in Pennsylvania and Texas, with similar contamination problems. All monkey shipments were halted and a general embargo was declared, lest the disease become established in the human population.[3] But back in Africa, nature has not been so benign. The Ebola strains there, notably the Zaire variant, have proven notoriously lethal in their pathogenicity.

What this virus has in common with several other primate microorganisms is a high degree of virulence and apparently recent movement from monkeys in the wild to the local human population. Among the monkey viruses that can cause serious and fatal human diseases are simian variants of hemorrhagic fever (related to Ebola); a herpes virus simiae (B virus); respiratory syncytial virus; encepalomyocarditis virus; and simian immunodeficiency viruses.[4] All but this last group of viruses have been linked definitively to human illness, and suspicion is strong that AIDS had its origins in the simian variant of the human immunodeficiency virus (HIV) (see Chapter 7). And like Ebola and Marburg, all (including HIV), cause particularly severe forms of human disease.

The fact that so many viral organisms among our nearest relatives can infect humans and cause serious and often fatal diseases points to a major pattern: the most lethal viral and perhaps bacterial illnesses are often the newest ones to "cross-over" to the human species. Additionally, as we saw in Chapter 2, many of the most lethal human diseases are those like plague that are carried to us by insects—arthropod "vectors" such as ticks or fleas that bear often highly virulent, disease-causing organisms.

Virulence and Vectors

Commensalism

A common misunderstanding of evolutionary theory is that all organisms that share a common host will evolve toward a benign interaction. According to those who hold this benevolent view, all parasitic and chronic infectious diseases should evolve toward "commensalism" (from the Latin, "living at the same table"). The idea behind this theory is that as organisms evolve together in the intimate proximity enforced by parasitism, they would of necessity tend to become mutually tolerant to ensure the maximal opportunity for the survival of both host and invader. Over time, then, those parasites that had the least adverse effect on their hosts would be the ones most likely to survive long enough to reproduce and spread their offspring to another host.

It is true that some organisms reach an evolutionary accommodation with their hosts, and establish a commensal relationship, where mutual tolerance is the rule. For these organisms, a benign symbiotic pairing keeps the two organisms, which once had an antagonistic relationship, in a permanent evolutionary embrace of mutual dependency. While this relationship holds true, for example, for certain algae and fungi living together as lichens, it hardly explains the relationship that humans have with most of the microscopic world. Notwithstanding our intracellular mitochondria, which appear to be a vestige of a former parasitizing microbe, most of the bacteria in our bodies exist as a permanent drain on our resources. Even our most compatible microorganisms, intestinal bacteria such as *Escherichia coli,* live in a state of dynamic equilibrium between neutrality and outright pathogenicity. A partial proof of the chronic negative burden posed by "commensal" and seemingly friendly organisms such as *E. coli* are experiments with antibiotic-fed chickens and germ-free mice, which show that intestinal bacteria generally lower growth rates and reduce vitality. Certainly many, if not most, of the microbial species that are outside of us contain members that are in a state of perpetual warfare for the bounty represented by our nutrient-laden bodies.

Transmitting Serious Infectious Disease

The benevolent theory of parasitism belies a still more powerful evolutionary reality: Virulent organisms need not mollycoddle their host in order to survive *if* they can successfully proliferate and reproduce before or even shortly after the host dies. In fact, as we will see, the most virulent organisms often retain an efficient means of transmitting themselves even after their primary host is infirm. This reality leads to a corollary: If selection favors the rapid movement of infecting organisms from one host to another, it is also likely to also encourage the genes for rapid growth–and most likely, virulence–in the pathogen.

The mystery of pathogenicity is that an organism that is so virulent that it kills its host immediately would also appear to be one that loses out on the transmission lottery–if the host is so sick that it cannot pass the disease on, how does the organism propagate? Evolutionary biologist Paul Ewald has suggested a radical answer to this seemingly intractable paradox. Ewald has proposed that virulent pathogens solve their transmission problems by achieving such high concentrations of organisms within an infected host and such high proliferative ability once inside a new one, that even minor contact or contamination becomes an opportunity for transmission.[5] This is especially plausible when insect vectors or environmental vehicles (such as water-borne infections) replace the more typical person-to-person disease spread. The introduction of a vector that can serve as a passive transport system for a microorganism often replaces that organism's need for elaborate transfer mechanisms and serves as a kind of *deus ex machina* that allows the pathogenic virus or bacteria to concentrate on its own reproduction.

Another Look at Nosocomial Infections

We can reexamine hospital-acquired infections in this light. Most nosocomial infections are characterized by high densities of microorganisms in the infected hosts, who serve as "reservoirs" of disease. Coupled with a wide number of supernumerary hosts (nurses, janitorial staff, and such) who become unwitting vectors of the illness-causing germs, a germ that establishes itself in the crowded conditions of a typical urban hospital can count on lots of help for its spread. In nurseries, for example, certain infants carry and disperse so many staphylococcal or haemophilus organisms that they are called "cloud babies." Once such a reservoir of infection exists, the movement of a deadly pathogen is no problem–a nurse touches each infant in a nursery up to twenty times a day, more if the infant is sick. And only under the strict hygienic controls of the neonatal intensive care unit is there much attention to interbaby transfer of germs.

Environmental selection for the survival of potentially virulent organisms is also encouraged in hospital settings because fecal contamination of surfaces is likely, especially where diarrheal diseases occur. Aerosols containing infectious droplets can be produced just by flushing a toilet or taking a shower. In the hospital, microorganisms are often subjected to intense selective pressures by the institution's own sanitation and disinfection services. Repeated exposure to the same surface disinfectants over months and years can allow resistant bacterial strains to emerge. Hence, common hospital germs (such as *Pseudomonas aeruginosa*) have come to thrive in slop pails and disinfectant solutions as well as in flower pots. Our previous discussion of nosocomial infections can be reexamined in this light.

As support for the hypothesis that natural selection over time leads to a more virulent pathogen, Ewald observes that short-lived epidemics in hospitals are associated with a lower mortality rate than are long-lived ones. According to Ewald, this is because the opportunity for selection of resistant and robust microorganisms is constrained by a "quick" episode of infection, whereas a long one, lasting for weeks to months, can exert a continuous selection pressure for more virulent and resilient microorganisms. Indeed, in such chronic epidemics, it is not unusual to find mortality rates approaching 10 percent.[6]

Virulence in the Body

These observations ignore a vexing question: Why should conditions of microenvironmental hardship and relative ease of transmission *necessarily* lead to greater virulence? One answer is that the ability to reproduce quickly and infectiousness go hand-in-hand. To the extent that "virulence" is often the cost to the host of the offending organism, replicative ability can explain much of the toll of the disease process. The Ebola virus, for instance, appears to replicate extraordinarily quickly in the endothelial cells that line the blood vessels. The subsequent destruction of the vessel walls is what leads to the hemorrhage and death of so many African victims. By contrast, the TB bacillus replicates extremely slowly (a matter of days) by bacterial standards, and except in profoundly immunodepressed patients, produces a correspondingly chronic, smouldering disease that weakens and eventually kills most of its victims.

Delayed Transmission

A corollary to Ewald's hypothesis is that where transmission from parasite or pathogen to host is "easy," the parasite can be more virulent. A recent finding in insects supports the notion that the availability of prey is proportionate to the virulence of the parasite.[7] If this result applies to higher phyla, it would mean that it would be theoretically possible to reduce the lethality of an infectious disease by reducing the number of available hosts (comparable to reducing prey density in predator-prey relationships) and/or delaying its transmission from host to host.

Obviously, decreasing the transmission of diseases has been an objective of public health programs. But now it might be possible to predict the result of increasing the difficulty of a new infection as one which also reduces the virulence in the infecting organism. That is, factors that *delayed* the transmission of a disease could also select for less virulent organisms. This reaction appears to help explain the low virulence of HIV-like viruses in Japan (for example, HTLV-1), where the rate of sexually transmitted disease in general is appreciably lower than in the United States. This theory suggests that simply reducing the rate of the spread of such sexually transmitted diseases as syphilis, gonorrhea, chlamydia, and even AIDS could begin to transform them into more benign pathogens with longer waiting periods (latencies) between infection and outright disease, as well as lesser virulence (the intensity of the resulting illness). In practical terms, this means that the condom can be seen as an agent of evolutionary change.

Person-to-Person Transmission

Natural selection tends to exert pressure on disease-causing organisms that rely on person-to-person transfer (and that have limited viability outside their hosts) to "go slow" and not cause life-threatening illness. The rationale for this evolutionary wisdom is self-evident: Organisms like the leprosy bacillus, which have long latencies between infection and full-blown illness were among the most successful and prevalent diseases of humans. In theory, long latency and low virulence ensures that an infectious organism has a chance to be transmitted before causing such serious or disfiguring illness that the host is destroyed. Such diseases have evolved with the human species for a long time. Wart viruses, syphilis treponemes, herpes simplex viruses, and the rhinoviruses that cause the common cold are but a few examples. Other ancient diseases, such as tuberculosis in particular, appear to defy this rule since they are notable for their infectiousness and relatively high virulence, ultimately handicapping or killing most of their victims where medication is scarce. But historically, the TB bacterium has had the capacity of being able to survive for protracted periods outside the human body, allowing it to retain its incapacitating power and still be transmittable.

Another aspect of virulence is the microorganism's ability to produce a toxin that poisons the host. As we will see in the chapter on autoimmunity (Chapter 8), many seeming "toxins" are actually a part of the defensive repertoire of their carriers. Organisms that produce toxins are usually not highly infectious, as infectivity and toxin production are uncommon traits. Also, as each trait requires a separate set of mutations at different parts of the genome, a dual-threat germ thereby "uses up" valuable genetic space. An organism that makes a toxin is thus potentially at a disadvantage among its compatriots in terms of its capacity for transmission. Nonetheless, exceptions to this corollary exist, especially among water-borne diseases. Here host-free transmission frees the microorganism to be as virulent as circumstances permit. This is true especially for water-borne transmission in areas where hygiene is poor. Under such conditions, as patients become sicker, they constantly recontaminate the water supply. As long as the organism has egress to an infection sink such as a contaminated watercourse from which it may contaminate more victims, it is freed from the constraints operating in person-to-person transmission.

Support for this idea comes from data that show a correlation between ease of water-borne transmission and lethality. Where pathogens that cause diarrheal diseases required person-to-person contact for successful reinfection, they were less virulent than when they were able to infect large numbers of persons simultaneously via a common water system.[8] This idea is also corroborated by the finding that the classic water-borne infections caused by the vibrio form of cholera and the diarrheal infections caused by *Salmonella typhii* are almost always more serious than are the less virulent enterotoxigenic forms of *E. coli* that generally require food or fecal contamination for transfer.

You may wonder how this evolutionary model can be true if the typical typhoid or cholera victim is so often bedridden, seemingly unable to actively transmit contaminated feces back to the watercourse where the infection is sustained. To answer this enigma, it is necessary to take a closer look at cholera.

Cholera as a Model

We are in the midst of the most recent of many global pandemics from cholera, a rapidly debilitating and dehydrating diarrheal disease. Cholera is caused by a water-borne vibrio, a microscopic, motile (swimming), comma-shaped bacterium. The disease itself occurs in four stages beginning with the invasion of the vibrio. During this incubation period, the patient typically has diarrhea, headache, and fever. Without treatment, the patient enters the second stage and typically develops severe purging, vomiting, and cramping accompanied by a worsening of the diarrhea. In the third stage, the patient may collapse completely.

The current outbreak began in Peru in January 1991, largely as a result of social upheaval, poverty, and the absence of social services that assure a safe water supply. (Such services had been guaranteed to the people by the Charter of Punta del Este in 1961, of which Peru was a signatory.) By 1992, the cholera epidemic had reached fourteen Latin American countries, affecting 390,000 people and causing some 4,000 deaths. The 3,000 deaths in Peru could have been even greater had not many communities rallied together to provide rehydration programs and sanitize water supplies.[9] After the outbreak swept through South America, the epidemic spread back to the African continent where it had last been introduced 20 years before. In Africa, social upheavals indirectly created the circumstances for the reemergence and flare up of cholera, an endemic disease for many nations lacking effective sanitation. In the 1970s and 1980s, massive social dislocation occurred, resulting in millions of persons living as refugees in densely populated camps. The breakdown of sanitation during this period also encouraged the survival of cholera vibrios on leftover rice and other foodstuffs. Funeral practices may also have contributed, as the women who prepared the bodies of the cholera victims also prepared the food served to the mourners.[10] When conditions improved and the camps broke up, many sick, but still ambulatory refugees took cholera with them.

As of mid-1993, cholera was reported in thirty of the forty-six African countries and was particularly prevalent in Mozambique, Malawi, Zimbabwe, and Zambia. The largest epidemic of cholera is currently threatening Southeast Asia following a massive outbreak in Bangladesh which began in December 1992. By the end of March 1993, cholera had been responsible for 107,297 documented cases of severe diarrhea and 1,473 deaths.[11] Many others undoubtedly went unreported.

The causative organism for this outbreak was an entirely new strain of *Vibrio cholerae,* called O 139. Even developed countries are within the global reach of this antibiotic-resistant organism. (A case of this highly lethal disease was reported in California in a traveler who returned from a trip to India.) This new agent greatly expands the definition of cholera-like diseases and represents a serious threat to spread worldwide, creating the potential for a new pandemic. Faced with this new threat, the World Health Organization (WHO) has asked all nations to report immediately to WHO all illnesses caused by this strain. Concern is intensified because persons who have previously gotten cholera or have been vaccinated against it are not immune to this new strain.[12] Thus, *V. cholerae* O 139 is part of the growing number of organisms that pose novel and uncharted threats to public health.

Cholera owes its lethality to a combination of factors. Because of the typically high densities of bacteria in contaminated waterways, cholera vibrio need not depend on the survival of its victim for propagation. A person suffering from cholera need only contaminate bedding or clothing that will be washed in the nearby stream to spread the disease. Contaminated bedding and towels reseed watercourses as they are washed, thus also contaminating the water used for cooking or other household purposes. Thus, even after cholera victims are weak and bedridden, they can still contaminate others with vibrios distributed through fecal contact.[13]

What is the solution of the water-borne contamination/virulence equation? Epidemics such as the one in Peru can be stemmed through decontamination of the water supply and assurance that clothes and bedding from sick persons are isolated from those of the rest of the family and washed in boiling water. Contamination may still occur in susceptible family members, but the wholesale contamination of a common watercourse used by thousands can be stopped.

Substitution of purified, disinfected drinking water may select for less virulent but still contagious forms of similar bacteria. In fact, this has proven to be so—as water supplies were progressively purified from the 1950s through the 1960s in the African subcontinent and the Mediterranean basin, the less virulent form of cholera, the El Tor form, replaced the classic *Vibrio cholerae*. But the 1980s and 1990s outbreaks in Africa and Peru reflect the deteriorating or nonexistent water disinfection programs in those countries coupled with reliance on waterways for washing and sewerage.

A parallel look at tuberculosis provides a model for understanding the forces that shape virulence in person-to-person versus water-to-person transmitted diseases.

Tuberculosis in Epidemic Form

Discovered more than 120 years ago by the Frenchman, Adrien Veillon (1864–1931), and isolated on March 24, 1882, by the German physician and Nobel laureate, Robert Koch (1843–1910), the tuberculosis bacillus *Mycobacterium tuberculosis* was considered the scourge of its time. By the turn of the century, TB had killed almost one-quarter of all Englishmen and comparable numbers of persons on the continent. Significant control was not achieved until the 1960s when Selman Waksman, a microbiologist at Rutgers University, discovered streptomycin, the first of eleven antibiotics with antitubercular activity. By the end of the decade, TB was considered a diminishing threat in the United States as case loads fell to historic lows.

But today, TB is undergoing a global resurgence. In 1990, more cases of TB caused by this bacillus and its near relative *Mycobacterium avis* were reported in the world than at any time in recorded history. In 1990, statisticians for WHO counted 8 million active cases and 2.9 million deaths worldwide, making TB the leading cause of death and disability among all infectious diseases.[14] Since 1985, TB has been growing at an exponential rate in the United States, with 39,000 more cases between 1984 to 1990 than were expected by the CDC from 1983 trends.[15] Today, 27,000 people in the United States currently have active cases of TB, up 20 percent since 1985.

Events that were unimaginable just a decade ago now recur with disturbing regularity. In 1989 to 1990, at a New York State correctional institution, a swift and fatal TB epidemic killed thirteen inmates.[16] Between 1990 and 1992, a half-dozen metropolitan hospitals reported outbreaks within their walls, each causing multiple deaths. These events all stem from a previously preventable and controllable disease. Why?

While many factors contribute to this alarming situation, one in particular–the neglect of proper procedures to control this organism when it infects AIDS patients–stands out as the most serious and avoidable omission. It is here, in the immunologic wasteland of AIDS, that powerful, new evolutionary forces are shaping this age-old enemy. The current resurgence of TB in Africa and in urban centers in the United States–and in South America and Asia–is being fueled by the AIDS epidemic. The weakened immunologic environment of an AIDS patient virtually assures free rein for the adaptable TB bacillus and provides greater opportunity for microevolution than in an immunocompetent host.

HIV creates an "evolutionary vacuum" in which almost any and all new variants of an original infecting organism can thrive, especially in hosts with profoundly impaired immunity. Such untrammeled opportunity for change is particularly dangerous in the case of TB. When TB organisms infect an immunodeficient host, be it the very young, the elderly, or the immunosuppressed, their survival pattern is different than in an immunocompetent patient. In immunologically intact hosts, the TB bacillus owes much of its survival advantage to a highly protective waxy coat or envelope and to its ability to sequester itself in cells of the immune system known as macrophages. It hides in these cells, reproducing inexorably even as the immune system works to stifle its survival. In immunologically depressed hosts, such subterfuge may be unnecessary, and the more dangerous active forms of infection, where the bacillus occupies the lungs, liver, and muscles, can prevail. As populations of the TB bacillus expand, the patient becomes symptomatic. The lungs are weakened, deep coughing becomes more prevalent, and bloody, contaminated sputum is produced. Liver function wanes as special inclusions called granulomas form and destroy surrounding cells. With this expanded growth, the TB organism is liable to undergo genetic changes that include new, more virulent subtypes. This growth pattern is particularly relentless when it occurs in an AIDS patient only imperfectly treated with antibiotics.

A depressed immune system permits the reactivation of old centers of TB infection as well as vulnerability to new infection. An AIDS patient carries 7 to 10 percent *a year* risk of acquiring TB, a rate that is hundreds of times normal.[17] And when a TB infection becomes disseminated in an AIDS patient, antibiotic regimes that might have curtailed the TB organisms in an immunocompetent host commonly fail.[18] Because they lack an effective T-cell-mediated immune system, AIDS patients are exquisitely vulnerable to the most severe types of pathology we have shown to be associated with persistent TB: disseminated spread, lung involvement, granulomatous changes in the liver, and destruction of the large muscles, notably the psoas muscle. (Granulomas are particularly striking to a pathologist because they include so-called giant cells comprised of macrophages with multiple nuclei, as well as other cellular mediators of the immune system.) Normally microscopic, granulomas can expand to egg size, destroying surrounding tissues on the way.

As shown in Figure 3, TB normally has a maximum case fatality rate in immunologically intact patients of between 1 and 10 percent. However, with an AIDS-crippled immune system, the fatality rate can be anywhere from 60 to 100 percent. Typical reports of the death rate of AIDS patients with TB cluster between 72 and 89 percent. As suggested by Figure 3, this staggering death rate is attributable in large part to the emergence of antibiotic-resistant TB. Recurrence after apparent recovery is also higher—up to thirty-four times so—for HIV-positive patients compared to those who test negative the HIV organism.[19] While reported rates for recurrence are typically less than those shown in Figure 3 for patients who have completed a full course of TB treatment, figures as high as those in the figure have been reported in subgroups of patients for whom treatment has been inadequate or in whom antibiotic-resistant TB has emerged.[20]

Multiple Resistance

Resistant strains of TB appear for much the same reasons resistant strains of other bacteria have emerged—because they have been subjected to selective pressures that have led to survival instead of annihilation. An ominous early report from the CDC should have been a warning of this disastrous public health threat. In 1982 and 1983, an outbreak of antibiotic-resistant TB swept through nurseries and schools in four western states.[21] Other reports appeared in 1985 that indicated that TB could

Figure 3: Progression of Multidrug Resistant Tuberculosis

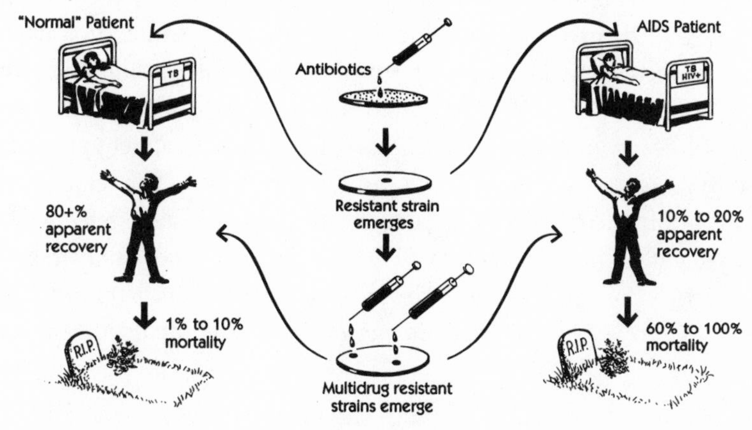

not only mount resistance to isoniazid (the standard drug of choice) but also to rifampin, a drug used prophylactically to treat children and adults in the surrounding community.[22] By 1993, at least half of all TB cases in New York City showed single- or multi-drug resistance.

The emergence of multiply resistant TB proved doubly catastrophic for patients infected with HIV. When an AIDS patient is mistakenly given only a prophylactic dose of isoniazid when he *already* has a silent case of TB (a common occurrence), the level of antibiotic in his bloodstream is insufficient to kill all of the TB organisms. Instead, the suboptimal dose kills off some of the most susceptible substrains, leaving behind a more robust TB germ to propagate. As the patient gets sicker, he may be given rifampin and isoniazid in the hopes of gaining a therapeutic foothold. But again the treatment is likely to be ineffectual, exerting a further selective force for survival of resistant tubercle bacilli. And so it goes, until the patient is a walking factory of highly infectious TB organisms, all multiply resistant to antibiotics. In time, treble and occasionally quadruple antibiotic resistance is possible. The next patient to get this infection (occasionally even one of the medical personnel treating the patient) now begins her battle at a terrible disadvantage—her treatment must overcome the background resistant strain already present.

This scenario is hardly fanciful. In New York City in 1991, one-third of the tested TB strains were already resistant to isoniazid, and 15 percent were resistant to isoniazid and rifampin.[23] The causes are simple—neglect or disregard of evolutionary rules and potential. This assertion is buttressed by patterns of antibiotic drug use documented in a newly issued report from the National Jewish Center for Immunology and Respiratory Medicine. Reviewing all of the records of TB from 1989 through 1990, two pulmonologists charted the actual treatment programs given to patients with classic pulmonary tuberculosis. The team found that the antibiotic protocols and treatment programs were defective for twenty-eight of the thirty-five patients (80 percent) with an average of almost four errors per patient.[24] The most common errors were just those most likely to lead to resistant forms of TB. These included:

- A treatment program begun with suboptimal doses or schedules for drugs
- A single new drug added to a failing treatment regimen instead of starting a crash program with multiple drugs
- Little or no follow-up to ensure compliance when patients lapsed from their treatments
- Inappropriate use of isoniazid for TB prevention

These errors, multiplied from patient to patient, virtually ensured that resistant TB would emerge and necessitate an extraordinarily expensive and sometimes fatal course for the patient. The researchers documented costs of $180,000 per patient when salvage therapy was needed to rescue a faultily treated patient. And each treatment failure increases the threat of contagion and further evolution toward virulence.

Given the ability to incubate indefinitely and reproduce without resistance in HIV-positive hosts, TB organisms undoubtedly have evolved at a high rate. As one research team observed, "Infection with HIV also appears to have facilitated the capacity for multidrug-resistant strains of tubercle bacilli to produce explosive, lethal outbreaks."[25] The danger of such outbreaks among AIDS patients is that the outbreaks thwart public health efforts at containing the epidemic by permitting the survival of large numbers of antibiotic-resistant TB organisms in potentially infective hosts. This, in turn, creates a greater opportunity for the spread of the most resistant and infectious organisms. Given the special risks posed by AIDS patients for disseminating antibiotic resistant and virulent strains of *Mycobacterium tuberculosis*, some clinicians have proposed that they be quarantined or otherwise constrained in their social contacts. However, this draconian measure is unjustified for patients under "observed therapy," a procedure developed by the Denver Health Department in 1965 for directly delivering and observing the actual oral ingestion of medications by TB patients.[26]

These observations suggest that the evolutionary potential and natural course of infection with initially nonresistant and/or particularly virulent strains of TB must be considered in designing therapy. Confidence that simultaneous treatment with four antibiotics, the current procedure, will assure control should be tempered with a dose of reality. The old adage that multiple resistance to four antibiotics is evolutionarily impossible because of the rarity of the mutations responsible for each mutation was disproven for antibiotic resistance in other bacterial strains.[27] Remember that evolutionary forces continue to work on the bacterium as its survival and propagation continue unopposed by effective therapy. This reality is underscored by the finding that a relative of TB known as *Mycobacterium avis* and a new resistant strain of TB itself have evolved to the point where they inactivate one of the body's last remaining defenses against them, a key chemical mediator of the immune system known as the tumor necrosis factor.[28] Historical precedent and even minimal respect for evolutionary potential dictate that clinicians reject the notion that TB will remain susceptible to *some* combination of treatment. Already, about 1 percent of infections remain intractable to *any* combination of antibiotics.[29]

Recommendations

Given this evolving threat, four specific recommendations have been made in the last year to limit the prospect of further deterioration of an already serious medical crisis.[30]

1. Begin *all* treatments for new TB patients with four drugs: isoniazid, rifampin, pyrazinamide, and ethambutal.
2. Test all strains of TB for their susceptibility to antibiotics and constantly adjust treatment programs accordingly.

3. If drug resistance occurs in a given patient, call in the experts and commence a crash program of control.

4. Assure that the patient takes all medications by direct observation of all doses administered.

5. Guarantee that *full* course of treatment is taken (up to 6 months).

These steps are an incomplete battle plan no matter how well intentioned. Tuberculosis control should begin with blocking transmission and assuring that a significant portion of the at-risk population—especially AIDS high-risk groups—is vaccinated with an agent that confers reasonably strong immunity to potentially infected hosts. A good bet is a modified version of the classic bacille Calmette Guérin or BCG. Childhood immunization with this agent is currently only routinely done in some Canadian provinces, notably Quebec.

With the advent of AIDS, the TB organism is in a new battleground where the immune system is a passive bystander. It is crucial to recognize that without the ability to raise an effective immune response, TB will continue to be a highly fatal disease for AIDS patients. Special treatment regimes should thus be commenced early and intensively for AIDS patients who fail to show tuberculin reactivity (a sign of a preexisting immune reaction to TB), including new and relatively untried antibiotics such as rifabutin, which has recently shown activity against the *Mycobacterium avis* complex. Ultimately, control of TB may have to await control of the immune depression that comes with AIDS—or, ideally, control of AIDS itself.

7 AIDS

AIDS is the single greatest threat to well-being facing the world's population today. This is so because of its continuing ability to be transmitted to young people and their offspring both sexually and through body fluids, but above all because of its lethality. It is the most deadly disease facing young people aged 22 to 45 in most of the developed countries of Europe and North America. Throughout the Third World, it challenges parasitic disease as the greatest debilitating illness for the population as a whole. Presently, AIDS is making its greatest inroads in Africa where over 7 million people are believed to be infected.

Because of its newness in the human population and its high mutation rate, it is likely that the human immunodeficiency virus (HIV) that causes AIDS is undergoing evolutionary changes even as this is being written. As we have seen, with microorganisms that cause human disease, newness per se often demands rapid evolution—or extinction. Whenever an unprepared population is put at risk and then rapidly winnowed by an agent for which no preexisting or transplacental immunity exists, *both* the microorganism and its host population are forced to evolve. The size of the host population is important because as the number of affected persons increases, so does the number and potential genetic variety of viruses carried by them. The opportunity for selection goes up accordingly, as long as genetic variation exists among the viral particles that move from host to host. With hindsight, many epidemiologists believe that it was factors intrinsic to its evolutionary novelty and its mutability that account for the variety and adaptability of the human immunodeficiency virus today.

Modes of Transmittal

In 1978, when I visited the Sutro Baths in San Francisco to warm up in the steam room after a particularly frigid skin diving trip, I had no idea that I might have been an unwitting witness to a very fatal evolutionary game. As Randy Shilts so persuasively documents in his book, *And the Band Played On* (New York: Viking/Penguin, 1993), sometime during this period it is plausible that one or more of the persons who served as the epicenters of AIDS on the West Coast was propagating the virus sexually. The centers for much of this activity were places like Sutro Baths, where promiscuous heterosexual and homosexual sex was commonplace.

During the period from 1970 through 1983 or so, the gay and sexually liberated community of San Francisco encouraged and reveled in sexual freedom. In the late 1970s, it was not uncommon for a single sexually active male to have unprotected sex with ten to thirty partners in a week, and (as noted in early Centers for Disease Control reports), as many as a thousand partners in a year was not uncommon. As the frequency of sexual contacts increased at places like Sutro (which doubled as a sexual mecca *and* a steam bathhouse), the yet to be discovered human immunodeficiency virus (HIV) was probably undergoing an extreme form of natural selection.

Any type of sexual activity that bypasses the traditional vaginal route of exchange of bodily fluids will put sexually carried organisms into contact with mucosal membranes that are ill prepared to resist viral or bacterial invasion. Because seminal fluid contains both new cells and foreign antigenic material, the vaginal mucosa has probably evolved to be accommodating to natural secretions while remaining hostile to foreign organisms that may be transferred with each ejaculate. In the rectum and colon, by comparison, the body accommodates some four hundred different bacterial species, providing many of them a "safe haven" especially in the lower intestinal tract. But one researcher has hypothesized that the anal-genital route of exposure puts a new set of microorganisms in contact with intestinal mucosa unprepared to resist invasion or penetration, especially by the human immunodeficiency virus.[1]

Certainly, the physical and immunologic barriers of the mucosa are qualitatively different in the anus and the vagina, leaving the anal tissues at higher risk of damage. Nonetheless, epidemiologic data show that AIDS is also readily transmitted through heterosexual sex, especially from men to women. That is, penile-vagina intercourse provides virtually no barrier to the transmission of HIV. Overall, it is the rate of intercourse and the number of partners as well as infection through contaminated needles that determines the likelihood of spread of AIDS, not the form of sexual contact.

Viral Evolution

The "loose" sexual mores of a drug-using community make for a "loose" virus in an evolutionary sense. With increasing rates of body fluid exchange (such as through shared needles and/or profligate sex), viral evolution toward virulence is strongly favored. Conversely, constraints that would ordinarily encourage viral passivity, nonvirulence and nonpathogenicity (such as delayed transmission) and "protected" sex or drug use are effectively lifted. As the frequency of sexual exchange increases, those HIV strains with the greatest speed of replication, shortest waiting period ("latency") before causing symptoms, and the highest virulence will be selected. That is, viruses with these characteristics would be assured the earliest opportunities for transmittal. As long as HIV-positive persons transmitted the virus through contaminated semen in the first 3 months or so of the projected latency period, and those infected do so in turn, no effective barrier to the evolution of the short latencies characteristic of virulence would exist. And as a corollary, as long as the virus that caused the most serious disease symptoms was being transmitted before its carriers became so incapacitated that they were no longer sexually attractive, no diminution on the virus's destructive potential could be expected.

Bathhouse Politics

In 1983, while a health professor at the University of California at Berkeley, I advocated that the bathhouses be closed as a symbolic demonstration of the need to constrain the high risk of contagion from HIV and other sexually transmitted diseases. That effort was stymied by well-meaning civil libertarians who objected to the use of public health policy power to restrict freedom. While I respect those concerns, I still believe that had a broad educational campaign been initiated at the outset of the epidemic and the bathhouses closed more expeditiously, many deaths would have been averted. I also believe that a sensitive but intense program of follow-up calls to HIV-positive and AIDS patients by the contact-tracing programs then mandated by law for sexually transmitted diseases would have blunted the AIDS epidemic early on. The alternative of providing "compassionate messages" in the early educational campaigns only reinforced the belief that safe sex was optional.

In the early years of the epidemic (about 1981 to 1983), resisting contact tracing on the spurious grounds that AIDS was not "exclusively" sexually transmitted and protecting civil liberties by leaving the bathhouses open was part of the political agenda of a group that did not want to be singled out as the focus of a death-dealing disease.

Unfortunately, the belated closing of the bathhouses in 1984 (Sutro was among the first) did little or nothing to foreshorten the life of the epidemic. Seroconversion rates (which measure the prevalence of new cases of antibodies to HIV and hence its infection rate), remained essentially unchanged during the period 1984 to 1986 after the baths were closed. By the mid-1980s, anonymous sex occurred as often in bars, sex clubs, and the privacy of the bedroom as in the epicenters of the baths. Condom-protected "safe sex" became a byword in San Francisco at this time, and belatedly received the urgent attention it deserved. Prevalence rates of sexually transmitted diseases, a bellweather for HIV, dropped accordingly. As a postscript, public health advocates were still voicing similar arguments in 1993 to those used in the early 1980s to justify the closure of video booths or sex clubs where some unsafe sex still occurs.[2] But unless and until personal responsibility for curtailing behavior that puts others at risk becomes the norm, detrimental evolutionary changes in microorganisms will persist.

Limiting Sexually Transmittable Diseases

For any sexually transmittable disease, it is critical for a community to encourage behaviors that limit unprotected sex since such limitation also slows any evolutionary changes in the infecting organism. By limiting sexual contact, forces that select for less virulent agents with longer latency periods are brought into play. In theory, as the opportunity for transmission drops with diminished contagious sexual contacts, only those disease-causing organisms that have delayed onset and relatively mild manifestations are selected. And if the evidence to be reviewed below holds up, it looks like such a change has begun on the West Coast of the United States.

Changing patterns of sexual behavior may also have led to the increase, persistence, and current prevalence of chlamydial infections, a nonlethal sexually transmittable disease (STD) that accounts for about a third of all cases of STD in the United States.[3] This disease produces few symptoms in its early stages in women who can become chronic chlamydial carriers. Teenage sex and multiple sex partners has led to this disease becoming established widely in the United States.

Chlamydia and AIDS are but two of nearly fifty different sexually transmitted diseases. Clearly, primary prevention of transmission is the most important means of reducing the incidence and dampening the virulence of any sexually transmitted organism. Efforts in this direction are now under way by the Division of Sexually Transmitted Disease/HIV Prevention at the Centers for Disease Control (CDC), which focuses on prevention rather than treatment as the first line of defense. The agency is investing broadly in community-based programs that carry risk-reduction messages directly to teenagers and other high-risk groups. But, even so, federal officials are still only indirectly impacting the AIDS epidemic.

For example, the CDC is still pulling its punches in its AIDS information campaign. There is no information on how to prevent HIV transmission or on the value of condom use in current televised messages about the risks of AIDS.[4] Only by slowing the rate of transmission of this deadly disease will the virus be encouraged to evolve toward longer latent periods and clinicians be given the breathing room they need to develop more effective treatments. What is needed is nothing less than an evolutionary strategy to change the whole complexion of the AIDS epidemic.

Background of a Killer

The death-dealing infections produced by the current form of the HIV organism pose a critical question to the medical profession: Why does

AIDS remain such an intractable and fatal disease? Clearly it owes much of its lethality not to its own toxicity, but rather to its ability to destroy a portion of the host's immune system. That is, unlike some major disease-causing bacteria, such as the staphylococcal and streptococcal species, HIV produces no toxin of its own. Rather, it has acquired its particularly lethal characteristics as a result of its remarkable ability to cause the decay and eventual loss of immunological competence in a critical part of the immune system—the part that produces cell-mediated immunity. The cellular portion of the immune system includes the lymphocytes known as T cells which normally handle intracellular pathogens like HIV. By first invading and then killing one subset of these T cells (the so-called helper or $CD4^+$ cells), HIV knocks out the core of this system, providing the virus with a virtual safe haven from immunological assault. By virtue of their ability to live inside both lymphocytes and macrophages, HIV strains that have stripped the cellular immune system of its power and become nearly invulnerable since an antibody response cannot reach within the cell itself.

By a quirk of fate, I was on the first team that discovered that the immune system could be impaired by RNA viruses, the same group which includes the immunodeficiency virus. In 1969, I proposed to Dr. Phyllis Blair, my postdoctoral supervisor at the University of California, Berkeley, that one of the reasons for the success of the mouse mammary tumor virus (like HIV, an RNA virus) in producing breast tumors in animals might be linked to its ability to destroy the particular portion of the immune system associated with resistance against deviant cells. This work, published in 1970,[5] showed that the mammary tumor virus could indeed depress the T cell portion of the immune system, and invited further study of RNA viruses as potential immunotoxicants. However, given the relative absence of interest in RNA viruses some 24 years ago, little follow-up was sparked by this early discovery. This has proven unfortunate, for we have since learned that the key to AIDS lethality lies in the special ability of HIV to destroy the critical helper cells of the cellular portion of the immune system.

Even in the first "asymptomatic" stages of HIV infection, when cell counts of these critical $CD4^+$ lymphocytes remain high (about 500 million per liter of blood), previously unrecognized signs signal the erosion of immune competence. Follicle inflammation reminiscent of teenage acne may appear on the face along with seborrheic dermatitis on the chest and other skin infections.[6]

As the blood level of $CD4^+$ cells continues to drop, more opportunistic infections gain a foothold. When the level drops below 200, diseases such as *Pneumocystis carinii* pneumonia, the hallmark of full-blown AIDS, commonly arise. Tuberculosis and the fulminant infection caused by the *Mycobacterium avis* complex soon follow, along with fungal overgrowth, thrush, and other invasive diseases. These often catastrophic illnesses provide the major causes of death in AIDS patients. Anywhere from 6 months to 10 years can elapse from initial infection until such full-blown symptomatic diseases erupt, but the average latent period is estimated to be between 3 and 4 years and growing, as the significant delays in transmission cited above are extending the virus's ability to remain dormant.

Origins of the Immunodeficiency Virus

It remains an evolutionary enigma how such a lethal organism could come to produce a uniformly fatal disease, seemingly without hope of control through some innate resistance mechanism, in such a broad cross section of the human population. Part of the answer appears to be related to the relative newness of HIV as a human pathogen and to its route of entry into the human body.

It is likely that the human immunodeficiency virus has spread from a near-relative primate species to humans only within the last four or five decades. The monkey-eating habit of some cultural groups of central African countries such as Sierra Leone and the Ivory Coast provides a tantalizing clue to how such passage could have occurred. By shooting and butchering monkeys and other primates, people would be likely to be contaminated by blood-borne infectious agents such as the SIV organism. As one observer notes, "Scratches, bites, and the mixing of blood or other body fluids [between monkeys and humans] is likely in these circumstances. . . . Those who have studied the relation of simian diseases to man have long feared such an event."[7] Thus, these human populations were probably repeatedly exposed to primate and monkey viruses.

The earliest reports of AIDS in human patients can reliably be traced to 1959–1962, when a sea captain who picked up cargo in Africa returned to England with a mysterious fatal infection. His serum was reanalyzed years later and showed the HIV antibodies characteristic of AIDS. Sporadic reports continued over the next two decades. In 1969, a young boy in St. Louis was found to have HIV-positive serum after dying of pneumocystis carinii pneumonia. Then, in 1981, the first reports of a "gay disease" appeared out of Los Angeles and New York: Kaposi's sarcoma, previously a disease limited to elderly Jewish men, had appeared inexplicably in young, sexually active homosexual men. (It now appears that Kaposi's is a distinct disease, also sexually transmitted, which is different from AIDS.)

HIV clearly follows the pattern of an infectious organism that has only recently taken up residence in a new host. The introduction of a new viral agent from one species to a related one commonly causes a more fatal disease in the new host than in the old one. This has proven true for other immunodeficiency viruses related to HIV that have moved among primates other than humans. At least once before the new introduction of an HIV-related virus (from sooty mangabey monkeys to pigtailed macaques) was coupled with the dramatic appearance of virulent types of the virus with greater amounts of genetic diversity than in the original strains.[8] This research and others support the idea that the human immunodeficiency viruses (HIV-1 and HIV-2) are not new, but rather old ones that became more deadly as they moved to humans from monkeys or apes.[9]

The relationships among such viruses are shown in a "family tree" of AIDS-related viruses. As shown in Figure 4, the nearest neighbors in an evolutionary sense of HIV-1 and 2 are primate viruses that include a chimpanzee simian immunodeficiency virus and a Cameroon strain of HIV. More distant cousins of HIV exist in the green monkey and mandrill. Both are simian immunodeficiency viruses.

HIV's Relationship with Other Pathogens

Paradoxically, the success of the HIV organism responsible for AIDS may be related to the success of other infectious conditions in the human host. Where malaria is endemic, AIDS appears to have taken on a particularly virulent form. This strange confluence can be explained by the functional codependency of the immune system and the immunodeficiency virus.

Figure 4: Evolutionary Relationships of Immunodeficiency Viruses

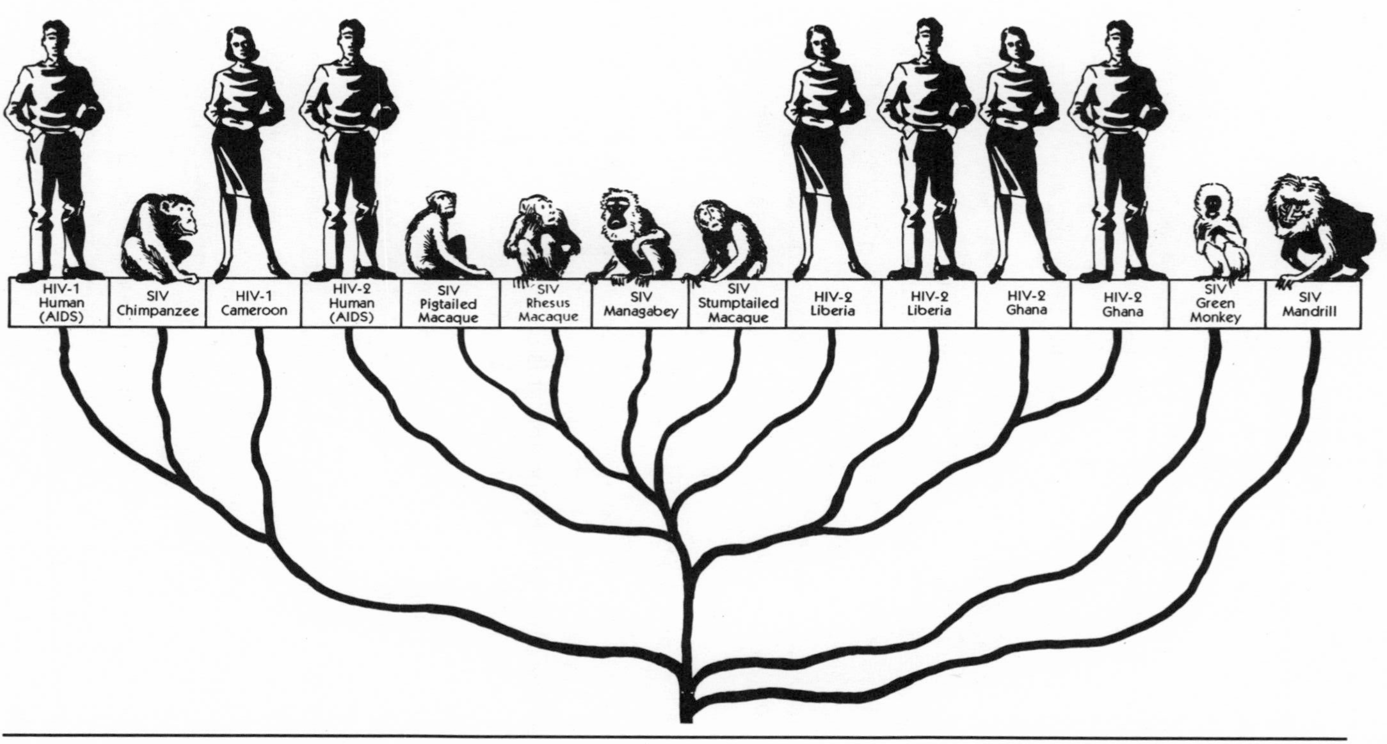

As long as the immune system is quiescent, the HIV organism finds few if any susceptible cells to infect. Even after successfully infiltrating such cells, as long as the immune system lies fallow, the virus cannot replicate easily. So-called "resting" T cells provide a poor host for viral replication. But if the immune system is activated or turned on by infecting organisms such as the malarial parasite, more and more cells become available for viral replication. When activated by malaria, the immune system, so finely tuned to respond to foreign organisms, becomes a kind of doomsday machine in the presence of the immunodeficiency virus.

Soon after infection, the body appears to launch an abortive burst of immune activity. This response ensures that still more T cells will be activated, providing a further stimulus for viral replication. (As we will see in the next chapter, the virus itself may possess a "superantigen" that directly activates such a wide range of potential host immune cells.) In the face of this unsuccessful immunologic assault high levels of virus in the blood decline as HIV retreats to lymphoid tissues.

Widespread Distribution

AIDS is currently so widely dispersed around the world and so prevalent in some sectors of tropical Africa that public health officials call it a pandemic. To a lay person, this understated term appears innocuous enough, but it makes public health officials cringe because it means that virtually everyone is at risk. The general consensus of experts attending the Ninth International AIDS Conference held in Berlin in the summer of 1993, is that AIDS is now out of control, leaping ahead some 20 percent between 1992 and 1993. In 1994, it is expected to infect some 2.5 million people worldwide not counting Africa, where the disease is out of control in some equatorial countries. As many as one out of three men who visit health centers in Zaire and Uganda are commonly found to be HIV-positive. In a decade, the AIDS epidemic is expected to affect more than 30 million persons.

New cases of AIDS are concentrated in the developing countries where about 90 percent of all new infections are currently occurring. The epidemic is particularly explosive in Southeast Asia. According to WHO, in Thailand the number of HIV infections jumped from 50,000 to more than 450,000 in just the 2 years between 1990 and 1992. Because its victims are almost invariably young (patients between the ages of 22 to 44 are commonly the most severely impacted) and die within a few years of manifesting the symptoms of the disease, and because up to one-third of all children of HIV-positive mothers are also doomed to die of AIDS, this disease will have significant evolutionary implications for the next generation.[10] At its present incidence rate and lethality in certain communities, the HIV organism is inexorably selecting out the most vulnerable subpopulations and leaving behind a residuum of resistant people.

Sporadic reports have already appeared of persons who harbor the virus but who lack evidence of full-blown disease symptoms. But the greatest evolutionary changes currently happening are those that are reshaping the genetic makeup of the virus itself.

Dissemination and Virulence

AIDS is still traveling easily and widely, cresting with the wave of social disruption that currently splits societies in sub-Saharan Africa and regions of Southeast Asia and India. Evolutionary biologist Paul Ewald believes that the high level of virulence of AIDS in mid-central and East Africa evolved rapidly as a result of the increase in multipartner sexual contacts precipitated by the destruction of the traditional social fabric that occurred in the 1970s.[11]

Various other social factors contributed to the explosion of AIDS. Civil war, starvation, and the in-migration of many Africans toward the centers of commerce in urban areas assured a breach in traditional monogynous or polygynous (but nonetheless limited) sexual contacts fostered by tribal traditions. New road building coupled with urbanization offered new opportunities for sexual contacts and for much wider and faster transmission of AIDS. Truckers carrying goods across great distances and single men from among the new wave of migrant workers coming to the cities encouraged the growth of prostitution, particularly in Zambia and Zaire.[12] As many as 80 percent of the prostitutes in central cities in Zambia have developed HIV seropositively, potentially spreading the virus in all unprotected sexual contacts.

Aggravating an already explosive epidemiologic situation is the free and widespread use of hypodermic needles for self-treatment with antibiotics and, to a lesser extent, for drug use. This use of old hypodermic needles provides a direct route for the HIV organism to gain access to the blood stream. On the west coast of Africa, where sexual contacts are less widespread, a parallel epidemic of an HIV varient known as HIV-2 is less virulent and has a lower prevalence than does the primary HIV-1 epidemic. Some writers have commented that the fact that two relatively dissimilar viruses (HIV-1 and 2) appeared virtually concomitantly and produced major epidemics points to a common social pattern for their joint origin.[13] But HIV-2 appears to be adapted for a slow rate of spread, allowing its hosts to harbor infectious levels of the virus long before it produces any outward evidence of disease or immunologic deficiency. This pattern fits Ewald's predictions that infrequent sexual contact, in diminishing the potential rate of spread of HIV, selects a more "patient" and benign organism. Only those HIV organisms that have reduced virulence and long latencies can survive the delayed contacts between infected and uninfected partners.[14]

How does the AIDS virus accomplish this feat? By evading the immune system and finding a suitable "hiding place." This is, in fact, what the HIV organism appears to do. We have already seen that HIV can survive intracellularly; that is, inside certain cells. In actuality, it slips into a long-lived cell of the immune system by binding with a ubiquitous surface protein. Once inside, it merges its genetic material with that of the cell's. (Since HIV, like other retroviruses, uses RNA as its genetic material, this is accomplished by a process of "reverse transcription" whereby RNA is transcribed into DNA and then integrated with the host cell's chromosomes.) By also coding for substances that dampen the immune reactivity of the host, the HIV organism can chance periodic escapes from its cellular enclave, constantly shedding small numbers of viruses into the bloodstream where they serve as potential agents for further dissemination.

For the human immunodeficiency viral types, some trade-off between the long intervals between replication and release, which demand that the virus find a safe haven, and the ease of transfer among sexually active persons, which ensures virulence, must exist. The more often the host of the virus engages in sexual activity, the more opportunities are created for any quickly replicating virus to find a new host. Evolutionary biologists therefore make a prediction: HIV virulence should be related to the frequency of sexual contact.

And the example of HIV-1 and HIV-2 in Africa provides a test of this prediction: The virulent strain of HIV has evolved almost exclusively in central and East Africa, where social conditions fostered rapid exchange of sexual partners. On the west coast of Africa, where social conditions were more stable and sexual promiscuity less pronounced, the more benign HIV-2 prevails. In Senegal, where HIV-2 is the most common source of AIDS, infection leads to AIDS at an extremely slow rate, implying the existence of a long-latency virus. By contrast, in the Ivory Coast, where the capital city of Abidjan underwent substantial social upheaval, sexual activity was likely more intense, and the strains of HIV-2 appear to be correspondingly more virulent.[15]

This pattern also appears to be reflected by changes in the virulence of AIDS in the United States. In the last few years, the latency between infection and full-blown disease has increased in the major epicenters of AIDS where *protected* sexual contacts have been most vigorously encouraged. In San Francisco, the average latency between infection and full-blown symptoms of AIDS may be as long as 10 years, whereas only a few years ago it was about 5 years. Clearly, something is changing either within the virus or among the hosts it infects. The best bets are on the likelihood of the virus changing, given the extraordinary genetic mutability of the AIDS-causing organisms.

Viral Evolution from Within

Given the scope of HIV's genetic variability, it is important to consider the evolution the virus may undergo *within* a single person. We have already seen that, like other RNA-based viruses, the HIV virus is a "retrovirus" that relies on the host's own DNA to make copies of itself. But being an RNA virus also provides HIV with a remarkable capacity for mutational change. In fact, its rate of mutation is several magnitudes greater than that of our own cells. Understandably then, new variants of the HIV organism can often be found within months after the initial infection. And during such an intense evolutionary incubation period, it is not unlikely that some variants might arise that are more likely to be transmitted than is the original HIV strain.

An example is a variant of HIV that has a predilection for replicating inside the macrophages of the immune system rather than inside the more usual $CD4^+$ cell host.[16] This finding, if generalizable, has profound implications–it may mean that those persons who harbor the macrophage strain are "high-risk" transmitters because macrophages, being migratory, can show up in many different anatomical sites and secretions. It may also mean that current vaccine efforts may be missing their proper target.

Other microevolutionary phenomena that accompany HIV infection affect treatment strategies and the clinical outlook. Patients whose HIV strains suddenly begin producing colonies of fused cells (syncytia) face a drastic acceleration of their downward clinical course and require much more aggressive therapy than do nonsyncytial formers. New infections become more common, and resistance to opportunistic diseases rapidly fades. The details of this shift are critical to understanding the difficulty in targeting this rapidly evolving virus.

What we know is that, as a result of random genetic change, some HIV variants acquire the ability to force the cells they infect to fuse, forming vast arrays of cell mats known as syncytia. (A syncytium is a group of fused cells that share a common outer membrane.) During infection, about 50 percent of patients aquire the syncytium-forming strain of HIV-1. When this strain arises, it signals a rapid acceleration in the rate of loss of $CD4^+$ T cells and rapid progression of AIDS to its fatal endpoint. Tragically, the HIV-1 virus remains relatively susceptible to control using the most common drug of choice (AZT or azothymidine, also known by its brand name, Zidovudine) only as long as it remains nonsyncytium producing.

Until recently, all AIDS patients were routinely put on AZT in an attempt to slow down viral replication. While this treatment is often initially successful, it does not prevent the burst of new viral growth that commonly occurs about 6 months after the onset of treatment.[17] This rebounding population often contains AZT-resistant strains, including the syncytium-forming variants marking the end of the effectiveness of this treatment strategy.[18] Parallel resistance to drugs that are used to complement antiviral agents has also been reported. Resistance to alpha-interferon, one of the body's natural antiviral agents, emerges after short-term treatment with Zidovudine.[19] So does resistance to the more commonly used multiple-drug therapies. These shifts in viral populations following AZT, ddI, or ddC therapy obviously greatly reduce the likelihood that present-day medications and treatment plans will achieve an ultimate cure. This is particularly true because, as we have seen, the virus appears to be vulnerable to chemical attack only during its early stages following transmission.

Reconsidering a Viable Control Strategy

A change in treatment philosophy and strategy is clearly indicated. As we saw with antibiotic-resistant bacteria, the pattern of suppression of high organism densities followed by a recrudescence of a newly resistant infecting pathogen reflects a classic evolutionary pattern. Chronic, often suboptimal chemotherapy that causes cell death in a highly mutable population creates an optimum environment for evolutionary change. The original population of viruses is likely to contain small numbers of variants that otherwise are displaced by the concomitant presence of a dominant viral type. But the dominant type is often the sole target of chemotherapy, permitting the resistant minority population to expand after the dominant population is suppressed. Simply doubling the number of therapeutic agents, (that is, adding ddI or ddC to AZT) has not improved this picture, perhaps because new mutations to all three drugs can arise readily among the hundreds of new HIV variants generated in the course of several months of growth under therapy.

The hypermutability of the HIV organism also greatly compounds the task facing the immune system. Among other problems, the immune response to HIV has to be quick enough and specific enough to limit the infecting virus to prevent it from overwhelming the immune system itself. Achieving this end is severely hampered by the rapid changes in its surface makeup. As the virus expands, these changes make the AIDS virus a shifting target for any immunologic assault. In fact, HIV can mutate at a rate up to 1 million times that of typical DNA viruses,[20] making it so variable as to successfully elude virtually all of the immunologic attacks mustered against it to date. In fact, isolation of HIV-1 strains from individual patients routinely show up to a 2 percent rate of spontaneous deviation in the makeup of the viral coat.[21]

In a pioneering article that appeared in 1990 in the journal *AIDS*,[22] three University of Oxford theoreticians offered a prophetic view of the consequences of this genetic mutability. The team postulated that the high rate of mutation in HIV that occurs during viral replication could generate strains of the virus that would *perpetually* elude the host's antibody response. Since the virus also simultaneously decimates the CD4$^+$ lymphocytes, the authors used a computer to model the microevolutionary interaction between the immune system and the virus. Their theoretical construct predicted that great viral diversity would be generated, and that such diversity would eventually increase above the level where the immune system could hold the viral growth in check. They found that their model correctly predicted the observed behavior of the HIV organism—given a period of largely unrestrained expansion (as would occur during an initial burst of viral replication or following the development of resistance), the virus becomes a doomsday machine.

The dry technical jargon of their words veils the more tragic elements of their abstract finding: "The theory is examined via the development of a mathematical model which reveals that an increasing number of antigenically distinct viral strains may overwhelm the immune system of the host."[23] This, indeed, appears to be what happens in most if not all AIDS patients. As an AIDS patient's immune systems begin to collapse, one or more different viral strains can be found in the bloodstream. The model predicted that this increase in viral diversity should be observed only as long as the immune system is strong enough to exert selective pressure on the viral population—as soon as the system collapsed completely, succumbing AIDS patients would generally be found to have only one dominant HIV strain: the one with the highest replication rate.[24]

Variation in Transit

If evolutionarily selected variants of HIV are the rule, we should see genetic differences in the HIV strains that come to dominate one host versus those that arise in an infected partner. In fact, this pattern has been shown to occur in some preliminary tests of viral makeup between original infected hosts and their sexual contacts. In one key study, a mother's HIV strain differed some 8.5 percent from that of her daughter who had been infected in the mother's uterus.[25] This amount of variation carries potential immunological implications. If HIV can undergo evolutionary divergence from one host to another and from mother to daughter, it greatly reduces the likelihood of finding an immunologic common denominator that will thwart transmission and subsequent infection. In part to beat this system, current vaccine efforts are concentrating on relatively constant and vital regions of the HIV organism (for example, the hp 120 protein). But to date none have proven successful in controlling either the transmission or the outgrowth of variant HIV types.

Contagion from Opportunistic Organisms

As we saw in the discussion of tuberculosis, AIDS patients are commonly overwhelmed by the unbridled growth of opportunistic infections. These infections include fungal organisms, other viruses, and opportunistic bacteria including salmonella.[26] The organisms causing these infections *also* undergo rapid evolutionary changes during their initial period of explosive expansion in an immunologically compromised environment, and then again when suboptimal antibiotic treatments are given. Some of these selective pressures, as we saw for the TB bacterium, encourage antibiotic-resistant forms. But evolutionary theory also predicts that a microenvironment that favors outgrowth of a particular strain can also create a state of dependency on that environment.

Without treatment, newly arising variants of opportunistic infections in AIDS patients are likely to be adapted to an immunologically impaired environment. In practical terms this means that immunotherapy for opportunistic infections is highly promising, especially if it can be in an "adoptive" form where a nonimmunodepressed, compatible donor supplies cells or antibodies to attack the AIDS patient's infection. On the down side, this reality also suggests that the opportunistic organisms that evolve in AIDS patients will tend readily to infect other AIDS patients or other patients whose immune systems are impaired.

This hypothesis has now been verified by clinicians who have followed AIDS patients through hospitals and waiting rooms where non-AIDS, but immunologically vulnerable, patients have also been present. And the picture is not a pretty one. The rare pneumonia common to AIDS patients caused by *Pneumocystis carinii* (known as PCP for short) has stricken at least five Swiss renal transplant patients who shared the same waiting room with AIDS patients. Similarly, PCP has shown up in cancer patients in increased numbers proportional to the increase in AIDS patients. The variant of the hepatitis B virus, which can cause a fulminant infection in AIDS patients, has also been transferred to immunosuppressed bystanders. And most ominously of all, multidrug-resistant TB has also been passed from HIV-positive carriers to similarly weakened but HIV-negative patients.[27]

These findings raise a major ethical dilemma—what constraints if any should be placed on AIDS patients to limit the likelihood of their spreading their secondary infections? The gravity of this reality was brought home graphically to me at the University of Illinois Hospital in Chicago where I did my ethics rounds. I was presented with the case of an indigent, advanced AIDS patient who wanted to be cared for by his family. What would otherwise be a simple act of compassionate acquiescence by the physcians tending him was complicated by one additional feature of his disease—he had active, multidrug-resistant TB.

While some forms of prophylaxis are protective of TB contagion for family members (for example, prophylactic rifampin), this was deemed unsuitable in his case because of the multidrug resistance. His own treatment for TB had been rocky, with periods of noncompliance. The medical staff wanted him committed and placed in isolation rather than face a budding new epidemic should his family members become infected with TB. But both his family and the patient himself wanted home hospice care above all else. The mother was willing to take the risks, and to take whatever precautions were necessary. In the end, I negotiated an agreement whereby his younger siblings would be cared for by a relative and the mother would get nursing instruction and attention to monitor her own status vis-à-vis TB. She was more than willing to accept her personal risk but did not want her children infected.

Quarantine?

But this case highlights a major dilemma—if AIDS patients are indeed evolutionary crucibles for new and more risky diseases, should not some steps be taken to limit their social contacts? Tuberculosis in particular is a general threat since it does not require immune depression to infect a healthy adult and can then flare up in the population in epidemic form. My own view is that AIDS patients should be treated as contagious risks from the outset, and counseled confidentially about the nature of the hazard they pose to others. Their behavior can be monitored, especially as they take anti-TB medication, but incarceration or forced institutionalization is much too draconian a solution for the risks they pose to the general public. AIDS patients with TB should be treated as would any TB patient: with isolation, observed medication, and counseling. AIDS patients with other opportunistic infections should be taught to practice the highest standards of personal hygiene. And caretakers should be screened to exclude those who may be immunologically compromised or otherwise at special risk.

All of this is, of course, fine in abstract. But the reality of AIDS, particularly in prisons, is much more grim. Inmates and guards alike are constantly at risk of acquiring fatal TB from their constant contact with infectious patients. The answer, of course, is not to require all AIDS patients to be quarantined, as is currently done in Cuba and in the United States for Haitian immigrants. Hospitalization and compassionate care are the only proper responses.

New Treatment Strategies

Opportunistic Infections and Windows of Opportunity

A corollary to the evolutionary approach is that understanding the forces that drive natural selection can provide the insight for novel and effective therapeutic approaches. We now understand that in the immunologically compromised environment of an AIDS patient, an otherwise treatable infection may undergo such radical expansion and microevolution as to become life-threatening. An example is herpes simplex, the cause of genital herpetic lesions. Resistant forms commonly emerge after sequential courses of intensive antiviral therapy with acyclovir (a drug that normally controls herpes type 2), leading to death in many AIDS patients.[28]

Recognizing that evolutionary events will occur during antimicrobial therapy also provides a window of opportunity to control such otherwise intractable infections. For instance, using a different antiviral drug, such as foscarnet, can deflect the selection pressures that drive acyclovir-treated herpes into resistant forms. A course of foscarnet can "buy time" in an evolutionary sense, allowing the herpes virus to mutate *back* to its original, acyclovir-susceptible form.[29] While not always successful,[30] this discovery can limit the spread of often fatal herpes lesions. If foscarnet does not always control the lesion-causing organism, a second antiviral agent can be tried.[31]

The acyclovir/foscarnet data provide a novel model for treating HIV. Selection followed by counterselection can potentially create a kind of evolutionary "whiplash," catching a newly mutated strain off-guard. But by relying solely on a limited repertoire of antiviral agents such as AZT, ddI, and ddC, HIV resistance to one or all agents is likely. Were an entirely different group of antiviral agents that target different parts of the HIV genome available to put counterselective pressure on resistant forms (much as foscarnet does to acyclovir-resistant herpes), it is theoretically possible to catch HIV off-guard and control its replication. Even more radical is the idea of using selection to cajole or coerce the virus into acquiring so many different mutations that its own replication is hindered.

An example of such an approach was employed by Yung-Kang Chow, a young Harvard medical student working at Boston's Massachusetts General Hospital. In 1993, Chow announced a strategy for overcoming antibiotic resistance of HIV that capitalized on its well-known ability to mutate. Keep in mind that the first generation of chemicals brought to bear on the AIDS epidemic have been those agents that inhibited the enzymatic machinery to make the genetic material needed by the virus to make additional copies of itself. As each new agent was brought into play, the virus adapted to their toxicity through rapid genetic changes that reduced the target site or otherwise limited the inhibiting ability of the drugs. This strategy proved invaluable to viral survival even as a second generation of drugs was introduced that thwarted viral replication. Within a few weeks, even this direct inhibition was stymied by new mutations.

Knowing that each mutation needed to overcome antiviral toxicity weakened the virus's replicative ability, Chow's team put a tissue culture strain of HIV under intense selection pressure, driving it to simultaneously acquire mutations in the same part of its genome to three separate antibiotics, including both enzyme and replication inhibitors.[32] The result of this superintense selection pressure was to drive the "successful" strain to oblivion: Once the virus had acquired all three mutations, it was no longer able to replicate successfully, dooming its long-term survival even as it escaped the control of the killer antibiotics.

Or so it seemed. But less than 6 months later, the Harvard group rescinded its "major discovery," acknowledging that their HIV strains had at least one mutation that they themselves had introduced independently of those generated by the antiviral drugs.[33] Such a disclosure dampens the enthusiasm for this approach, but it does not diminish the general wisdom of the idea. These preliminary evolutionary experiments suggest some tantalizing approaches for controlling the AIDS virus itself.

Other Solutions

In spite of the repeated failures of chemicals to control AIDS because of the emergence of drug resistance, many researchers remain intent on finding a magic bullet for controlling HIV.[34] As I have intimated, this approach will likely fail unless it considers all of the avenues for escape programmed by HIV's astonishing evolutionary capacity. The most innovative strategies, and the ones advocated in this book, are those that integrate treatment with a deep understanding of the evolutionary complexities and vulnerabilities of the HIV organism.

The patterns of therapeutic failure point to commonalities in the resistance of AIDS and bacterial and fungal infections. One useful approach in these latter instances has been to chart judiciously the timing and emergence of resistant forms and to adjust treatment protocols "on the spot" to keep up with newly emergent resistant types. To date, this approach has been used sparingly if at all for HIV. This need not be so. Newer techniques of DNA analysis, like the polymerase chain reaction, permit the specific gene sequence that causes resistance to AZT to be charted.[35] Utilizing this technique more widely could permit patients to be checked in advance to determine drug resistance or susceptibility patterns of their HIV. If we can perform random testing for drug metabolites on a high-intensity schedule, certainly we can monitor for genetic changes in HIV and adjust our treatment modalities accordingly.

With this kind of window into the viral genome, it may even prove possible to undertake some new and dramatic genetic engineering approaches to AIDS monitoring and treatment. It would theoretically be possible to use "directed" mutation techniques to force the AZT-resistant HIV organism to back-mutate at the site in question, or to derive treatment protocols that fine-tune antibiotic regimes to the susceptibilities of HIV variants.

A second idea for control of AIDS is suggested by the back-and-forth resistance seen in the herpes simplex virus that causes herpes. By using the known evolutionary potential of the HIV-1 organism, an environment that selects for well-studied resistant forms like that known to withstand AZT can be intentionally created. By then anticipating what forms are most likely to emerge following an initial round of therapy, the clinician can quickly substitute a more potent analog. This concept of "controlled selection" could also be used in theory to attempt to drive the virus into a weakened form that will either be prone to back-mutate into a susceptible strain or become hypervulnerable to an untried drug modality being held in reserve.

Another mechanism for resolving the dilemma of early emergence of resistant strains is to use combinations of drugs, a strategy used early and successfully in treating cancers, particularly childhood leukemias, and in treating recalcitrant infections. An example would be the trial initiated in 1990 for combining ddC (2,3 dideoxcytidine) and AZT (Zidovudine) in treating AIDS patients.[36] Unfortunately, early data from this trial presented at the Ninth International AIDS Conference in summer, 1993, showed no real advantage of the combination to either drug used alone. Other variations on this modality have been tried only tentatively since the early 1990s,[37] but few have proven as successful as originally hoped. New approaches that utilize drugs that target different stages of the HIV replication cycle are logical candidates.

At least one research team suggests that strategies to control AIDS be modeled after successful strategies for cancer control. By focusing simultaneously on three to four different stages in the cell replication cycle, it is possible to "outwit" the virus and curtail its growth as if it were a dividing tumor cell.[38] By converging therapy on a critical link in the chain needed for viral replication, the HIV organisms may be provoked into making a fatal (to the virus) combination of mutations. But even as this strategy was being heralded as a "breakthrough" in treating AIDS, one reviewer cautioned that HIV is "a highly mutable and wily opponent . . . that may be able to avoid checkmate with a large array of alternative moves."[39]

Obviously, concurrent efforts to restore the compromised immune system are needed if controlling AIDS through chemoprevention or treatment is to show any likelihood of success. At a minimum, strategies to strengthen the fading immune system's T cell capabilities appear essential. Two researchers at the University of Arizona Department of Nutritional Sciences have suggested using large doses of vitamin E therapy to strengthen the immune system.[40] Other equally obscure but untested approaches to bolster the flagging immune strength of AIDS patients have included ingestion of live lactobacteria[41] and the use of previously unrecognized drugs with immunomodulatory activity (such as Panax ginseng).[42] Both approaches could profitably be explored for stimulating the besieged immune systems of AIDS patients—especially if other specific treatment modalities were directed at controlling the source of the immune depression itself.

As a patient's immune system's repertoire of responses plumets, an AIDS patient becomes as vulnerable as a dying leukemia victim to virtually every potential new pathogen. The successful experience of rescuing even a few such leukemia patients provides a useful but as yet untapped model to fight late-stage opportunistic infections in AIDS.

A still more radical proposal is to use the known responses of HIV to selective pressures to drive its evolution toward a more benign form. We have already explored the simplistic idea of sending out more condoms and encouraging "safe" (and more limited) sexual contacts to delay transmission and therefore select for less virulent forms of HIV. This approach remains a crude but essential first step in blunting the epidemic. But to really bring HIV under control, it will be necessary to control the conditions of its spread still further—and to capitalize on the residual host reactions to the virus as means of limiting and shaping its evolutionary drift. For instance, it may prove possible to render an AIDS patient "noninfectious" (such as through the use of passively administered blocking antibodies), even though his disease remains uncontrolled.

Radical Therapeutic Suggestions

No matter how promising these suggested approaches may appear (and some may not), the repeated failure to find a "solution" to the AIDS epidemic makes it clear that some radical new strategies are essential. Several new proposals include the following:

1. Intentionally substitute more benign viral agents along the chain of contagion to compete with the more virulent forms of HIV.

2. Develop a program to identify and reach the highest risk patients (those with the most virulent, antibiotic-resistant strains of HIV) and exert

the strongest possible social suasion selectively to limit *their* likelihood of spreading the virus.

3. Develop vaccines that exert selection pressure on the virulence as well as the survival of the HIV organism.

4. Design interventions that provide better protection at the level of intercourse.

5. Engineer genetic resistance to AIDS in a suitable stem line of bone marrow cells and use them to replace the AIDS patient's own immune system.

6. Prevent the immune system from becoming activated following an initial viral infection to limit or preclude intracellular replication of HIV.

7. Enhance the "first lines of defense" against AIDS along the lines of my proposal for limiting infectiousness.

The first suggestion is highly speculative but evolutionarily rational. In a little mentioned sidebar to the studies that document how continuous treatment with AZT selects for AZT-resistant form, some HIV strains have emerged with continuing sensitivity to this drug.[43] It would be conceivable to isolate and propagate such a resistance-resistant (that is, quasi-permanently sensitive and genetically crippled) variant of HIV and then use it to intentionally seed a patient whose own infection was resistant to AZT. This "benign" viral therapy would be analogous to the early (circa 1960s) use of an avirulent strain of staphylococcus known as 502 A in an attempt to induce an overgrowth of the more benign form so it would displace the more pathogenic strain.[44] By creating evolutionary competition within the host for lymphocyte space, it might be possible to use the benign, susceptible AIDS strain to overcome the otherwise lethal, resistant one. Should the treatment fail, the built-in susceptibility to AZT might provide a fail-safe switch to undo the experiment. Obviously such a radical approach should only be attempted after extensive review and informed consent of the patients at risk.

The second idea requires social engineering to accomplish and is fraught with ethical problems of coercion and discrimination. Nonetheless, by focusing on the highest risk transmitters of HIV and offering incentives for safe sex and compliance with treatment modalities, some steps in the direction of reducing the viral spread (beyond just general advice to practice safe sex) may be achieved.

The third idea expands on current vaccination strategies to develop immunization approaches that greatly limit the likelihood of virulent HIV strains from persisting. To do so means identifying the common cell membrane receptors that permit the invasion of the $CD4^+$ cells or the basis for the "superantigen" capacity (see Chapter 8) that may give HIV the ability to perpetuate its immunologic damage.

The fourth suggestion acknowledges that increasing the resistance of women to sexually transmitted HIV is of paramount importance at this stage of the epidemic. Today, fully half of all new cases of AIDS are occurring through heterosexual sex. A physical barrier for women (for example, the female condom) has already been tested and approved by the FDA. But a more specific method of increasing resistance is needed to provide a better barrier to transmittal. One idea is a highly effective antiviral douche. The present spermatocide nonoxynol is only a weak viricide. Another is to reinforce the barriers that exist at the level of the vaginal mucosa. By boosting the mucosal immunity of potential AIDS patients it may prove possible to reduce the likelihood of initial HIV penetration of this first contact area.[45] In theory, it should prove possible to enhance vaginal mucosal immunity by selectively boosting the IgA-type immune response, perhaps to the gp 120 protein. Even seaweed derived carageenan may protect against vaginal infection.

The fifth suggestion is an extension of the "pathogen-derived-resistance" principle championed by J. C. Sanford of the Department of Horticultural Sciences at Cornell University.[46] In Sanford's plan, human blood cells would be protected against AIDS by designing a series of genes to protect the cells against viral invasion and/or growth. A related plan was proposed by Dr. Julianna Lisziewicz, a scientist at the National Cancer Institute, who proposed ways to genetically engineer cells to block HIV replication.[47] I am suggesting an extension of this idea in which genetically engineered cells would be returned to the patient after abolishing most or all of the indigenous infected cell population.

The sixth idea was championed at the 1993 AIDS conference by Anthony S. Fauci, director of the National Institute of Allergy and Infectious Diseases. Dr. Fauci proposed using an immunosuppressant drug called cyclosporin A to block the activation of the immune systems of HIV-positive individuals, which appears to provide an expanded T cell population for HIV to infect.[48]

The seventh idea embodies the belief that the earliest possible detection of transmission provides a kind of "golden hour" of opportunity to thwart successful transmission. A blitzing, right-after-the-fact treatment with massive AZT has been proposed as a blocker of viral replication. This approach has been tried with apparent success in blocking HIV colonization of needle-stick victims, although isolated examples where even immediate AZT treatment has failed are sobering reminders of the plasticity of the virus. Something akin to a postcoital contraceptive that would provide prophylaxis against AIDS in the event of an unprotected, high-risk encounter (for example, after rape) might provide an internal environment sufficiently inimical to viral invasion to abort an infectious encounter.

Ethical Observations

I would stress that all of these ideas are only that – suggestions and novel or quasi-novel approaches to control a disease that is out of control worldwide. AIDS has already threatened fundamental social institutions. Immigration rules have been tightened by fearful countries such as Japan and Singapore, even as the United States continues to ban the immigration of persons ill with AIDS. Discrimination and exclusion, bias and denial, all have warped effective planning to control this epidemic. Even the early attempts at providing free syringes to limit needle sharing (a pattern of drug use currently responsible for up to a third of new AIDS cases in the United States) were thwarted by short-sighted political representatives who believe that such a policy would only encourage drug use. While legal constraints theoretically limit the heavy hand of government in forcng persons to be tested for AIDS or demanding that contacts be divulged, the specter of greater governmental intrusion into the lives of high-risk groups remains just over the horizon. Impoundment by the United States in Guantánamo, Cuba, of AIDS patients from among Haitian refugees; forced quarantine of AIDS patients in Cuba; barriers to the free movement of HIV-positive persons; exclusion of gays and compulsory HIV testing in the military; and continued homophobia all speak to a persisting civil rights dilemma. Clearly, ethical resolutions will have to accompany clinical ones if this epidemic is not to get the better of us.

Evolutionary Perspectives

The present evolutionary situation is anything but reassuring. As the HIV-positive population burgeons toward 30 million, the opportunity for still greater evolutionary drift and change in the viruses associated with this disease increase accordingly. A vast reservoir of human hosts now provides a living evolutionary laboratory for a virus that knows no bounds. What will happen over the next 20 years is still speculation. But one thing is sure—unless the conditions of spread and dissemination of the HIV organism are curtailed and dramatic new policies put into place to thwart its rapid dissemination, it will remain a virulent disease. Only through instituting policies that limit the transfer of the active virus or that ensure that its recipients are protected against viral replication will this scourge be stopped.

As we look at AIDS through an evolutionary lens, it is useful to remember that the vision of this disease provides a bidirectional look at selective forces. Not only can we see AIDS evolving from its primate origins, we may also use AIDS as a lens to look at human evolution. The paramount lesson of AIDS—that without an immune system, we succumb rapidly to opportunistic infections—also provides a way of looking at the evolution of the immune system itself.

The most recent thinking has, in fact, turned a new light on the apparently self-perpetuating destruction of the immune system as the core problem confronting the body following an HIV infection. As long-time AIDS researcher Dr. Anthony Fauci, director of the National Institute of Allergy and Infectious Diseases, has said, "Even if you knocked off the virus early, you could still have damage to the immune system."[49] The hub of this self-destruction is likely to be found in the evolutionary roots of the paradoxical phenomenon of autoimmunity, the topic of the next chapter.

8 Attacks Against the Self

Given its primary role in defense against infectious diseases generally, and its remarkable ability to limit the growth of some cancers and viral conditions more specifically, it does not seem unreasonable to ask why the immune system turns against the body. In fact, the complete story of how the immune system comes unraveled during an infection with HIV ultimately involves understanding the paradox of autoimmunity. Why would a system that has evolved to protect the body have retained the capacity to engineer its own self-destruction?

Voyages of Self-Discovery

One of the first historical reports of an apparent case of autoimmunity has an unexpected leading character. In 1493 when Christopher Columbus returned from his second voyage of discovery, he was plagued with a strange bout of arthritis and eye trouble. His joints were stiff and sore, and his eyes were so red and inflamed that they were reported to actually be bleeding.[1] One other salient medical fact about the Columbus voyages: It is almost certain that Columbus and his crew brought back syphillis to the Old World since an epidemic originating in Portugal and Spain swept the European community from 1492 to 1495. Other sexually transmitted diseases, notably trichomonas infections, may also have been picked up by Columbus's crew during unauthorized shore leaves. How do these sexually transmitted diseases relate to the captain's health problems?

Medical detectives have assembled enough details about Columbus's symptoms to relate them to a contemporary disease, a rare disorder called Reiter's disease. This condition was originally described by a Hans Reiter, a German physician. Reiter described a Prussian lieutenant who developed diarrhea followed by arthritis, inflammation of the whites of the eye (conjunctivitis), and an inflammation of the urethra (urethritis). Remarkably, Reiter associated this condition with a prior infection with a spirochete.[2] With hindsight, we can now guess that Columbus had acquired either a form of trichomonas or a diarrheal disease that predisposed him to developing what we now recognize as an autoimmune disease.

What makes this condition so important is that it is the first report of what is now recognized as a host of conditions in which prior infection with a microbial organism leads to an attack by the body's immune system on its own components. Organisms as diverse as the *Chlamydia trachomatis* spirochete; the *Yersinia enterocolitica* bacterium; and *Salmonella, Shigella,* and *Camplylobacter* bacteria (common causes of diarrhea and ulcers); and even the Lyme disease organism, *Borrelia burgdorferi,* can all trigger an autoimmune reaction that includes symptoms of arthritis in both children and adults. Even some parasitic infestations have been reported to give rise to autoimmune disorders that include symptoms of arthritis.[3]

This constellation of otherwise unrelated diseases poses a mystery: first, why does the body "self-destruct" following what appears to be a successful immunological effort at expelling an intruder; and, second, why is it in the intruder's evolutionary interest to cause an autoimmune disease? Both of these seemingly intractable questions pose an evolutionary dilemma. If the body's success in fending off a relatively innocuous invader such as the trichomonas organism routinely leads to serious secondary illness, why did natural selection not eliminate those persons who presumably had a genetic propensity for this maladaptive reaction? The corollary to this question is why is the immune system such a double-edged sword in the first place?

In 1900, the great German immunologist, Paul Ehrlich coined the phrase "horror autotoxicus" to describe the dreaded possibility that the immensely potent cellular destructive capabilities of the immune system could be turned against the self.[4] To understand how such a circumstance could arise, it is useful to look at the evolution of the immune system within the body.

Evolutionary Processes and the Immune System

The immune system incorporates its own form of natural selection in honing its capabilities to recognize the diverse chemical forms of the outside world. In 1955, Niels K. Jerne, then at the California Institute of Technology, first suggested that the immune system might undergo a process of natural selection as it was exposed to antigens. He believed that lymphocytes capable of responding to foreign substances would be stimulated to grow and expand their antibody production while those that did not encounter their respective antigens would lie fallow. Four years later, Sir Macfarlane Burnet built on Jerne's concept by proposing that the immune system works by allowing the emergence of a *single* antibody-producing cell from a host of genetically different white blood cells (the B cell line as we know it today).[5] The factor that determined which cell line or clone would be allowed to proliferate would be the antigenic stimulus itself. Today, four different gene families have been uncovered that permit the evolution of some 1,920,000 different antibody types.[6] This diversity permits a wide spectrum of antigens to select for their respective antibody-producing cells. Though subject to modification as more experimental data became available, the basic features of the clonal selection theory have remained intact over the ensuing 35 years.

Like Darwin's theory of natural selection, Burnet's theory posits two key elements: (1) that enough genetic variation exists in the cells of the immune system to permit selection to operate; and (2) that following selection, descendants of the selected clone are somehow encouraged to survive and proliferate. In theory, the survivors are programmed by virtue of the unique genetics to make but a single type of antibody. Newly developed data have refined this theory to show that only cells that express the antibodies with the strongest binding capabilities–ultimately those that prove most effective–survive.[7] It is now clear that stringent selective forces also operate during the reaction of the immune system to ensure that useless or nonoptimal antibody-producing cells are eliminated. Thus, the immune system actually hones and sharpens its effectiveness as it reacts to antigens from putative invaders or otherwise undesirable agents.

But for the immune system to work without damaging the body—that is, to "tolerate" the self—it must be so designed as to forbid the emergence of self-reactive cells that could hone in on the body's own constituents. Given the constant emergence of potential self-reacting cell lines, clearly something more than a simple "absence of encouragement" of potentially autoaggressive cells is needed to assure tolerance.[8]

While Burnet postulated a mechanism of self-tolerance through elimination of autoreactive clones, it is only in the last decade that the full features of his theory have been confirmed. Self-tolerance occurs through the elimination of potentially self-reactive cells. Early in their development, potential autoimmune cells of the B cell or antibody-producing lineage encounter and bind many antigen molecules from the body itself. At this one critical moment in their development—and at this moment only—such binding sends a signal to the nucleus that causes that specific B cell to die. Potentially autoreactive B cells thus undergo a "programmed cell death" during early development that ensures that none will be around to react to the body's constituents later in life.

The T cell line of lymphocytes, which will eventually carry out the cell-mediated immune functions of surveillance, parasite and virus control, and graft rejection, pass through the thymus as they differentiate. Here, they go through a cellular gauntlet similar to the one traversed by the B cells. Wherever they encounter the body's constituents, those T cells that have matching receptors die off. Like their B cell counterparts, if maturing T cells contact parts of the body's own cellular makeup that lock onto and match their own surface configurations, they are given a kind of molecular "kiss of death" and expunged from the roster of potentially reactive cells.[9] In theory, this process of clonal deletion ensures that no potentially reactive T cells will be around later in life to attack the body. But this system only works as long as the body's own constituents or antigenic mimics of those constituents do not inadvertently restimulate the system or spontaneous mutations do not recreate an antiself receptor on a reactive T cell.

Autoimmune Diseases

When this system of self-tolerance does fail for some or all of the reasons just enumerated, antibodies may be produced by B cells against some of the body's own cellular constituents. Unless this attack is intensified and the T cell line of lymphocytes are called into play, the affected person may be under siege, but not yet sick. In persons with myasthenia gravis, which attacks the muscle-nerve junction, autoimmunity will develop from the very onset of antibody production.

Some of the classic autoimmune diseases and their targets are listed in Table 2.

What can explain this plethora of disorders, affecting virtually every organ system of the body? For one thing, these autoimmune diseases can be separated into at least two main groupings: (1) diseases in which cellular and/or humoral immune responses are primarily directed against single organs (for example, the beta cells of the pancreas in diabetes; the thyroid gland in Hashimoto's thyroiditis; bone marrow in pernicious anemia), and (2) those in which multiple organ systems are involved (for example, systemic lupus erythematosus or rheumatoid arthritis). Immunologists believe that the organ-specific autoimmune diseases are the result of the *de novo* appearance or activation of a single, "forbidden clone" of genetically unique, self-reactive lymphocytes. When this occurs, some factor or factors act to break the tolerance that customarily exists to protect us against Ehrlich's horror autotoxicus.

For instance, one clone of lymphocytes recognizes and produces antibodies to a particular antigen known as PM-Scl. Reactivity against this particular antigen is associated with forms of connective tissue autoimmunity known as scleroderma and polymyositis in about half the affected patients.[10] In scleroderma, rheumatogists believe that an immune response against collagen and the centromere portion of the cell (necessary for proper cell division) leads to skin tightening and eventually to multiple organ attacks and, ultimately, kidney failure or progressively fatal lung destruction. A clue to scleroderma's origins comes from the fact that the T and B cell clones that appear to be activated react against antigens associated with chromosome separation during cell division via the anticentromere antibodies[11] or with certain regions of the DNA molecule itself.[12] Such reactions could interfere with normal cell division and/or

Table 2: Major Autoimmune Diseases and Their Targets

Diseases	Affected Structures
Rheumatologic Conditions	
rheumatoid arthritis	joints, connective tissue
mixed connective tissue disease	collagen, joints
scleroderma	skin, heart, lungs, gut, kidney
CREST syndrome*	blood vessels, skin, esophagus
Sjögren's syndrome	liver, kidney, brain, salivary gland, thyroid
polymyositis	muscle tissue
dermatomyositis	skin, muscle
systemic lupus erythematosus	DNA, platelets, kidney, skin
Endocrine Disorders	
Grave's disease	thyroid
Hashimoto's thyroiditis	thyroid
insulin-dependent diabetes	pancreas
Addison's disease	adrenal gland
polyglandular endocrine disease	multiple glands
Dermatologic Diseases	
pemphigus vulgaris	skin
alopecia areata	hair follicles
Neurologic Conditions	
myasthenia gravis	nerve/muscle acetylcholine receptors
multiple sclerosis	brain and spinal cord myelin
Nephrologic Conditions	
Goodpasture's disease	kidney
Gastrointestinal Diseases	
Crohn's disease	intestinal tract
primary biliary cirrhosis	bile duct
fulminant acute hepatitis	liver
Hematological Abnormalities	
pernicious anemia	gastric parietal cells
idiopathic thrombocytopenic purpura	platelets
autoimmune hemolytic anemia	red blood cell membrane
Reactive Disorders	
juvenile arthritis	joints
juvenile-onset diabetes	pancreas
rheumatic fever	mitral valve
Reiter's disease	joints, eyes, urethra

**CREST stands for calcinosis, Raynaud's syndrome, esophageal hypomotility, sclerosis, and telangiectasias.*

expression of DNA in critical cells such as fibroblasts known to be involved with collagen synthesis and thereby lead to the manifestations of scleroderma. At least one other antigen, known as Scl-70, has been implicated as a factor that contributes to the impaired collagen synthesis characteristic of scleroderma patients.[13] Clearly, the situation in this and related autoimmune diseases is exceedingly complex, as many other antibodies directed against self components ("autoantibodies") and specialized targets such as the membranes around the cell's nucleus (antinuclear antibody) are eventually found in reactive patients.

A clearer situation exists in systemic lupus erythematosus (SLE). Lupus affects about 1 in every 1,000 females in this country (it affects females about nine times more frequently than males). Racial differences also exist, with individuals of African American ancestry being more commonly affected than other groups. This disease ultimately involves many organ systems, causing arthritis, skin rashes, inflammations of organs, blood disorders, and neuropsychiatric abnormalities. Newly designed tests have shown that a single antiself antigen coded by genes present on the eleventh chromosome is associated with this disease, particularly in African Americans.[14] Antibodies against this antigen occur in about 35 to 50 percent of SLE patients, and in almost all with Sjögren's syndrome. These autoantibodies can be isolated from the kidneys of affected patients and probably account for much of their symptomology.

In insulin-dependent diabetes mellitus, the beta cells found in the pancreatic islets of Langerhans that produce insulin are often the target of powerful antiself reactions. Evidence for the active involvement of an autoimmune reaction early in this disease can be found by examining the blood from preclinical diabetics. Many are found to have circulating antibodies and T cells that react against pro-islet beta cells, suggesting that an immunologic assault on the pancreas is imminent.

A more complex situation arises when the targets of autoimmunity start out localized but are eventually spread among many organ systems. This can occur in autoimmune thyroiditis, where pernicious anemia also occurs; and in Sjögren's disease and mixed connective tissue disease, where autoreactive cells against multiple antinuclear antibodies arise. In such circumstances, a wide spectrum of reactive clones of lymphocytes appear to be progressively activated and produce autoantibodies directed against antigens shared in common among several different organ sites.

Even where a single clone of self-reactive cells is initially activated, subsequent evolution of the disease may envelop more and more diverse targets. In multiple sclerosis (MS), autoreactive cells that destroy a protein (myelin) that helps insulate nerve cells may be supplanted by a wider range of autoreactive cells. Where full-blown MS occurs, burgeoning colonies of T cells react to an expanded group of myelin basic proteins in a phenomeon known as "determinant spreading." This reactivity may even spill over to involve unrelated proteins, including the classic antigen associated with blood poisoning and lockjaw, the tetanus toxoid.[15] One explanation for this broad range of reactivity is that the initial damage wrought by the autoimmune attack in MS leads to the development of still more antibodies from an overly vigilant immune system. This idea is supported by finding antibodies to distant relatives of myelin, including a group of antigens that surprisingly include the tetanus toxoid mentioned above.[16]

The Superantigen Story

This wide constellation of reactivity in MS and other multitarget autoimmune disease hints at the existence of some mechanism that can activate an incredibly diverse range of reactive T cells, not just those directed at the targeted self-antigen. The best candidate with this capacity is a group of substances called superantigens, so named for their extraordinary ability to provoke a broad array of immunological reactions. A superantigen is a substance produced by a living cell that activates a large number of different clones of T cells, including many that were previously among the "silenced" self-reactive clones. As shown in Figure 5, a superantigen has the ability to activate at least 1 in every 50 T cell lymphocytes, whereas a normal antigen will customarily activate only 1 in every 10,000 or 1,000,000 lymphocytes.

A substance thus becomes a superantigen by virtue of its ability to bind to and activate a wide spectrum of the lymphocyte mediators of immunity. This ability is conferred on the antigen by a peculiar capacity to serve as a molecular bridge between large numbers of different T lymphocytes and the cells that activate them. These activating cells are called antigen-presenting cells. A superantigen binds to a special site expressed on the surface of antigen-presenting cells and also to the surface

Figure 5: Consequence of Exposure to Normal Antigens and Superantigens

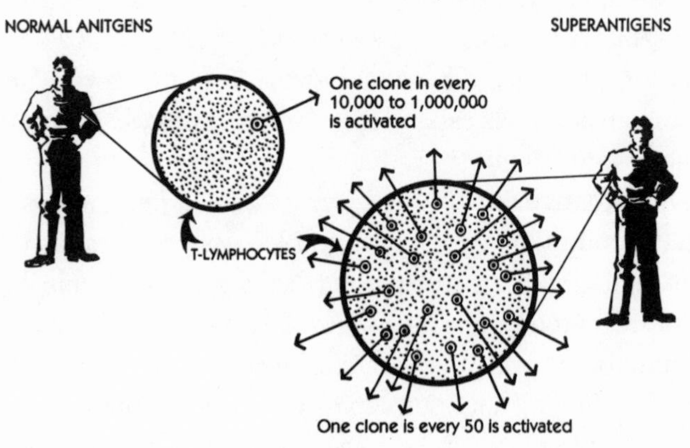

of the one in fifty or so of the billions of T cells in the body that has a matching variable receptor site. In so doing, superantigens form a kind of "C-clamp" or lock that holds the two cell types in intimate proximity. This binding is the *sine qua non* of immune activation–when it occurs, the T cell is irrevocably committed to attacking the presented antigen, wherever and whenever it is encountered.

A superantigen is in essence a very indiscriminate matchmaker. Instead of the usual binding of specific activating cell and only one lymphocyte target, a superantigen links together many thousands of activating cells with many thousands of T cells, each of which would normally respond selectively to only a single antigenic type. (Indeed, some superantigens can perform this multiplicity of activations without an intermediary antigen-processing cell.) When a superantigen conscripts thousands of T cells, it commits each one to "active duty" (that is, to commence their immunologic activities). The resulting immunologic assault is a scattershot attack on a host of antigenic targets. The consequences to a person who has the misfortune of unleashing all of these activated lymphocyte clones are profound.

Symptoms of a broadside immunologic assault can be legion, including those of the type of reactive arthritis that afflicted Columbus–aches, weakness, inflammation of mucosal surfaces in organs such as the urethra or eyes, and so on. Others may experience the generalized malaise that accompanies certain bacterial infections or the more extreme reactions caused by the massive release of intercellular mediators such as the tumor necrosis factor (one of a group of intercellular hormones or cytokines that arise during inflammation) that accompany the wholesale activation of the immune system. The type of shock that accompanies certain staphylococcal infections, particularly the toxic shock syndrome associated with the use of some tampons, can be explained by a superantigen-mediated release of cytokines triggered by a staph toxin.[17]

In fact, superantigens in the garb of bacterially produced endo- or exotoxins have been proposed as the major causes of septic shock and many of the rheumatoid diseases that are now thought to be mediated or initiated by microbial agents.[18] Another association exists between bacterial toxins and autoimmune disease. Researchers at the University of Massachusetts at Worcester have demonstrated in rats that a staphylococcus enterotoxin activated T cells in a tissue culture that then produced autoimmune diabetes when reintroduced into otherwise healthy hosts.[19] This discovery demonstrates that naturally occurring bacterial by-products can activate normally quiescent, self-reactive T cells and thereby provoke autoimmune disease.

Some researchers believe that they can see the signature of a superantigen-mediated self-reactive immunity in the wide spectrum of symptoms that accompany certain autoimmune diseases. One group of researchers at Cornell University Medical College and the University of Utah College of Medicine has postulated that a generalized dysfunction of the immune system must occur in conditions such as systemic lupus erythematosis (SLE) to account for the myriad symptoms common to almost all SLE patients. A typical patient may have the classic butterfly-shaped rash over the bridge of the nose, joint and muscle pain, and evidence of autoimmune damage to internal organs such as the kidney. To explain the broad attack on body parts so characteristic of SLE patients, the team hypothesized that a sweeping activation of self-reacting T lymphocytes occurs that chronically stimulates the antibody-producing arm of the immune system.[20]

From the perspective of the host, the ability of superantigens to provide self-reactive immunity appears totally aberrant. Once superantigens have triggered an immune reaction, the body "remembers" those antigens just as it does the special characteristics of an inciting bacterium or virus following immunization. Hence, any further stimulation from damaged tissue or encounters with another group of bacteria carrying similar antigens can reactivate the autoimmune state.

This memory system in the immune system would explain why diseases such as SLE undergo periods of remission and recurrence or "flare ups." Lupus symptoms may abate after the initial offending microorganism has been cleared. However, some time later, another infection or stress can release a further barrage of provocative proteins that reactivate the self-reactive clones of the immune system, jump-starting the disease process all over again. A quiescent immune system can thus flare into action again, recreating the original symptoms as antibody-producing and self-reactive immune cells once again proliferate to control the real or imagined invader.

This polyclonal activation of the immune system also explains how other, nonbacterial provocative agents could produce autoimmune phenomena. For instance, the ability of silica to produce scleroderma can now be explained by noting that this mineral provokes the release of superantigen-like substances.

Silicone-containing breast implants, which incorporate silica in their outer envelopes, can also produce a unqiue constellation of autoimmune disease symptoms in an indeterminate number of women, especially those whose implants rupture and spill silicone gel into the body. Given the immunostimulatory and inflammatory effects of silicone gel itself, the combined presence of bacteria and/or inflamed tissues associated with silicone implants is a formula for inducing autoimmune disease. The subclinical infections that commonly accompany breast implants containing silicone could also provide a nidus for superantigen release, as many superantigen-like exotoxins are elaborated by staphylococcus and other bacteria commonly found in and around implanted prostheses.

If this model which I proposed in 1993[21] is true, over the next few decades, women who experience the rupture of infected and uninfected silicone breast implants will experience autoimmune disease in increasing numbers. Data are also being amassed based on a growing number of clinical reports (now in the hundreds) that link silicone with autoimmune conditions with the features associated with polyclonal autoimmune activation.[22]

Evolutionary Explanations of the Immune System

If the immune system evolved to protect us, how is it so often tricked into such seemingly maladaptive responses? Among the less palatable answers is that autoimmunity is simply a recurring error of nature that results from our common evolutionary heritage with so many other organisms. In this model, autoimmunity is the result of an otherwise effective immune response against an evolutionarily "primitive" invading organism that just happens to express an old antigenic configuration that we still possess on some part of our own anatomy. Another, more plausible, explanation is that autoimmunity is provoked by microorganisms as part of *their* adaptive repertoire to deflect the immune response away from themselves.

In the accident-of-nature model, an immunologic attack on certain bacteria or viruses inadvertently targets an evolutionarily conserved substance shared by both the infecting organism and its human host. The resulting reaction leads to a concomitant immune response against the invader *and* some constituent of our own bodies. This self-reactive state has been shown to occur in certain streptococcal infections, notably streptococcus A, which causes the notorious "strep throat" of rheumatic fever. Here an immunological attack on the bacterium leads to antibodies against *both* the strep and antigenic components of the mitral valve of the heart, joints, and nerve sheaths. This response can lead to later heart valve damage and inflammation (carditis), a kind of chorea, and/or polyarthritis, all causd by an autoimmune reaction. For this reason, pediatricians are particularly alert to "strep throat" in their young charges and use antibiotics aggressively to suppress it quickly. While rheumatic fever was thought to be all but eradicated in the United States, a recent epidemic in Utah, Nevada, and Wyoming has given rise to great concern in the medical community.[23]

Professor Gian Franco Bottazzo, chair of the prestigious Department of Immunology at the London Hospital Medical College, believes that we have coevolved with one or more intrinsically "autoimmune" viruses that used to mimic our tissue antigens so closely that they were never recognized. Only recently have they diverged enough in their own evolutionary path to have provoked immunological reactions antithetical to their own—and to our survival. Bottazzo dates the existence of such a virus to the dawn of civilized history, but the emergence of its newly acquired autoimmune properties only since the beginning of the nineteenth century.[24] This model would explain the paucity of reports of classic autoimmune diseases in the medical literature until the early 1800s.

An alternate explanation for the involvement of superantigens and multiple organ sites in autoimmune disease is that many different components of related organ systems may express similar antigens. This antigenic sharing could have arisen as a result of multiple organs having common embryonic origins in the same germ layer. The presence of common antigenic determinants would then explain how an immune reaction could affect multiple sites, since the T cells that target one organ would also potentially target all those with similar determinants.[25]

But why would evolution have selected for the presence (or retention) of autoantigens among bacteria and viruses? Consider this idea: when one of our own tissues becomes an innocent bystander to a broadside attack against an invader, it serves as a kind of immunologic decoy, absorbing antibodies and attracting T cells, thereby drawing fire away from the intended invading target. The antigens provoking such a response could eventually become selected among a given group of microorganisms as a strategy for an invading organism to avoid being "hit" by a battery of immune reactions. In this sense, for bacteria and viruses, shared antigens serve an analogous function to the incendiary flares dropped by jets to draw heat-seeking missiles away from themselves.

But what about the concurrence of antigens on bacteria and normal body constituents, as occurs in streptococcal type A organisms and the mitral heart valve. Originally, this commonality could have been selected as a form of "molecular mimicry." If microorganisms can express surface features that duplicate those on some body constituent, it may serve as a kind of subterfuge to *avoid* setting off an immune reaction. Since the body tends to be tolerant of its own tissue antigens, veiling themselves in molecularly similar garb could have been a successful evolutionary ruse for bacteria just as it is for viceroy butterflies who color themselves to mimic their poisonous monarch counterparts. The body normally will not fight a look-alike bacterium as vigorously as it will a foreign-looking one.

Evidence for this predicted absence of an immune response to molecular microbial mimics, or at least for a dampened response, can be found in nature. Ironically, this dampened immune response may be evolutionarily advantageous to the bacterium but disadvantageous to the human host. After a salmonella infection, those patients who have a *weak* immune response against the bacterium tend to be the ones who get Reiter's disease, while those who completely eradicate the disease with a full-blown response tend to remain arthritis-free.[26]

This weaker immune reactivity could reflect the existence of a partial tolerance to the bacterium coinciding with the expected tolerance to a patient's own, cross-reacting proteins. If true, this weakened reactivity would explain the adaptive advantage to the bacterium of mimicking the host's antigenic makeup. Since a weak immune response provides a "safer" environment for the salmonella, selectively infecting and proliferating in human hosts who share molecules with them provides a means of surviving even as their noncross-reacting compatriots are eliminated by a more effective immune response in genetically different humans. The fact that the host subsequently develops an autoimmune disease would be immaterial to the perpetuation of the surviving bacteria, since they would already have been spread by a fecal route to the next source.

Molecular Provocateurs

An even more radical hypothesis, to be explored below, is that microorganisms evolved and kept superantigens in addition to cross-reacting autoantigens as a means to provoke the immune system into a wildly disparate set of reactions that preoccupy the host and miss the invader entirely. That is, superantigen immunological activation would commit so many different T cell clones that it would allow an infecting organism to escape an immunologic assault, even though such activation leads to numerous problems for the host. It is probably not coincidental that superantigens found in bacteria share similar characteristics with those found so far in some viruses.[27] Both groups of organisms may have kept the responsible genes as part of their repertoire for overcoming host resistance.

As we saw previously, among the best candidates for host-incapacitating bacterial superantigens would be certain endo- and exotoxins naturally released by the *Staphylococcus* and *Streptococcus* species as they invade and die in the body. (Endotoxins are found in the bacterial cell wall itself.) Several of the enterotoxins are known to produce high fevers, while others have the previously inexplicable property of stimulating cells to divide. Among the most potent stimulants are the toxins that produce toxic shock syndrome and the symptoms of scarlet fever. These substances also appear to work like superantigens, since they stimulate lymphocytes of the immune system, most notably $CD4^+$ and $CD8^+$ cells, as do the most potent superantigens.[28] An untried experiment in AIDS patients would be to use this much vaunted activation capacity of a substance such as enterotoxin B to *re*activate HIV-poisoned $CD4^+$ cells.

Juvenile Chronic Arthritis as a Model

As proof of the molecular mimicry theory of autoimmunity, many forms of arthritis appear to be provoked by bacterial or viral organisms that share some component their host's molecular makeup. Among the more devastating manifestations of this phenomenon are the juvenile forms of arthritis in which inflammation of the joints and surrounding spaces occurs in children before they reach the age of 16. An 18-year-old girl who used to babysit for us had had this condition since she was 9. The joints in her legs and arms were so badly inflamed and swollen that she had difficulty walking. Certainly, evolutionary mechanisms could not explain this suffering! But explain it they can.

From talking to our babysitter, I learned that she had experienced a severe bout of diarrhea just before she developed her first symptoms. With hindsight, we can now say that this infection, perhaps caused by an organism such as the salmonella bacterium, triggered her autoimmune condition just as the hypothetical bout with the same agent provoked Columbus's symptoms of Reiter's disease. It took an epidemic of food poisoning caused by *Salmonella typhimurium* to establish the validity of this connection between bacteria and juvenile arthritis. Following ingestion of a single contaminated food source at a banquet, 260 persons developed salmonella dysentery. Within 4 weeks, 19 persons (7.8 percent) of the original group had developed rheumatoid arthritis, mostly of the Reiter's type.[29] Certain other types of juvenile arthritis have now been confirmed as being causally associated with a preceding bacterial infection.[30]

But, you might argue, not all patients with juvenile arthritis report having a bacterial diarrhea or other infection. A partial explanation is that the precipitating infection that activates the immune system into an autoimmune attack may be subclinical and poorly recognized. In a recent study, about half of a group of children with juvenile arthritis were found to have a synovial immune response and accompanying antibodies against *Chlamydial* or *Yersinia* organisms but no overt evidence of their infection.[31] These data implicated both an immune reaction to these bacteria and the presence of a smouldering subclinical infection in the pathogenesis of their disease.

Molecular Mimicry

Studies such as this suggest that previously unappreciated bacterial reactions trigger autoimmune disease and are likely to become more common in the ensuing decade. In thinking through this relationship, it is useful to keep in mind that a transient arthritic flare-up can also occur after a viral infection such as rubella (German measles) or influenza type A. Here again, the infection appears to be subclinical in that patients never knew that they had an infection before developing the arthritis.[32] But even in many of these quiescent infections, the immune system is actively attacking the pathogen. For as yet unexplained reasons, in some but not all infected patients, the immune system's "fire" is spread to parts of the body (such as the synovial membranes of the joints) which appear especially vulnerable to immunological attack.

The bacterial connection with arthritis generally is made more plausible by the discovery that a high proportion of patients with particular forms of arthritis have antibodies in their blood to a component of the bacterial cell wall. This antibody appears to be especially common in patients with a form of spinal arthritis known as ankylosing spondylitis.[33] It now turns out that many patients with this rheumatologic disorder have had a history of a previous salmonella, shigella, or yersinia infection that preceded their illness.[34] While not proving a bacteriological origin of this disease, the occurrence of such cross-reacting antibodies is strong supporting evidence for a link.

These observations suggest that somehow reactivity against a virus or bacterium can produce reactivity against critical cell constituents expressed in our own bodies. The most plausible explanation for this occurrence is that bacteria and certain human joint tissues have common antigens, a form of the molecular mimicry discussed above. Such cross reactivity has been found between specific bacterial constituents such as cell wall proteoglycans and those that are crucial to the integrity of the joint, such as proteins of the synovial membrane (which lines the major joints of the body). While not the only explanation for bacteria- and virus-associated autoimmune diseases, antibodies directed against invasive bacteria do contribute to the damage seen in the joint synovial membrane which displays antigenic surfaces similar to those found on certain bacteria.[35]

Another clue to the development of reactive arthritis and related autoimmune diseases is that only certain individuals appear at risk for arthritis after infection with the triggering bacteria. These persons often carry certain genetic "markers" in their major histocompatibility complex system, markers that regulate self-identity and immunological reactivity. In humans, this system is determined by genes in that code for human leukocyte antigens known as the HLA series.[36] More than 90 percent of persons with ankylosing spondylitis express the genetic determinant, known as HLA B27, a marker found in only 8 to 10 percent of the general population.

While the associations between HLA types and disease continue to amass, no one is quite sure of the actual mechanism by which they contribute to susceptibility to autoimmunity.[37] One explanation is that different HLA genes alter the critical portion of the major histocompatibility protein displayed on the cell surface of the antigen-processing cells. This special protein takes the form of a long groove, much like the cleft in an apricot. It is along this groove that small lengths of potentially antigenic proteins (polypeptides) are held for presentation to immune cells. In theory, different HLA antigens may present different portions of the protein molecules that activate the helper T cells ($CD4^+$) and effector T cells ($CD8^+$).

The extent and variety of different antigens that can be displayed on the cell surface in any one individual is usually associated with evolutionary advantages. The more diversity present in the HLA genes, the greater the likelihood that any one antigen-presenting cell will successfully display a foreign protein fragment, say, from a novel bacterium. Diversity *per se,* then, would account for enhanced disease resistance.

Something like this is hypothesized to explain the appearance of new HLA alleles in the Indians of South America. As these populations migrated southward from their Paleolithic Arctic origins some 40,000 to 50,000 years ago and again in more recent waves of migration 17,000 to 20,000 years ago, they were likely exposed to novel diseases. Resistance to certain diseases is often coupled with a specific HLA gene. (Malarial resistance, for instance, is linked to HLA B53, which is discussed in Chapter 10.) Carrying *different* HLA genes on chromosomes inherited from each parent (heterozygosity) is associated again with heightened resistance to disease. Such heterozygosity has, in fact, been found among the Havasupai, a tribe of about 650 people who inhabit the Havasupai Gorge of the Grand Canyon in Arizona.[38]

But here, again, the same system that codes for adaptive reactivity can backfire and produce pathology. For instance, ankylosing spondylitis is also highly prevalent among such Native American populations, possibly reflecting the initial evolutionary advantages of carrying an HLA B27 gene that produces a high-intensity immune reaction to certain bacterial antigens. As much as 50 percent of Native Americans express this gene compared to no more than 8 to 10 percent of persons of northern European ancestry.

The molecular mimicry hypothesis for ankylosing spondylitis and other rheumatologic disorders has some experimental support. Some of the groove-like proteins displayed on the cell surface by HLA molecules actually mimic the antigens expressed by certain key bacteria. For instance, a bacterium known as *Proteus mirabilis* expresses a protein on its surface membrane that looks like the groove proteins coded for by HLA genes known as HLA DR1 and DR4. When either of these two HLA proteins are present and displayed on cell surfaces throughout the body (but especially in the lining of the joints), an immune reaction to the proteus bacteria can boomerang and involve cells of the body itself. In fact, carrying either HLA DR1 and DR4 signals a heightened susceptibility to rheumatoid arthritis. In England, DR1/DR4 positive arthritis patients generally have antibodies to proteus far in excess of the background level in the population as a whole.[39] Interestingly, the Epstein-Barr virus, which is associated with chronic fatigue syndrome and mononucleosis, also comes wrapped in a protein whose makeup shares amino acids in common with certain HLA proteins.[40] Here again, an attack on the Epstein-Barr virus may mistakenly involve the HLA proteins as well, producing tissue and organ damage throughout the body.

"Heat-Shock" Proteins

The strongest clue about a bacteria-arthritis-autoimmune connection comes from a seemingly obscure fact—the T lymphocytes from the immune system of patients with various autoimmune diseases are commonly found to react to a strange protein known as the heat-shock protein.[41]

The heat-shock protein is among an ancient group of protective substances found in organisms from every phylum. Such proteins "chaperone" other molecules to and from the cell nucleus and are involved in protein synthesis, transport, and folding.[42] As such, they are instrumental in the growth, activation, and survival of cells, especially when those cells are under duress.

At one point these ancient proteins may have served their hosts as part of the defense against radical environmental changes, where increases in temperature and free-radical-mediated stresses were common. When released, heat-shock proteins create physiological conditions that afford their hosts increased advantages in new environments. It is therefore reasonable to assume that natural selection favored bacteria that "learned" to elaborate these proteins under stressful conditions including heat itself.

All living organisms today share this molecular response as a holdover of an ancient mechanism for ensuring survival. In higher organisms, release of heat-shock proteins often occurs in response to the stresses associated with infection: intense inflammation, toxins, and tissue oxidative changes. Under stress, cells in our own body release a slightly smaller heat-shock protein that bears a striking resemblance to the parent molecule found in bacteria. For bacteria, production of heat-shock proteins ensured their survival under environmental stressors that would otherwise kill or reduce the viability of cells and ultimately the organism itself.

For humans, reaction to heat-shock-expressing cells in our bodies may have evolved as a mechanism for the immune system to detect and eliminate infected or otherwise stressed cells whose continued presence was inimical to the survival of the whole organism. Perhaps for this reason, the mammalian immune system "doesn't like" heat-shock proteins and responds to their presence as if reacting to a medical emergency.

Indeed, heat-shock proteins stimulate the immune system so powerfully that they serve as superantigens!

This last attribute of heat shock proteins may provide the "missing link" to understanding how bacteria can trigger autoimmune diseases and why the human body retains this adaptation, even as it appears to put itself at risk for a serious chronic disease later in life. Because so many pathogens signal their presence by releasing heat-shock proteins, a rapid cell-mediated reaction against bacterial or viral heat-shock proteins is likely to have evolved as an early part of the immune system. Later, that response was probably incorporated into the immunologic mechanisms used to defend the body against invading organisms generally. This rapid immune reaction to bacterial or viral heat-shock proteins thus provided a general "first line of defense" against invasion since it involved a reactive mode that did not have to await a formal immune response. As an example of the adaptive value of such a response, consider the mycobacteria. As a group, these primitive pathogens are among those microorganisms with the richest repository of heat-shock proteins. It would obviously be advantageous to "send out the troops" at the earliest contact with tuberculosis and related deadly bacteria.

But, while adaptive as a defense against potential pathogens, the same reaction can be turned against the body if it finds heat-shock proteins expressed in damaged tissues. Anyone who has injured a knee or hip as a youngster knows that it may well be the first site of arthritis if an arthritic condition occurs. This can happen because the cellular damage released heat-shock proteins that may have "flagged" that site. A later flare-up of immune responses stimulated by a bacterial or viral infection can bring about a localized response.

Another attractive model to explain the role of heat-shock proteins in arthritis is that microorganisms that display heat-shock proteins congregate in the joint space where the most intense reaction is concentrated. Tissue damage would then result from otherwise healthy cells in the joint lining receiving inadvertent "friendly fire" from the defending immune system. This model has heuristic appeal since pathogenic organisms have now been isolated from synovial tissue, the site of most severe reactive arthritic diseases. While some researchers remain skeptical of this association,[43] suggestive evidence for a causal association between heat-shock proteins and some autoimmune diseases has been obtained from animal studies. For example, a severe, destructive arthritis can be produced in an otherwise healthy rat by simply injecting it with heat-shock-reactive T cells that had been activated in *another* rat infected with the tuberculosis bacterium.[44] Conversely, blocking the immune reaction against heat-shock proteins by vaccinating rats against the mycobacterial heat-shock protein prevents or slows the appearance of arthritis.[45]

While proof of this kind cannot ethically be generated by experimenting in humans, T cells that react strongly to heat-shock proteins have been found "at the scene of the crime," that is, in the joints of patients who have rheumatoid arthritis or other autoimmune arthritic disorders.[46] Moreover, the T cells of the human immune system that react against the mycobacterial heat-shock proteins also react against human heat-shock proteins.[47]

Heat-shock proteins have also been proposed as the culprits in systemic lupus erythematosus (SLE) as well. Support for this radical hypothesis comes from observations that show that trace amounts of some heat-shock proteins (1:100,000,000,000 of their molecular weight) exert powerful stimulatory effects on the division of just those T cells known to be active in SLE.[48] Equally important, self-reacting autoantibodies for a number of stress proteins can be found in patients with both SLE and rheumatoid arthritis.[49]

Whatever their eventual proven contribution, heat-shock proteins in particular and superantigens in general clearly play a major role in human autoimmune diseases. For this reason, understanding their evolutionary *raison d'etre* is all the more important.

Evolutionary Perspectives

The first task is to explain how *both* partners of the evolutionary relationship—host and parasite—can derive benefits from having or responding to superantigens. We have already seen how, from the bacterium's viewpoint, elaboration of toxins that provoke a broad range of immune cells may help it circumvent an otherwise *specific* immune activation that would jeopardize its survival.[50] From the body's perspective, being able to "sound the alarm" in response to a common, ubiquitous toxin expressed on particular bacterial strains also makes evolutionary sense.

In fact, having a system that reacted to the superantigen known as bacterial endotoxin (a lipopolysaccharide found on the cell surface of all gram-negative bacteria) can be seen as an especially favorable adaptation. While an excessive response to endotoxin can cause a rapid fall in blood pressure, massive tissue damage from free radicals, blood clotting of small vessels (disseminated intravascular coagulation), and even death, some researchers have suggested that the endotoxin response is actually an adaptive one.[51] The fact that animals that react only weakly or not at all to endotoxin are extremely susceptible to bacterial infection strongly suggests that this broadly reactive mode of the immune system is an adaptive feature vital to our survival. Even the release of tumor necrosis factor, clotting, and shock that occurs after massive endotoxin release obscures the likelihood that these same reactions are probably beneficial when they occur locally and in small quantity. For instance, a local increase in blood coagulability can contain an infection.

Adaptive Qualities in Autoimmunity?

Even autoimmunity itself may not be all bad. In certain circumstances, according to Irun Cohen of the Weizmann Institute in Rehovot, Israel, a propensity to autoimmune reactions may be a vital component of the functions of the immune system, notably control of cancer and parasitic diseases.[52] The ability to go after cells that are only marginally different from the body–such as cancer cells that express tumor-specific antigens or antigenically distinct parasites–would indeed confer a survival advantage to people who had it. But, in this sense, the same capacity that gives the immune system an edge for zeroing in on deviant cell types may simultaneously give it "too sharp a tooth" when the body inadvertently exposes some of its own tissues to attack (for example, after damage to the thyroid gland) or when the immune system gears up for a massive assault provoked by superantigens and attacks its own tissues instead.

AIDS and Superantigens

This maladaptive reaction may explain part of what is happening in the case of HIV. We have already seen that for the HIV organism to be successful, it must find a suitable population of activated *and* dividing T cells to infect. Under most conditions, the specific targeted T cell in the body, the CD4⁺ cell, remains inactive. But the HIV organism, like its retrovirus cousin, the mouse mammary tumor virus, may produce a superantigen. (A simian immunodeficiency virus has already been found to express such a substance.[53]) Under superantigenic stimulation, thousands of otherwise quiescent $CD4^+$ cells would be activated. The resulting cellular divisions would put the body in a false state of alert—and provide a vast array of newly dividing $CD4^+$ cells for infection by the invading immunodeficiency virus.

Suggestive evidence that such a mechanism may assist HIV in gaining a foothold in its host includes the observation that HIV infection results in the selective loss of T cells with a particular variable region—just the site targeted by superantigens.[54] This observation fits nicely with the general finding that when superantigens are injected into a host (in this case, a mouse), superantigen-targeted T cells are the first to proliferate and then die.[55] Persons with active HIV infections may show the residuum of this process as they commonly carry an inactive, dying T cell population of the kind stimulated by superantigens.[56]

The fact that immunodepressed AIDS patients experience a Sjögren's-like autoimmune disease would be an immunological paradox but for the superantigen hypothesis. Until now, it seemed virtually inexplicable that AIDS patients whose immune systems are being systematically destroyed by viral infection can nonetheless develop an autoimmune condition. The explanation of this enigma makes sense if the human immunodeficiency virus (HIV) were found to express a superantigen—since superantigens can activate powerful $CD8^+$ T cells directly without the need for the decimated $CD4^+$ population.

Superantigens, were they proven to be present on human AIDS viruses would explain how HIV strains "use" the AIDS patient's immune system to their own advantage. Recall that the immunologic apparatus of most AIDS patients goes into a meaningless and ultimately self-destructive process of replication and decay, a process that circumvents an effective attack on the virus itself. Were this decay provoked by superantigens, it would explain much of the observed phenomena. In fact, the immune system appears to continue to decay even *after* significant numbers of the blood-borne virus are gone, apparently sequestered in tissue macrophages and lymph nodes. By setting in motion a seemingly self-perpetuating autoimmune assault on the immune system itself, the HIV organism vouchsafes its own survival.

Conclusions

Thus, provoking autoimmunity can be seen as an adaptive reaction from the microbial world's vantage point, even as it is generally inimical to well-being from a human perspective. For the host, autoimmunity may be a necessary evil, the price of eternal vigilance against an inimical world of competing organisms vying for supremacy. But when an organism such as the human immunodeficiency virus provokes this system, we pay a heavy price indeed.

Why so many people would remain vulnerable to autoimmune diseases generally—and, more critically, how this vulnerability can coexist with a general state of well-being—at present remain unanswerable questions. But, at a minimum, we may profitably reexamine how susceptibility to disease is shaped to find clues to lead us out of our present state of ignorance.

9 Vulnerability to Disease

Benefits and Risks of Immunologic Competence

One of the important adages of evolutionary theory is that adaptations for protection against one source of harm may generate vulnerabilities toward another. As we saw in the last chapter, one explanation for the prevalence of autoimmune diseases is that having a "high-strung" immune system may be adaptive in some circumstances. For example, it provides an early detection system for cancer; a surveillance system for damaged cells; and a seek-and-destroy system for parasites that hide within cells. The constant threat of malignancy and of bacterial or parasitic invasion maintain these adaptations in the immune system, but also make it vulnerable to inappropriate activation and hence to autoimmune diseases. The examples given in the previous chapter provide a model for visualizing how selective pressures keep resistance to many diseases in a state of dynamic equilibrium with vulnerability to others. In this chapter, I explore the genetic basis for this adaptive state.

Genetic studies provide an explanation for this equilibrium. The relatively high prevalence of many of the most common hereditary diseases, especially those due to recessive or X-linked genes, has an evolutionary explanation. For the most common disorders, recessive genes that are dangerous when present in a double dose are kept in the population by the selective advantage afforded individuals who carry the gene in a single dose. Carriers of many of the most common hereditary diseases, such as sickle-cell anemia, Tay-Sachs disease, and cystic fibrosis, are postulated to have better survival odds than do their normal compatriots when confronted with the threat of parasitic (malaria), bacterial (tuberculosis), or pulmonary disease, respectively.

Many more complex, polygenic human adaptations, such as skin color, heat-stress adaptations, and blood enzyme deficiencies, follow a similar pattern. Each evolved as a response to the selective pressures of environmental factors.[1] Light skin permits vitamin D to be synthesized after exposure to the weak ultraviolet rays of the extreme northern and southern latitudes. Sweat glands occur in higher density in individuals living closer to the equator to ensure more efficient cooling. And, as we will see in the next chapter, genetic mutations such as the glucose-6-phosphate dehydrogenase (G6PD) enzyme deficiency afford protection against malaria in certain equatorial regions.

Adaptations and Maladaptations

While these genetically determined traits are adaptive as responses to certain environment-specific stressors, each is maladaptive in environments that differ significantly from those that shaped their origins. Light skin in European emigrés to Australia predisposes them to melanoma. A high density of sweat glands puts the tropical African who migrates to a northern clime at risk for folliculitis, inappropriate heat regulation, and other disorders. And many of the sixty or more X-linked G6PD variants increase the susceptibility of male workers to acute hemolysis (rupture of blood cells) in the presence of high concentrations of camphor, carbon monoxide, or other noxious chemicals; and to more insidious hemolysis after eating foods, such as fava beans, which cannot be properly metabolized.

Lipids as a Model

If one of the tasks of evolutionary medicine is to explain the persistence of genes that predispose their holders to serious illness. Among the most difficult circumstances to explain is why there exists such an extraordinary prevalence of lipid disorders in Western populations. As much as half of all heart disease can be explained by genetic factors. Excessive levels of certain lipoproteins (a group of substances made up of a core of lipid globules surrounded by a protein shell), especially low-density lipoproteins, contribute to this heart disease risk, especially among Caucasians.[2] In many instances, the culprit appears to be a composite molecule known as lipoprotein (a), which, in addition to its lipid core, carries an additional molecule (a glycoprotein) linked to it by disulfide bonds. When present in excessive amounts, this molecule along with its congener Lp(e) are each associated with heightened risk of heart disease.

Under normal circumstances, Lp(a) has the special attributes of accelerating wound healing and cellular repair mechanisms, strengthening the matrix that holds blood vessels together, and preventing the unhealthy oxidation of lipids. Most interestingly, Lp(a) is found in appreciable quantities among mammals only in humans and guinea pigs. This has led Linus Pauling and his associates to suggest that Lp(a) evolved to replace the functions lost as ascorbic acid (vitamin C) disappeared from the constitutions of these two species. (Recall that both humans and guinea pigs require extrinsic vitamin C to survive.) When ascorbate (a form of vitamin C) is added to the diet of persons with ultra-high (and ultra-risky) levels of this lipid, its levels diminish. This observation has led Pauling to suggest depressing Lp(a) by massive amounts of vitamin C, a hypothesis partially confirmed by data showing that atherosclerosis in guinea pigs and humans can be partially reversed by ascorbic acid supplementation.[3] Thus, in the case of Lp(a) at least, the double-edged sword is sharply defined: one edge provides improved wound healing and other protections against bodily damage from chemicals, while the other edge generates a risk of heart disease.

The evolutionary explanation for this otherwise admirable adaptation is linked to Dobzhansky's rule described in Chapter 2. Recall that natural selection generally protects an individual only up to successful child rearing. As long as the first edge of this adaptation provides its benefits through this period, the second edge–revealed in the inimical consequences of heart disease–is the unavoidable evolutionary risk.

Maladaptations

Other illnesses are a result of the limitations imposed by evolution on the rapidity by which humans can adapt to novel environments. As a former Chicagoan, I can testify to the continuing maladaptive response humans have to the low light levels common in winter at northern latitudes. A specific disorder, known as seasonal affective disorder (SAD), is apparently related to a deficiency in the normal cycle of production of melatonin in reaction to light passing through the skin.[4] Even my five or six generations of forebearers who lived through Polish/Russian winters had not prepared me adequately for the long period of fog, gloom, and pale sun so typical of Chicago winters, perhaps because I grew up in much more temperate latitudes. I experienced periods of depression and excessive weight gain regularly during seven winters in Chicago!

The transmigration of whole populations from one environment to another might be expected to produce physiological upheavals of varying intensity and severity. One such event appears to have affected the African populations that migrated to the Caribbean. The relatively new arrivals at islands such as Curacao who came primarily from central Africa and now compose 95 percent of the island population appear remarkably vulnerable to systemic lupus erythematosis.[5] This maladaptation may be linked in as yet undefined ways to novel dietary or environmental factors that trigger this autoimmune disease in susceptible individuals.

We should not take any comfort in the expectation that since many of us grew up with the industrial revolution, we are necessarily preadapted to its by-products. As Herman J. Muller, the Nobel Prize winner who discovered the mutation-producing effects of radiation, observed some 30 years ago, "Today, we human beings are exposed to a great number of substances not encountered by our ancestors, to which we therefore have not been specifically adapted by natural selection. Among those substances are food-additives, drugs, narcotics, antibiotics, pesticides, cosmetics, contraceptives, air pollutants and water pollutants."[6] But this insufficient period for adaptation does not explain why humans are generally vulnerable to fiber or crystal mediated diseases such as asbestosis, byssinosis, and silicosis. These "industrial" diseases caused by asbestos, cotton, and silica have long historical precedence in human culture and occur naturally in the environment. The fibrogenic reaction to them, particularly in the lung, may be a vestige of a generally adaptive wound-healing response to chronic injury.

Muller's theory does explain why some people may develop poorly characterized chemical illnesses such as multiple chemical sensitivity or reactivity to formaldehyde, chromium, and toluene disocyante, each of which has produced classic sensitization and secondary immune-mediated diseases such as asthma. But the Muller theory does not account for the fact that some people are ultrasensitive to these chemicals.

At least four different kinds of chemical sensitivity have been described where the immune system appears only secondarily involved. Each condition has a common initating exposure pattern, but a different sequence. Following contact with a novel chemical in a newly constructed building ("sick building syndrome") or from abrupt exposure to high concentrations of solvents or other industrial chemicals (multiple chemical sensitivity syndrome), it appears that some individuals become sensitized so that even low-dose exposures reactivate symptoms of overexposure.[7] Two similar conditions lead to "reactive airway" diseases that resemble inflammatory lung disorders or asthma (discussed in Chapter 11). These still controversial chemical sensitivity conditions suggest that previously adapted organ systems may fail as the result of an unanticipated insult or environmental change that strikes particular genetically vulnerable persons. Such vulnerability may simply uncover presently unselected random variation in the human population. Differential vulnerability may also explain other diseases that are directly caused by chemicals, such as cigarette-smoke-induced cancer, benzene-induced aplastic anemia, or acute nonlymphocytic leukemias, conditions that presently strike the population differentially. In these conditions, a poorly adapted detoxification system may inadvertently activate the chemical into a carcinogenic intermediate in some but not all exposed persons.[8]

Diabetes

Vulnerability to Diabetes

As exemplified by SAD, the conditions indigenous to one environment are likely to select for relative constant hormonal values tightly entrained by environmental cues, be they light/darkness cycles or available nutrients. In this sense, many modern-day nutritional disorders may be seen as the failure of previously adaptive "set points" in the endocrine system, now out of kilter with contemporary circumstances. One important example is diabetes, in which insulin production in the pancreas in response to blood sugar is highly regulated genetically.

Diabetes is an endocrine disorder associated with absent or poorly controlled insulin release that puts its victims at risk for serious secondary health problems related to high blood glucose levels. One of these problems is an excessive proliferation of endothelial cells in the lining of small blood vessels, leading to blindness and heart disease. Another is poor infection control. Diabetes is particularly common in a society plagued by chronic overconsumption.

In major urban areas such as New York City, diabetes has undergone a dramatic upsurge, increasing in prevalence tenfold from 1866 through 1923 and continuing that trend to the present.[9] This pattern reflects the fact that diabetes is expressed primarily in persons who have adopted a Western, industrialized society diet. Only a small proportion of indigenous peoples who generally have maintained a high fiber, low fat diet have this disorder (see Table 3).

Diabetes Susceptibility

Ironically, many of these same nonindustrialized peoples, such as Fijians, Somoans, and Native Americans, are precisely the ones who become overweight and develop the highest incidence of diabetes *after* they adopt the diet of developed countries. This observation suggests a prior evolutionary explanation for the diabetic-predisposed phenotype. One predisposition that allows maturity-onset diabetes to be expressed more easily is having the ability to metabolize sugars rapidly and to store fat in periods of plenty. That is, the diabetes-predisposed physiology is one that allows its holder to binge and then go hungry for days at a time. Obviously, such an adaptation would have a selective advantage in Paleolithic times when food was scarce.

But what might have proven advantageous some 30,000 years ago may obviously lose its value as environments change. Genes that predispose to developing diabetes, particularly in its autoimmune form, have limited or no continuing adaptive value. But retention of the predisposing gene(s) can result from a "freezing" of the population's previously adaptive genetic norms. Such genetic stasis—a frozen snapshot in evolutionary time—could arise in the face of relaxed selection where environmental conditions no longer exert selective force in the particular genetic loci.

This model may explain how diabetes-predisposing genotypes may be retained by some but not all populations. Such a circumstance occurs

Table 3: Prevalence of Diabetes in Different Societies[10]

Major Nutrient Source	Population Group	Prevalence (in percents)
Gatherers	African nomadic Bryoas	0.0
Hunters and gatherers	Alaskan Athabaskans	1.3
	Greenland Eskimos	1.2
	Alaskan Eskimos	1.9
Vegetarians and fish eaters	New Guinea Melanesians	0.9
	Loyalty Island Melanese	2.0
	Malaysia, rural villagers	1.8
Grain, fish, and meat eaters	India, rural villagers	1.2
	Israel, Yemenites	0.1
	New Caledonians	1.5
	Polynesia, Pukapuka	1.0
	Fiji Islanders	0.6
Industrialized westerners	Australians, Canadians, Americans, and Japanese	3.0–10.0

in the retention of a high frequency of the HLA DR4 gene among Japanese patients with autoimmune diabetes. This gene is remarkably prevalent among diabetics in Japan, yet it appears to have little continuing relationship to diabetes in other social groups, such as the Swiss.[11] Such divergence can be explained by the relatively recent cross-over to a diabetes-promoting diet in Japan compared to Switzerland, or, as we will see below, to novel pathogens that have caught the Japanese genetic system off-guard.

Diabetes as an Adaptive Disease

When diseases come into being that appear to defy reason, it is often useful to consider the possibility that they are derived from conditions that once had adaptive value. Diabetes is a case in point. As we have seen, in diabetes, patients have lost the ability to regulate their metabolism of glucose and thus fail to adequately regulate its levels in the blood. Wasting, loss of energy, damage to the retina, and susceptibility to infections are just a few of the legion of pathologic changes that accompany this endocrine disease. As shown in Table 3, as much as 10 percent of the adult population of some developed countries may eventually develop some of the symptoms of this disease. Why should so many humans acquire a disease that throws their entire metabolic system out of order and ultimately causes a host of pathological changes that are potentially life-threatening? To understand this dilemma, it is useful to review the major features of the disease and to identify a model group that provides a potential window into its evolutionary origins.

Diabetes exists in two major forms: type 1, in which patients are typically dependent on insulin, and type 2, where patients are insulin independent but experience some of the problems of inadequate glucose control.[12] Many people in this second group tend to be overweight because they have lost the ability to regulate their fat metabolism and instead store excess amounts of fat, leading to obesity. This last, paradoxical observation provides a fascinating clue about the origins of this major metabolic disturbance.

The Pima Indians and Diabetes

The Pima Indians have a genetic makeup that appears to strongly predispose them to diabetes in modern society.[13] But what might have been adaptive early in the origins of these Arizona Indians was lost as these populations, particularly those of the Gila River Indian community, adopted Western life-styles. An extraordinary proportion—as much as 85 percent—of the adult Pima Indians now living in that community exhibit the symptoms of a form of type 2 diabetes. Adults are typically obese and have excessive blood levels of glucose. Because of their unique ancestry and the specialized circumstances of their contemporary environment, the Pima have provided a living laboratory for examining the origins of diabetes.

The Pima are descendants of the Hohokam group of Native Americans who first settled near the Gila River about 2,000 years ago. The archeological record indicates that the Hohokam practiced a subsistence economy of hunting and gathering supplemented by crops fed by an elaborate irrigation system. This successful adaptation to desert life continued until the early part of this century when the importation of European cultural traditions radically disrupted the Pima way of life. Most food is now purchased, diet has changed, and the Pima are plagued by obesity and diabetes. Why?

Some researchers today believe that it was the Pima's prior genetic adaptation to a rarefied environment and minimal staples that has put them at risk of these adverse reactions to their new life-style.[14] In past environments, the Pima probably relied on a genetically programmed metabolism that anticipated periods of enforced fasts and allowed for long, postabsorptive periods when food was plentiful. Their typical fiber-rich but energy-poor diet would require a slow metabolic rate to ensure that nutrients would be extracted slowly during passage of food through the intestinal tract. These periods would typically require the persistence of low circulating levels of insulin, especially during the nighttime hours. During times of abundance, high insulin levels would be released, allowing excess food to be metabolized.

Most people who develop diabetes do not respond to insulin normally. Pima Indians have a high "resistance" to utilizing glucose and consequently must maintain high insulin levels in their blood to keep glucose concentrations at appropriately low levels. These high insulin levels inhibit the breakdown of fat stores and the release of fat into the blood, allowing fat to be stored. That is, the high insulin levels encourage the buildup of fat "in reserve." Data show that even in Pimas with severe diabetes, fat storage and metabolism remain responsive to insulin levels.[15] This means that fat remains in storage (insulin has an antilipolytic, anti-fat dissolving effect), and obesity becomes likely as long as calorie intake continues at a level above that needed for daily activity.

Normally, the release of even small amounts of insulin stimulates the pick up and use of glucose from the blood, thereby lowering blood glucose concentrations. People eating a typical American meal can expect their insulin level to drop to fasting levels within a period of 3 to 4 hours after eating. Constant snacking or imbibing sugar-rich drinks can boost the insulin level artificially, leading to a chronic, high background level of insulin. As long as insulin is present, fats will continue to be produced and cholesterol generated without being broken down and utilized.

When insulin is present in too high a concentration, it can produce rapid lowering of glucose levels and dangerous hypoglycemia. Consequently, geneticists posit that some populations, such as the Pima, evolved mechanisms that allowed them to keep the adaptive value of high background insulin levels without their glucose-lowering effects. Such high levels would permit a relatively constant metabolism of ingested foodstuffs with deposition of fats in stores throughout the body at times when food was in excess. For the Pima, what was once a selective advantage to a people who lived at the edge of survival became detrimental in their new environment of relative abundance and ease.

Origins of the Diabetic Phenotype

A genetic makeup that permitted insulin to be in the blood without lowering glucose would also be advantageous during periods of starvation since it would allow relatively normal levels of glucose to be maintained in the blood even in the face of reduced caloric intake.[16] According to human geneticist James Neel, the genetic constellation now carried by some Native Americans such as the Pima constitutes a "thrifty genotype."[17] The necessary metabolic changes that brought this adaptation about nonetheless predisposed its Native American holders not only to resist insulin action, but to allow this resistance to build up fat stores and eventually, to produce diabetes.

Genetic factors alone do not explain why the Pima get diabetes. A series of studies of Pima Indian women with and without noninsulin-dependent diabetes mellitus showed that more children of mothers with diabetes (some 45 percent) developed diabetes between the ages of 20 to 24 than did offspring of mothers who were not diabetic during pregnancy (1.4 percent).[18] The fact that these data hold up even after factoring in whether the father was diabetic (it had no real effect on the numbers), clearly suggests that factors during pregnancy, perhaps insulin levels, have considerable influence on the manifestations of the disease.

"Why the Pima and not other Native Americans?" you might ask. First, other Native Americans are, in fact, also at increased risk of developing diabetes, although not nearly to the same degree as are the Pima. Since the 1940s and perhaps earlier, many Amerindian populations have experienced a veritable epidemic of adult-onset diabetes (the form associated with obesity and noninsulin dependence). While some researchers place considerable stock in nongenetic theories, for instance that chronic alcoholism explains this radical departure from physiologic norms,[19] most acknowledge that the unique genetic origins of the Native American populations have more to do with explaining diabetes than does their adopted life-style.

All Amerindians, in fact, probably descended from a few progenitor individuals who went through intense natural selection and population "bottlenecks" from which they were the sole survivors. These events probably occurred more than once during the major migrations across the ice-free corridor created in the Bering Strait during interglacial periods 17-40,000 years ago. During this time, it is reasonable to infer that intense natural selection favored those who had Neel's thrifty genotype, allowing them maximal efficiency in utilizing the scarce food sources typical of a midlatitude tundra environment. More recent migrants, notably the Athabaskan peoples who gave rise to what are now modern-day southwestern communities such as the Hopi, do not have the same diabetes patterns as do the earlier arrivals. This pattern suggests to some researchers that differential selective forces on the Paleo-Indian migrants, including their reliance on unpredictable big game sources, favored the thrifty genotype, but did not favor it among the later-arriving Athabaskans who had a longer period to adapt to the more plentiful and constant resources typical of warmer climates.[20]

Thereafter, surviving populations passed on the thrifty gene and some other unusual genetic combinations, such as those that predispose for arthritic conditions. This latter gene, called HLA B27, as we saw in the last chapter, puts its carriers at enhanced risk of a spinal degenerative condition known as ankylosing spondylitis.[21] As many as 80 percent of Native Americans carry this marker, in contrast to 8 to 10 percent of persons of European ancestry.

While this theory undoubtedly needs to be refined to account for different origins and subtleties in diagnosis (for example, type 1 vs. type 2 diabetes)[22] it provides a useful example of how selective forces shape disease vulnerability generally. The Neel model can help explain why the buildup of fat stores, especially in men with abdominal fat accumulation, may be beneficial under extreme circumstances (as in the evolution of the Pima) but can lead to an increased risk of heart disease,[23] as well as diabetes, when the environment is radically altered. It may also help explain how insulin resistance is maintained, since it may serve as a modern-day adaptation for conditions that foster inactivity and excessive food intake, since high insulin levels may paradoxically prevent further weight gain in already obese persons.[24]

Understanding the likely evolutionary origins of this disease can also help to explain the ability of nongenetic factors to shape differences in insulin-dependent diabetes mellitus.[25] Since generally only one out of every three pairs of genetically identical twins develop insulin-dependent diabetes, environmental factors clearly play a role in determining its onset. Data pointing to such factors include the observations that Finns have three times the incidence of diabetes (about 40 per 100,000) of their Estonian neighbors, and Icelanders have half the incidence of their founding populations in Norway.[26] A major determinant, according to researchers at the University of Texas Health Science Center in San Antonio, is the degree and rapidity of the acculturation by which traditional populations become Westernized or modernized. In keeping with Neel's hypothesis, rapid dietary changes including increased intakes of total and complex carbohydrates and fats coupled with decreased exercise appears to push newly acculturated native populations, such as Mexican American immigrés to San Antonio, into a diabetic or prediabetic mode.[27]

Autoimmune Diabetes

Diabetes and autoimmunity may be more closely linked than previously thought. Bacteria and viruses associated with autoimmune provocation, such as the Coxackie virus, are implicated in the origins of diabetes in childhood, a form that is usually more severe and insulin dependent than is the adult-onset type. As we saw with the diabetic Japanese with HLA DR4, data are also available that suggest that some forms of juvenile-onset diabetes associated with such bacterial or viral infection occur only in persons with the necessary HLA genes, a fact reminiscent of the story behind many autoimmune diseases.[28] A key cofactor predisposing to insulin-dependent diabetes is one of the HLA genes associated with antigen processing in the immune system. Both of the HLA markers known as DR3 and DR4 are strongly implicated since, in Caucasian populations at least, over 90 percent of persons who develop insulin-dependent diabetes or another form of autoimmunity that affects insulin itself express one or the other of these markers.[29] These data suggest that genetic susceptibility to an aberrant immune response coupled with an environmental trigger is necessary to precipitate insulin-dependent diabetes.[30]

Evolutionary Explanations of "Predisposing" Genes

But what could explain the rising incidence of this form of diabetes? One idea is that some kind of selection is favoring the transmission of just those genes that predispose toward diabetes.[31] Individuals who express these high-risk HLA genes may be better adapted to resist certain infections or to develop immunity to other more immediate threats than to be burdened by later disabling pancreas autoimmunity. Another explanation is that the presence of such HLA genes somehow preferentially protects fetuses during an immunologically hazardous stay in utero, thereby perpetuating the vulnerability genes into the next generation.

Other clues can be gleaned from examining endocrine abnormalities in animals. There is evidence that many other endocrine disturbances are, in fact, autoimmune and are caused by genetically predetermined, aberrant immunologic reactions to viruses and bacteria. In genetically predisposed rats, spontaneous diabetes has been shown to break out following viral infections, presumably the result of an autoimmune response to antigens shared in common between a given virus and the beta cells of the pancreas.[32] As we saw in the previous chapter on autoimmunity, the plausibility of this linkage is underscored by the plethora of autoimmune disorders that are similarly triggered.

Typically, complexity rather than simplicity reigns. More than one autoantigen is clearly implicated in the immune reactions against the islet cells, and even cow's milk may contain an environmental mimic of an islet cell antigen, leading to a contemporary theory (discussed below) that explains how childhood ingestion of cow's milk can lead to diabetes.[33] Immune reactivity to the milk antigen would then involve the islet cells, leading to the early stages of insulin-dependent diabetes. Clearly, while not all diabetic patients have such an allergic response to milk protein,[34] the presence of powerful antibodies to the pancreatic cells helps to explain why they cease functioning in so many. But if the approach of this book is valid, the important question to ask is not how but why a given factor has come about that contributes to or causes a human illness. This approach helps explain that the two leading hypotheses to explain diabetes—the viral model and the cow's milk allergy model—are, in fact, interrelated by a common evolutionary thread.

The Virus Theory

Why would a virus, such as the Coxackie virus associated with childhood-onset insulin-dependent diabetes in humans, "want" to produce a life-limiting condition like diabetes? Of course, there is no such thing as "intention" or "willing" in the nonconscious living world. The answer must be sought in evolutionary theory. Here, one may invoke one or both of two standard explanations for apparent adaptations: (1) the virus simply "blunders" into a preadapted system—in this case the T cell arm of the immune system—which by chance attacks antigenically common targets in the virus and coincidentally in the pancreas; or (2) the virus has acquired a close molecular mimic of a self-tissue antigen as a result of selection to *avoid* immunologic assault, since the body would normally be anergic or nonreactive to its own cells and hence to the virus.

A more complex explanation may also come into play—could it be that a virus or bacterium that provokes a reactive autoimmune disorder actually thrives better in the environment created by the disorder (for example, the heightened blood glucose levels of insulin-resistant diabetes)? In this sense, producing diabetes is in the "interest" of the bacterium, even as it proves inimical to its host. This idea is underscored by the fact (known too well to infection-prone diabetics) that high blood sugar levels encourage the growth of bacteria.

The Milk Theory

Similarly, there is no teleological reason why the artificial substitution of cow's milk for human milk should lead to a cross reaction that jeopardizes the pancreas. If an "allergy" to cow's milk does explain diabetes, it could again be an atavistic reaction that previously had adaptive value for nondairying peoples. If herding and dairying are evolutionarily ancient traits, as archeological data suggest, then human populations were subjected to selective forces that preferentially favored genes that made for compatibility with the herding life-style.

For instance, the prevalence of the gene for lactase deficiency, a condition that makes the digestion of milk from any source difficult, is clearly associated with the lack of a dairying history in the affected populations. Groups that acquired an artificial source of milk retain a functional lactase gene complex into adulthood while groups that only recently took up dairy herding and do not drink milk past nursing or later childhood (many African tribal peoples) commonly lose lactase functioning as they become adults.

If ingestion of cow's milk were detrimental, as the insulin-dependent diabetes model suggests, then an evolutionary biologist would ask why genes to protect at-risk populations did not arise accordingly. Shouldn't cross-reacting antigens between cow's milk and the beta cells of the pancreas have been selected *against,* leading to the preferential survival of individuals with noncross-reacting beta cells? Since this does not appear to have happened, perhaps it is worth examining if there is some advantage to having a genetic linkage between cow's milk ingestion and autoantibodies against the beta cells.

A novel explanation is that selection for breast-feeding and optimal utilization of milk early in life left behind a vulnerability to dairy-related diabetes with all of its pathological consequences. The modern literature is rampant with studies that document the tremendous advantages afforded populations with extended breast-feeding. Populations that breast-feed have longer interpartum intervals and healthier children by virtue of antibodies carried in the mother's colostrum and the superior nutritive value of human milk. Hence, a relatively strong selection in favor of breast-feeding would have accompanied human populations into modern times. No selection would favor cow's milk ingestion, leaving reactivity against bovine antigens intact. Thus, it may be that diabetes was originally a simple accident of residual reactivity against dairy antigens. Such reactivity would partially explain the observation that the recent reduction in breast-feeding in many industrialized countries coincides with a relatively abrupt increase in diabetes.

Rebuttal

The countervailing reality must also be explained by evolutionary theory. Clearly, negative selection for susceptibility to diabetes must also exist since diabetes is particularly inimical to the developing fetus *and* to maternal survival. The greatly overweight fetuses favored by a glucose-rich intrauterine environment and diabetes itself puts extreme stress on a pregnant woman. If diabetes is simply an atavistic, negative physiological state in today's environment, why has it remained so prevalent? The answer again requires evocation of Dobzhansky's rule, since it is *adult*-onset diabetes that is now prevalent. Childhood diabetes can be explained by the same immunological rationales that explain the *raison d'être* for autoimmunity discussed in the previous chapter. Previously adaptive genes that made for rapid, "thrifty" metabolic conversion and storage of dietary carbohydrates persisted differentially in pre-agricultural peoples. Immune-response genes such as HLA DR3 and DR4 became established in industrialized society in part as a defense against certain communicable diseases. And in those societies the relatively ancient practice of dairying has probably winnowed out milk allergy–susceptible and hence diabetes-prone families. But in groups with only a recent history of cow's milk ingestion (like many African peoples), genetically based immune responses to this "new" antigen persist and can lead to diabetes. A prediction of this latter hypothesis is that the occurrence of lactase deficiency in childhood (a measure of lack of dairying activities in a given culture) is correlated with childhood diabetes.

Conclusions

These models of diabetes provide an example of the interactions between evolutionary forces that previously selected for an adaptive predisposition but that now work against well-being. Other diseases may also owe their resurgence to previous advantages that only recently have become detriments to good health. We can see, then, that otherwise counterintuitive susceptibility to disease can be explained by at least three different evolutionary mechanisms: (1) inadvertent or selectively neutral events (for example, the cross reactivity between otherwise adaptive gene products on healthy cells and bacteria or viral antigens); (2) the negative value of a particular susceptibility state being counterbalanced by its more immediate positive advantages; and (3) the positive selection in the past for adaptive genes that no longer have adaptive value (for example, the atavistic holdovers of genes that predispose to diabetes).

As we will see in the next chapter, in other diseases it is the normal genes that predispose to illness and mutations that afford protection. The clearest example of the evolutionary emergence of disease resistance is malaria.

10 Malaria

Any disease with a long enough history with the human species is likely to shape the genetic makeup of the population it affects. This is especially true for a disease that strikes the very young and has wide prevalence throughout the population. The archetype of such a disease is malaria.

The Evolutionary Origins of Malaria

This mosquito-borne parasitic disease has played a dominant role in human evolution for as long as 40,000 to 50,000 years. These dates mark the earliest evidence of the agrarian revolution in Africa, and with it the ecological disturbance that appears to have given rise to the disease in humans. Since that time, culture and disease have been in lockstep, moving in tandem as humans first cleared tropical rain forests for yam cultivation and malaria-carrying mosquitos gained a foothold in the resulting forest clearings.

According to a theory first developed by U.S. anthropologist F. B. Livingstone in 1957–1958, the African populations who first practiced agriculture put themselves at risk for contracting malaria by creating the environments most favored by the *Anopheles* mosquito.[1] These mosquitos, especially the *A. gambiae* species which can carry both the human and chimpanzee malarial parasites, lay their eggs in water in and around forest clearings, especially in sun-dappled ponds or slow-moving streams. These are precisely the conditions created by the yam culture peoples who inhabited the area now covered by southcentral Nigeria some 12,000 to 16,000 years ago. According to Livingstone, it was the Kwa-speaking peoples from this region who were hit hardest by malaria and subsequently developed the first genetic adaptations (sickle-cell hemoglobin) to protect themselves against malaria's depredations. In theory, as these populations expanded into the forest to cultivate yams, they simultaneously expanded the habitat of the anopheles mosquitos that previously had only infected forest primates. This hypothesis is reinforced by the discovery of the existence of common gene sequences in malarial parasites between humans and the chimpanzees who previously occupied these forests.[2]

It is now clear that malaria, like other major epidemic human diseases, was favored by ecosystem disruption that allowed the spread and concentration of insect vectors. The subsequent massing of human populations made possible by yam cultivation particularly and agricultural practices generally, provided susceptible hosts for the expansion of the parasite. A partial proof of this hypothesis about ecosystem disruption is the existence of populations in otherwise high-risk malarial regions, such as the Dyaks of Borneo, who live "in harmony" with their landscape and who have very low rates of malaria.[3]

The Selective Pressures of Malaria

Once adapted to one group of humans, it is evident that the malarial parasites readily spread to other populations, eventually encompassing all of the Mediterranean basin and even spreading to southern Great Britain with the advancing Roman legions. As the parasites spread, they exerted powerful selective forces on those populations since malaria itself causes often incapacitating disease and in cases of high fever, sterility in those men most severely affected. In time, genetic factors that conferred protection by lessening the severity of malaria or by diminishing the likelihood of its acquisition began to appear in the most heavily infected populations. These "resistance" genes usually affected the oxygen-carrying blood pigment hemoglobin, for it is in the red blood cell that the parasite undergoes its most critical differentiation. By modifying the structure or composition of hemoglobin molecules, genes such as those for sickle cell or thalassemia type hemoglobin molecules produce a resistant blood type that limits the reproduction of the parasite. This resistance appears due to lower oxygen tensions inside the affected red blood cell, subsequent "sickling" or collapse of the cell, and greater ease of phagocytosis (which destroys the resident parasites). Sicklers with the homozygous form of the hemoglobin S gene carry many fewer parasites in their blood when infected than do nonsicklers with normal hemoglobin. Heterozygous carriers with a single copy of the gene have intermediate resistance to malaria.

Other genetic defenses have evolved against malaria, including those for variants of an enzyme carried in red blood cells known as glucose-6-phosphatase (G6PD). Persons with deficient G6PD have less glutathione inside their red blood cells, a necessary nutritive constituent of the parasite's own metabolism. Another defense is a variant of the Duffy blood group antigen, known as Duffy negative. A high percentage of all African Americans and indigenous peoples of sub-Saharan Africa lack the Duffy group serotype. The Duffy antigen itself appears in positive hosts on the surface of red blood cells and seems to be the erythrocyte receptor for *P. vivax*. Effective invasion of the red blood cell by this malarial parasite and its monkey malarial relative (*P. knowlesi*) appears to require the presence of this antigen. Duffy-negative persons who lack the receptor are resistant to malaria. A recent therapeutic strategy has been proposed that uses substances that preferentially bind to this receptor and block access of the plasmodium to the red blood cell.[4]

Over time, such adaptations provide for the emergence of populations of people who carry the most effective forms of genetic resistance against malaria. High and sometimes maximal gene frequencies for these and related variants were built up by natural selection and were acquired by Old World populations of early Mediterranean, north Indian, sub-Saharan and West African populations where malaria was endemic.[5] Similar genetic adaptations are absent in New World populations—and in the monkeys that inhabit the rain forests in newly exposed malarial regions.[6] This makes the current expansion of malaria into South and Central America, Southeast Asia and Malaysia a major source of concern since few natural resistance mechanisms exist in at-risk populations there.

Today, upward of 400 million people, mostly in rural tropical areas around the world, are at risk for malaria. The World Health Organization's most recent statistics carry reports of some 6.5 million "formally reported" cases annually. Certainly, this is an underestimate of the true prevalence of this debilitating disease, especially since no statistics were included from tropical Africa because of incomplete reporting.

A Contemporary Overview of Malaria Control

Following the widescale use of pesticides such as DDT during and after World War II, there was hope that this scourge had been eradicated. But within a decade this optimism was shattered as more and more of the mosquitos that carry the disease developed pesticide resistance. By 1980, about fifty-one different anophele mosquitos, the principal vectors of malarial parasites, had developed resistance to DDT and other pesticides.[7] Since the 1960s, the cure and prevention of malaria have also been gravely compromised as more and more strains of the causative organisms (parasite members of the *Plasmodium* genus) have become resistant to the mainstays of malarial therapy. In 1969, WHO recognized the futility of total malaria control, citing economic, administrative, socioeconomic, political, and technical reasons. Instead of the massive mosquito abatement programs of the 1950s and 1960s, WHO shifted emphasis to a multipronged local attack that emphasized prevention and wider use of antimalarial drugs for treatment and prevention. However, this shift in focus proved ill-fated since it amounted to a mass relaxation of the environmental forces that however artificially were keeping the disease and its vectors at bay and substituted antibiotic control, a risky effort at best given the adaptability of the malarial parasite. Between 1976 and 1978, antibiotic-resistant malaria resurged in Southeast Asia and has been increasing slowly in South and Central America ever since.

As predicted from medical experience with antibiotics, the greatest setback in the antimalaria campaign has come from the undue reliance on standard drugs of choice for universal treatment of malarial patients—and from the use of these same drugs for prophylaxis of at-risk populations. In an anticipatable response to constant selective pressure, resistance to chloroquine and other antimalarial drugs have appeared worldwide in the major parasite species (*P. falciparum*). By 1984, WHO charted chloroquine-resistant malaria throughout the rain-forested areas of Central and South America, sub-Saharan Africa, Madagascar, India, Malaysia, and particularly in southeast Asia.[8]

Of greatest concern is a tendency for the appearance of multiple resistance to chemotherapeutic agents once chloroquine resistance has occurred coupled with an apparent increase in the ease of mosquito-borne transmission in resistant strains.[9] The story of the factors that shaped the emergence of this resistance and how evolution-wise strategies might have avoided this quandary—and be used to counter the present threat are the major subjects of this chapter.

The Causes of Malaria

Malaria itself is a particularly pernicious and devastating disease characterized by night sweats, weakness, and high fevers. It is caused by one of four species of the protozoan parasite known as a plasmodium (*Plasmodium falciparum, P. vivax, P. malariae,* and *P. ovale*). The falciparum form of malaria can cause a fatal, debilitating disease in susceptible persons, while the other three forms cause a milder, though still debilitating disease. The *P. vivax* form of the disease is particularly prevalent in sub-Saharan Africa.

The disease is transmitted to humans by the bite of a female mosquito in the anopheles group. The saliva which accompanies the bite carries the sporozoites that start the malarial cycle. Once in the body, the injected sporozoites migrate to the liver. After 1 to 2 weeks, they leave the liver, emerging as "mesozoites" that then invade the red blood cells, where they divide exponentially. Periodically, they burst through the cell membranes and fill the bloodstream, where they invade still other red blood cells. This periodic resurgence of new parasites from red blood cells produces the characteristic periodic fevers and sweats that identify a malarial patient as acutely ill. Eventually, if enough red blood cells are engorged with parasites, they can clog venules, giving rise to kidney failure and brain damage.

At any time after the initial infection (when the blood-borne parasite is present), a new cycle of infection can be initiated by the bite of a new mosquito. *Plasmodium* completes its life cycle in the gut of the mosquito by reproducing sexually, taking about 2 weeks to once again reach the salivary glands. In the *P. vivax* and *ovale* forms of malaria, the parasites can lie dormant in the liver for months or years after an initial infection, becoming an active disease long after patients consider themselves cured.

That malaria can have a devastating effect on a population, particularly one that has undergone recent dislocations due to civil strife, economic dislocation, or war is best evidenced by the postwar situation in Vietnam. Between 1984 and 1989, malaria underwent a dramatic resurgence in southern Vietnam. In this 5-year period, malaria affected 393,102 persons, up 64 percent from the previous 5-year period. The doctors who observed this upsurge believed that both the high incidence and relatively high death rate (some 1,069 deaths, up 129 percent) were due to the dispersal of previously unexposed persons into new economic zones and to the lack of health services, particularly among the ethnic minority populations.[10]

Resistance

The Differential Value of Resistance

If a significant portion of the population is genetically adapted to limit proliferation of one or more of the stages of the parasite's life cycle (sickle-cell-trait prevalences as high as 38 percent have been charted in some malarial regions of India), malaria may fail to become established in the "holoendemic" fashion needed to ensure self-perpetuation. But, usually, enough unprotected persons remain in the population to allow parasite invasion. And malaria thrives in densely populated areas where the gene frequency for the typically recessive protective genes is low. (In each generation there is a relatively constant porportion of vulnerable persons with normal hemoglobin types, based on the proportion of heterozygotes, a phenomenon known as Hardy-Weinberg equilibrium.[11])

Resistance factors such as the Duffy negative configuration (usually present in no more than 10 to 20 percent of the population) are especially advantageous since they act to thwart infection at the earliest stages of the disease—the erythrocyte phase. Any limitation of parasite numbers during this stage also carries a secondary benefit to the remainder of the at-risk population. That is, to be successfully picked up and carried by more than one or two members of the population at a time, the malarial parasite must proliferate in its host so vigorously that a mosquito biting anywhere on the body is likely to pick up a minimal infective dose of malarial organisms. The necessity of a high density of parasites in all blood-bathed tissues makes for a very uncomfortable host, especially in the tertian forms of malaria where parasites are periodically released from the red blood cells in massive numbers. With sufficient numbers of infectious organisms circulating in the body, even bedridden malarial patients remain capable of transmitting malaria as long as they are unprotected from the bite of a mosquito species that can carry the malarial parasite elsewhere.[12]

So, one way to achieve a modicum of control of epidemic malaria is by preventing the access of anopheline mosquitos to infected persons. In fact, various cultural solutions have been "selected" in malarial regions of the world to achieve just that. Ingenious strategies to limit mosquito bites have been adopted early on by many of the earliest preliterate societies where malaria was endemic. For example, to limit access by mosquitos, the Igbo peoples of equatorial Africa built mosquito-proof houses for their sleeping quarters. Typically, the house had no windows and only one small, close-fitting door. At bedtime, the family slept in this small shelter until dawn—when mosquitos cease their nighttime predations.[13] Similarly, in northern Vietnam's hill country, where the mosquito vector that carries malaria seldom flies higher than about 9 to 10 feet, the indigenous peoples build their homes on stilts, keeping their living room a minimum of 10 feet above ground.[14]

Genetic Resistance

Today, the genetic vestiges of the process of selection for malaria resistance are still apparent. As we have seen, some 11 to 12 percent of African Americans and even higher percentages of people from the Indian subcontinent and some areas of the Mediterranean basin carry the classic resistance factor against malaria—the hemoglobin S or sickle-cell hemoglobin gene known as HbS. This gene, found on chromosome number 11, determines the structure of part of the beta chain of the hemoglobin molecule. It is but one of more than forty-eight variants of hemoglobin that confer an advantage against malaria for their carriers.

According to cultural anthropologist William Durham of Stanford

University, who has performed the most exhaustive review of the HbS/malaria hypothesis, the only places in Africa where the HbS gene is present in appreciable frequency are just where one would expect that having this allele would have conferred a selective advantage to the holder; that is, in and around areas of the countryside where slash and burn agriculture was practiced.[15] Recent studies based on the time of divergence of variants of the HbS gene in African populations suggest that the progenitor of this gene arose 50,000 years ago, suggesting that agrarian practices may be even more primitive than first suspected, or that the agricultural revolution hypothesis for the origin of malarial selective pressures is wrong.[16]

The similar advantage in malarial regions of the world conferred by variants of G6PD has also led to the spread of this gene. More than three hundred such variants exist, most of which are carried on the X chromosome. A genetically based deficiency in this enzyme is carried by an estimated 400 million people throughout the world. Women who have a single dose of a varient gene for G6PD on one X chromosome with a normal gene for G6PD on the other appear to be resistant to malaria, conferring a selective advantage for their own survival and for that of their children.[17] (Half the female offspring of such women will carry the G6PD variant, as will half the males.)

Another genetic factor that confers resistance to malaria has also apparently been selected from among the genes of the major histocompatibility complex. HLA B53 and the DRB1 and DQB1 alleles appear to confer some survival advantage in malarial regions because their prevalence is high among persons in West Africa at risk for malaria.[18] The HLA B53 gene appears to provide a key antigenic marker that allows the immune system of the carrier to recognize the surface of the parasite when it is in the liver and then to produce an effective response against it.[19]

Intensity of Selection Pressure in Malaria

Malaria is such a pervasive and devastating disease when it enters a population that virtually any selective advantage will be favored. To appreciate the intensity of the selection pressure exerted by a malarial infestation in a populated region, one need only find a previously uninfected group with new exposure. This happened in the central highland plateau of

Madagascar, a traditional mosquito-ridden enclave that until recently had been virtually parasite free. Sometime in the last 20 to 30 years, the malaria parasite was introduced. In this newly exposed population, a research team from the Pasteur Institute of Madagascar found that virtually *everyone* who was bitten by a mosquito (average bites per person was only 1.5) developed malaria. At the peak of the mosquito season, 53.8 percent of the population was found to have parasites in the bloodstream.[20] Obviously, any gene(s) that protected against the morbidity and mortality of this parasite would provide a great selective advantage. Even if the gene(s) only reduced the severity of the fever experienced by the victim, it would have a selective advantage since it would forestall the sterilization of infected men.

We have already seen that genetic selection for the HbS gene reduces the depredations caused by malaria. Another example comes from the Indian subcontinent. In southern Nepal, the Tharu people in the Terai region are constantly exposed to malarial parasites as they gather wood and tend to their fields. In spite of this exposure, the native Tharu are remarkably resistant to malaria. Compared to other, non-Tharu, people who live in the same environment, the Tharu are seven times more resistant to malaria. The intensity of this exposure helps to explain the extent of genetic resistance. Remarkably, the Tharu have acquired the same adaptation that confers this resistance to many Mediterranean people—the gene for alpha thalassemia. (Alpha thalassemia is a disease in which there is overproduction of one of the chains of the red blood cell pigment.) More than half of the Tharu carry both alleles of this gene, making them homozygous for alpha thalassemia. While such persons are often anemic and run the risk of liver disease, they apparently have such an increased survival advantage over their nonthalassemic neighbors as to enjoy greater reproductive success from generation to generation. Researchers studying this remarkable phenomenon calculate the relative resistance conferred on a Tharu with this genetic makeup to be near 90 percent![21]

Evolution at the Parasite Level

Drug Resistance

The dramatic advantage conferred by genetic adaptations is in marked contrast to the lack of success in controlling the present malaria epidemic with antibiotics. Neither a chemoprophylactic nor chemotherapy program is currently enjoying much success, as the malarial parasite has developed resistance to the traditional and newest antimalarial drugs with disturbing frequency. As with the prior dependency on chloroquine, reliance on chemoprevention has ensured that selective pressures continue to create new strains of malaria.

This problem is particularly vexing in tropical African countries where malaria remains holoendemic, that is, present and prevalent among the population as a whole. Between 1978 and 1989, virtually all of the subequatorial African nations reported resistance among malarial strains to choloroquine, the traditional drug of choice. This resistance appeared in virtually every country at risk during this period. In part, this disastrous consequence can be attributed to the increased reliance on chloroquine for universal prophylactic (preventive) uses. But the real finger of blame points to inadequate treatment coupled with excessive reliance on this drug over other therapeutic modalities.[22]

In the African nation of Benin, researchers have noted resistance to chloroquine since 1986, when there was a sudden increase in resistant strains. This emergence of resistance corresponded to the widespread distribution of chloroquine in the population in a misguided attempt to allow public control for prophylaxis.[23] Self-medication was often made with sub-optimum dosages and sporadic treatments. Further exacerbation of the resistance problem happened between 1977 and 1982, when a chemosuppression campaign was attempted in the northern part of Tanzania (the Mara region). Typified by widespread use of chloroquine, this campaign led to increasing levels of resistance to both chloroquine and subsequent drugs.[24] Such findings show that when drugs are used prophylactically in a poorly thought-out program to prevent malarial propagation, resistance is a predictable consequence.

A similarly explosive appearance of chloroquine-resistant malaria erupted among schoolchildren in Gabon between 1984 and 1985.[25] Overall, the spread of choloroquine-resistant or amodiquine-resistant malaria moved from East Africa in 1980–1983, to Central Africa in 1985, and to West Africa.[26] While the true cause may never be known, it is likely that the dramatic increase in reliance on a chemoprevention and chemotherapeutic control strategy generated extreme drug pressures that selected for resistant malarial types.[27] Further exacerbation of the problem resulted from travel to and from affected areas, leading to the importation of resistant strains in various geographic locales throughout tropical Africa.

Therapeutic Failure

The major drugs used to treat malaria and the pattern of resistance to them are summarized in Table 4.

Where resistance to malaria is found for individual drugs, combinations such as quinine with tetracycline or fansidar with quinine have been used with moderate success.[28] This partial therapy is still problematic because fansidar itself is toxic. Fansidar is made by combining two previously effective drugs, pyrimethamine and sulfadoxine. Currently (1993–1994), the falciparum plasmodium has shown a high level of tolerance to pyrimethamine, so that resistance to the combination drug is now rampant.

Quinine is difficult to take orally and is toxic to the liver. Fansidar is more easily given to patients but is not as effective as chloroquine in treating the vivax form of malaria. A substitute drug, mefloquine, has proven an effective chemoprophylactic drug when used against chloroquine-resistant *P. falciparum,* but some physicians have questioned its safety even as others tout its effectiveness.[29] A new "standby" substitute drug called halofantrine has been proposed for self-treatment by travelers in malarial regions where resistance to Fansidar occurs.[30] But the concept of allowing self-treatment is flawed because it invites the emergence of resistant strains, and, as I will discuss below, because it raises the specter of inequitable protection.

Emergence of Resistance

The failure of so many drugs to control malarial parasites over the long run reflects the fact that the malarial parasite, like its bacterial counterparts, has evolved mechanisms to evade chemical control. The emergence of resistance to chloroquine, the traditional drug of choice, is particularly disturbing because it was the mainstay and virtually only consistently effective treatment for falciparum malaria for more than 40 years. In fact, there is essentially no equally safe and efficacious substitute for this drug in the pharmacopeia today.[31]

In Africa, the loss of chloroquine's efficacy began during the late 1970s. By the early 1990s, chloroquine resistance had spread to the

Table 4: Resistance to Malarial Therapeutics

Drug	Date Resistance Reported
chloroquine	1978 to present (worldwide except for Central America and the Middle East)
amodiquine	1985 to present (West Africa)
fansidar	1985 to present
quinine	1985–87 to present
primaquine	1987 to present
mefloquine	1970s to present (Cambodia, Thailand, and West Africa)
doxycycline	1990s
chloroquanide hydrochloride	1990 to present (Southeast Asia and Papua New Guinea)

furthest reaches of the planet where malaria occurs, including Indonesian New Guinea. In a study undertaken there by a team of U.S. and Indonesian researchers, forty-six villagers with the vivax form of malaria (caused by *Plasmodium vivax*) were tested for resistance. A large dose of chloroquine given to all forty-six appeared to control the disease, but in 22 percent, an ominous recurrence doomed the treatment regime. Even when the dose was increased and extended for 8 weeks of follow-up, parasitemia (parasites in the bloodstream) developed again. Interestingly, all of the recurrences were in children younger than 11 years, with over 70 percent of the children under 4 showing treatment failure.[32]

This last observation suggests a mechanism for the emergence of resistance to chloroquine. Children with relatively poorly developed immune systems likely serve as unusually fertile environments for parasite survival. The resulting burgeoning population of parasites is a reservoir of genetic variability that creates ample opportunity for natural selection.

Corroborating studies that show that African children 2 to 10 years old are both highly parasitized and carry low innate resistance come from studies performed in Kinshasa, Zaire.[33] Additionally, the parasite may lie fallow in the liver (the so-called hypnozoite form of the parasite), permitting relapses up to a month to several years after apparently successful therapy.

Exportation of resistant organisms via international travel greatly accelerates the normally slow evolutionary process. During the same period (1978–1986) when cloroquine resistance was emerging locally, a worldwide outbreak of resistance occurred, extending even to Vanuatu in the Pacific Ocean. In Vanuatu, up to 60 percent of the plasmodium strains isolated in recent years have proven to be resistant to cholorquine.[34]

Resistance and Pharmacologic Imperialism

The greatest public health danger, belatedly recognized during the late 1980s, is that continued ineffective treatment programs coupled with suboptimal dosage scheduling could lead to the emergence of resistance to *multiple* chemical agents, a phenomenon already too well known among bacterial diseases. At the core of this problem is the overuse of therapeutic drugs for prevention, or chemoprophylaxis. Both the World Health Organization and the Centers for Disease Control have endorsed chemoprophylaxis, even as they acknowledged a poor benefit/risk ratio for most of the proposed drugs.[35] Neither group appears to have considered the long-term consequences of encouraging travelers to use the same drugs for prophylaxis that the residents of the visited countries rely on for treatment. Widespread adoption of prophylactic strategies, especially when done at suboptimal doses is likely to encourage the emergence and spread of resistant strains. For this reason, I question the soundness of recommendations that limit consideration of benefits and risks solely to the traveler.[36]

It is true that if only one or a handful of travelers adopted a self-protective regime, the medical consequences to the indigenous population as a whole would remain inconsequential or nonexistent. But as soon as both citizens and visitors use the same drugs for critical care *and* for guaranteeing a "safe trip," the seed for therapeutic failure is planted. This happens because the same organism that is being controlled by high therapeutic doses in a sick patient will be subject to the oftentimes inadequate and hence selective effect of lower doses in a traveler (who doesn't forget to take a "protective" vitamin or pill once in a while?). Travelers to regions where the disease is endemic are also unlikely to be either genetically or immunologically prepared to resist infection, further intensifying selective pressures. Moreover, travelers often carry disease-causing organisms from place to place, increasing the likelihood of spreading resistant organisms. Ethically, the costs to the indigent population of potentially losing an effective malarial treatment for patients with active disease must be balanced against the potential value to the casual traveler of avoiding malaria. Considering that simple protective measures (mosquito repellants, adequate clothing, sleeping with mosquito nets, and so on) are all relatively easy and efficacious prevention measures exist, routine advocacy of potentially toxic prophylactic treatment appears unjustified.

If prophylaxis is essential for some reason, different drugs should be used than those the visited country relies on for disease control in its population. This solution, if implemented, would reduce the contribution that ineffective protective treatments are likely to make to the emergence of further parasite resistance.

The Malaria/AIDS/Lymphoma Link

Other diseases common to West Africa have a tantalizing connection to the growing focus of malarial invasion. The prevalence of malaria in the West African epicenter of the HIV organism has suggested to several researchers that coinfection with malaria predisposed several African populations to HIV.[37] Evidence supporting this radical hypothesis is circumstantial but provocative. Other viruses, notably the Epstein-Barr virus (EBV) have been shown to propagate favorably in persons who harbor the malarial parasite.[38] Part of this advantage for viral infection may be conferred by the evolutionary adaptation of the malarial parasite to dampen the inflammatory response and weaken the immune system. Such an adaptation ensures a longer period in a carrier state for the parasite, greatly increasing its opportunity to be passed on. Even as it dampens the immune system, a state where blood-borne parasites flare up periodically encourages proliferation of host lymphocytes. Since the EB virus, like HIV, thrives in an immunodepressed environment but replicates and is carried by cells of the immune system (here the B lymphocytes), it is reasonable to conclude that having malaria also increases the number of virus particles and increases the likelihood that some infected lymphocytes will become transformed into lymphomatous cells.

A converse relationship also proves important—the Epstein-Barr virus's ability to cause a florid, lymphoproliferative disease is linked to the immune dysfunction associated with malaria. One such disease, Burkitt's lymphoma (a tumor of the lymph system rare outside of Africa), is thus almost always associated with the presence of the malarial parasite.[39]

What Can Be Done?

Any effort to control the malarial parasite must take these concomitant ecological realities along with the evolutionary potential of both the host and the parasite into consideration. Rudimentary attempts have been made over the years to try to limit the emergence of resistant strains by coupling use of one antimalarial agent with at least one or two others. As an example, when the Walter Reed Army Institute of Research (pioneers in malaria studies) developed a drug called Lariam, it recommended that the drug be used in conjunction with two other drugs to minimize the emergence of drug resistance.[40] Nonetheless, the evolutionary progress of the parasite has so far outstripped that of its pharmacological antagonists. In the words of one 1985 reviewer, "The rate of advance in the chemotherapy of malaria has been slow in comparison with the steady spread of drug resistance."[41] These failures have occurred in the main because of the absence of collective agreements among countries for the best use of effective evolutionary strategies.

A case study of a successful campaign shows that without such perspective, even brute force may prove ineffectual. On the Island of Mayotte in the Indian Ocean, when a malarial epidemic broke out in 1984, comprehensive pesticide spraying (four times yearly) coupled with larvicidal activities directed against the mosquito and filling in of mosquito-breeding ponds proved only partially effective. Ironically, it was only when the chemical control of the plasmodium parasite was *reduced* that the infestation was brought under control. Success was ultimately attributable to observing the WHO recommendations against routine chemoprophylaxis in all but high-risk pregnant women, and encouraging personal mosquito protection. This led to a reduction of resistant strains and a successful campaign resulting in only three cases some 2 years after the epidemic began.[42]

The substitution of a *cultural* control for a chemical one has been a tried and true method of keeping pace with the evolutionary adaptations of the *Anopheles* mosquito. As we saw with Igbo and northern Vietnamese villagers, simply knowing enough about the habits of the mosquito to avoid its biting periods proves to be an effective strategy. The newest confirmation of this simple strategy comes from the Gambia. To control malarial transmission, the native population was encouraged to use mosquito netting impregnated with a low-toxicity, naturally derived pesticide (permethrin) each night as a bed cover. This method proved to be highly protective against transmission, reducing both the morbidity and mortality from malaria some 63 to 70 percent. In fact, the addition of a chemoprophylactic regime to children afforded no further reduction in malarial deaths over that achieved by netting alone.[43]

Vaccines

Because of the dual evolutionary tragedies of insect vector resistance to pesticides and malarial parasite resistance to drugs, some solution outside of the evolutionary endgame is critical. Only through the most intensive international efforts will malaria be brought under control. The greatest current hope towards this elusive goal is the development of a vaccine. In the words of one researcher at the Wellcome Tropical Institute, such a development is now both "a challenge and a necessity" because of the decades of repeated failure to control malarial epidemics through chemicals alone.[44]

Since a typical malarial infection proceeds through a series of stages (detailed at the beginning of this chapter), a vaccine in theory could be targeted at any one or several of the most vulnerable periods in the life cycle. And because each form of the parasite uses a different portion of the *Plasmodium* genome, each characteristic type bears a different surface configuration and hence becomes a different target for a vaccine. Two of the more promising vaccines include a erythrocyte vaccine directed at the asexual phase of the parasite and a circumsporozoite vaccine, which targets the surface configurations of the first parasite invaders introduced at the time of the mosquito's bite. A further development, which is intended to limit transmission of malaria, is directed at the stage where the parasite forms sexually differentiated gametes in the blood. (A summary of each of these vaccines is available.[45])

Recently, an international team of researchers capitalized on the phenomenon of genetic human resistance factors. The team isolated antigens of the pre-erythrocyte stage of *Plasmodium* as a basis for an antimalaria vaccine.[46] They did so by utilizing the fact discussed earlier that persons who carry the HLA B53 gene resist malarial parasites through an immunologic means. Recall that B53 presents a critical portion of the parasite's coat to the appropriate T cell in just the right configuration. The researchers were able to isolate the particular coat antigens that provoked the strongest protective response by actually catching the B53 protein in the act of antigen presentation and extracting the malarial coat antigen from its groove site on the HLA molecule. These ingeniously derived antigens will, in turn, form the basis for as yet untested but highly promising vaccines.

Although any malaria vaccine is limited by its necessary focus on only one stage of the life cycle of the parasite, this new approach serves as the most rational to date. In essence, researchers have capitalized on several thousand years of human evolution by using the protective HLA marker as the antigen-sorting device for vaccine development. In doing so, tropical medicine has for the first time incorporated a human evolutionary strategy into a rational program for disease protection. By modifying an adaptation previously available to those with the requisite genetic makeup (the HLA B53 allele), clinicians who develop the first successful antimalarial vaccine will in effect be spreading an evolutionary strategy available only to a select few to all those at risk for infection who lack intrinsic genetic resistance to the disease. This is a prime example of evolutionary medicine at work.

11 Evolution and Asthma

While pathology results from the failure of adaptation, many new diseases arise from previously adaptive reactions gone awry. Old adaptations often provide the scaffolding on which new diseases are built. As we saw with some forms of autoimmunity, evolutionarily ancient reactions that originally evolved to protect the body can form the basis for modern-day diseases. Understanding how an adaptation evolved and what selective forces shaped its original functions often provides the key to understanding its subsequent maladaptive role in disease.

This idea has its roots in the late 1940s and 1950s, when Hans Selye, a Canadian physiologist, developed the provocative idea of "diseases of adaptation." (See *The Stress of Life*, 2nd ed. New York: McGraw-Hill, 1978.) In Selye's view, much if not most of modern-day illnesses could be traced to a distortion of previous adaptations. Selye focused on the stress response which can lead to serious overuse or depletion of the body's reserves and resistance. While some of Selye's ideas have had to be updated (ulcers are nowadays attributed to the bacterium *Helicobacter pylori* and not to stress per se), his basic principles have stood the test of time. A fundamental corollary of Selye's basic concept is that the underlying cause of disease in specific organ systems may be found by uncovering the body's original adaptive purpose in locating a particular reaction at that site. What follows is an exploration of this idea as applied to a contemporary example, asthma.

Asthma as a Model

One of the mysteries of illness is that some "diseases" appear to strike otherwise healthy people indiscriminantly. A case in point is allergies, and, more particularly—the form of allergy known as asthma. Allergies result from a particular form of immune reaction in which a special class of antibodies known as IgE form against natural and synthetic chemical antigens. An allergic reaction typically unfolds as a result of these antibodies triggering the release of various chemical mediators, especially histamine. These events are discussed in detail below in the context of one form of allergy known as asthma.

Asthma, from a Greek root meaning "breathlessness," is associated with a tightening of the chest as the result of an increase in airway resistance, and is usually associated with wheezing and less often with a cough and excess sputum production. In children under 16, where asthma strikes most often, about 90 percent also have an allergy, while about half of asthmatics over 30 also have an allergy.[1]

Asthma is generally regarded as a form of allergy in which the immune system has become sensitized to antigens in the individual's surroundings. It is divided into two types of diseases: an "extrinsic" form in which an inciting agent can be identified; and an "intrinsic" form in which no substance capable of producing the necessary antibodies can be found.[2] This latter form is sometimes associated with "neurogenic inflammation" in which chemical agents provoke the release of neuropeptides that produce asthma's major symptoms in parallel fashion to those produced by the more common mediators of immunologic reactions.[3]

Treatment for the resulting bronchial inflammation and hyperreactivity is generally symptomatic, including use of steroids and bronchodilators that relieve the symptoms produced by the bronchial constricting chemicals such as histamine that are released during an asthma attack.[4] The most appropriate regimen and the possible risks associated with steroid treatment are presently hotly debated, since asthma-related dependency can contribute to deaths triggered by some of these pharmacologic agents.[5] Given these uncertainties, nonpharmacologic means of treatment that prevent or mitigate asthma (for example, by reducing exposures to provocative agents or neutralizing the immune response) are presently favored.[6]

The Scope of the Problem

To the over 40 million Americans who suffer from allergies or asthma, it goes without saying that these two diseases can make life miserable–they include the congestion, itching, sneezing, and generalized malaise of allergies, and worse, the sudden constriction of the chest in an asthma attack that makes breathing a chore or potentially life-threatening. In the last decade, asthma episodes have been reported with increasing frequency, leading some observers to believe that we are facing a new wave of this disease.[7]

Most of us know asthma from its symptoms–after exposure to some external provocation, breathing becomes more difficult or, less commonly, a cough develops with wheezing. The triggering event can be anything from an irritant chemical, cigarette smoke, or even just dry, cold air. But usually there is an inciting chemical that sensitizes the patient and provokes the production of the IgE antibody as in more general allergies. The hallmark of asthma is constriction of the passages to the lungs, the result of a highly reactive bronchial tree. Some allergists and pulmonologists, who see many cases of this form of hyperresponsiveness, refer to asthmatics as having "twitchy lungs."

As of 1993, symptomatic asthma is estimated to affect some 4 to 5 percent of the U.S. population, producing some 10 to 12 million cases in any one year at a cost of $6.2 billion.[8] In the United States, hospitalizations for asthma have risen 145 percent since 1970, mirroring similar trends in industrialized countries around the world.[9] More critically, the prevalence of asthma appears to be sharply increasing, especially among children, up some 60 percent in the last decade alone.[10] Certainly, something is afoot, as the death rate from asthma in the United States has doubled in the last 15 years, killing some 4,500 annually.[11] And a disproportionate number of these deaths occur in African Americans, who have three times the death rate of whites.[12]

Immunologic Parameters of Asthma

Given its traditional role in defending the body, it is ironic that the major culprit in classic allergy and asthma is the immune system. During an asthma attack, a complex array of cellular and chemical agents is activated in a cascade of reactions that is mediated by the IgE antibodies and includes both an immediate and a delayed set of reactions.[13] Paradoxically, attempts to control asthma by suppressing immunological functions can exacerbate the course of the disease by increasing vulnerability to infection generally.

The Protective Adaptation of Allergy

If the immune system plays such a dominant role in allergy and asthma, how do scientists explain the body's subversion of such an otherwise adaptive system into an agent of discomfort, malaise, and, in the extreme, death?

One explanation is that the allergic and asthma responses evolved initially to protect us against parasitic organisms. A good sneeze or wheeze can expel or repel a potential invader. Biochemist Margie Profet of the University of California, Berkeley, champions the view that allergy did evolve as such a system, serving primarily to rid the body of toxins.[14] In support of her hypothesis, she notes that most natural toxic substances (for example, bee venom) are highly allergenic. Many if not most toxins from plants as well as venomous insects provoke the type of immunity mediated by antibodies of the IgE class: When such antibodies are elaborated, they bind with specific antigens expressed by the toxic molecules. As we saw in our general discussion of allergy, where the antigens are bound to the surface of cells in the immune system, their interaction with antibodies commonly triggers the release of powerful vasoactive and physiological substances that change the permeability of blood vessels and provoke intense reactions in the surrounding tissues. Chemical mediators of the IgE response are in part spilled into the body by a unique reaction–the bursting of a group of cells known as mast cells, which are found in the lungs, the mucosa of the nose, and throughout the skin. When a mast cell breaks open after contact with antigen-binding IgE molecules, it spills granules directly into the tissue surrounding it and thereafter into the bloodstream and connective tissues.

These granules contain highly potent chemicals such as histamine, bradykinin, prostaglandins, and enzymes. While each mast cell is microscopic, they are densely represented in the target tissues of allergic reactions–there are as many as 20,000 of them in each square millimeter of lung tissue and about 5,000 per square millimeter of nasal mucosa. When their granules "blow up," massive amounts of histamine and other mediators are released, producing powerful effects on the surrounding tissues. These effects begin with the swelling and itching known to mosquito bite sufferers, culminating with tearing and sneezing; and, in the extreme form of allergy known as anaphylaxis–diarrhea, vomiting, and hypotension. In the lungs, these chemicals cause swelling, constriction of the muscles in the bronchi (the main branches leading to the lungs), and release of fluid. According to Profet, an evolutionary perspective on these reactions suggests that they are vestiges of mechanisms that originally served to expel or dilute offending toxic substances.

Certainly, this is the theme of every section on inflammation given in pathology courses. The hallmarks of inflammation–pain, heat, swelling, and an influx of leukocytes–are said to serve to dilute possible toxins and draw defensive cells to the site of injury. The resulting dilation of blood vessels lowers blood pressure and slows the dissemination of any toxic by-products throughout the body. But Profet's model fails to explain why these defensive reactions of the immune system do more damage than good. Generally speaking, toxins are not "expelled" by the allergic reaction, and inflammation is the cause of much of the pathologic damage that accompanies the invasion of microbes and foreign substances. Profet's mistake is to regard the entire system as one intent on eliminating offending substances from the body, rather than one geared to prevent their access in the first place.

Allergy as a Gatekeeper

My own view is that the selective forces that shaped the immune system were so potent that the body produced a system remarkable for its ability to keep offending substances from interacting with their cellular targets. Allergies in general and asthma in particular become serious, life-threatening diseases only to the extent that extensive antigen-antibody reactions are allowed to occur. If part of this reactive system worked to *prevent* antigens from entering the most sensitive tissues in the first place, an allergic/asthmatic reaction would actually be beneficial. More critically, if by the exclusion of highly antigenic materials, the asthma response also kept highly toxic molecules from entering the body, it would serve as a first line of defense against toxin-mediated diseases.

Actually, chemical sources associated with asthma generally provoke but do not induce extrinsic asthma. Air pollutants, particularly cigarette smoke and sulfur and nitrous oxides may irritate sensitive lungs and precipitate asthma attacks. However, clinical studies show that short-term exposures to these pollutants do not generally initiate an asthmatic response.[15] However, when asthma patients are chronically exposed to air pollutants, asthmatic symptoms are greatly exacerbated, particularly among children. Studies done both here and abroad demonstrate clearly that asthmatic patients experience aggravation of their symptoms when in polluted environments.[16] A few chemicals, notably toluene disocyanate and similarly reactive agents, can induce an asthmalike response.[17] But overall, the data on environmental agents and asthma strongly suggest that direct irritation of the lungs triggers preexisting asthma, but does not get at the root question of what causes the hyperreactive lung in the first place.

Events Underlying "Twitchy Lungs"

To understand how asthma might be aggravated by air pollutants, it is important to review the complex series of reactions in the lungs and respiratory passages in an evolutionary context. When an asthma-precipitating agent interacts with antigen receptors in the lungs, fluids are released, bronchioles constrict, and air resistance goes up, making it difficult to expel residual air and draw a complete breath. The characteristic wheezing of an asthmatic child reflects this state of hypersecretion and increased airway resistance that limits access of airborne pollutants to the lower lungs. The existence of such a complex and coordinated series of reactions in the lung suggests that at one time such reactions had an adaptive function. But what was it?

To uncover the true role of asthma, one must look first at the plethora of substances that can induce it.

The "Causative" Factors of Asthma

The number of different agents that are associated with asthma attacks today are legion. (A partial listing is shown in Table 5.) A simple glance at the extraordinary diversity of symptom-provoking agents suggests that identification of any common factor among such a plethora of agents will be a most formidable task. The sheer number of potential inciting agents seemingly makes the search mind-numbing.

Table 5: Substances Associated with Induction of Asthma[18]

Substance	Occupation
Products Associated with Baking or Food Processing	
Wheat or buckwheat	Millers, bakers
Grain products or dust	Farmers, farm workers, grain handlers
Flour	Bakers
Hops	Brewery workers
Tamarind of flax seeds	Millers, baggers, handlers
Green and roasted coffee bean dust	Roasters, baggers, handlers
Castor beans	Millers, baggers, handlers
Tea dusts	Tea sifters and packers
Vegetable gums	Candy makers
Soybean dusts and flour	Unloaders, handlers, processors
Rye flour	Bakers
Wheat gluten derivative	Bakers
Garlic powder	Spice factory workers
Green leaf tobacco	Tobacco harvesters
Linseed	Oil extracters
Psyllium seed	Pharmacy workers
Potatoes	Farmers, factory workers
Colophony (rosin)	Electronics workers
Ipecac dust	Pharmacy workers
Freesia and sunflower pollens	Flower growers, flower shop workers
Cotton, flax, and hemp	Textile mill workers
Other Agricultural Products	
Tobacco dust	Cigarette factory workers
Wools	Textile factory workers
Poultry feathers, droppings, or eggs	Poultry processers, farmers
Animal danders, urine	Farmers, farm workers, laboratory workers
Seafoods	
Prawns, crabs	Prawn and crab processors
Sea squirt fluid	Chinese food processors
Oysters, shell dust	Oyster shuckers, pearl processors
Fish glue	Bookbinders
Insects and Insect By-products	
Beetles	Museum workers
Locusts	Laboratory workers

continued

Table 5: Substances Associated with Induction of Asthma, *continued*

Substance	Occupation
Cockroaches	Schoolchildren and lab workers
Bee moths	Fish bait breeders
Housefly maggots	Anglers and bait breeders
Grain storage mites	Farm workers
Grain weevils	Lab workers, farmers
Mexican bean weevils	Pea and bean sorters
Moth and butterfly scales	Entomologists
Silk worms	Silk workers
Sewerworm flies	Waste processors
Silkworms	Silk makers
Crickets and grasshoppers	Bait processors
Microorganisms and Fungi	
Alternaria species	bakers
Aspergillus species	Grain processors, bakers
Fungal spores (various species)	Farm workers
Mushroom spores	Mushroom cultivators
Moldy compost	Nursery workers, gardeners
Pink rot fungus	Celery pickers
Cladosporium	Farmers and farm workers
Humidifier sludge	Homeowners
Wood Dusts	
Western red cedar	Woodworkers
South African hardwoods	Carpenters
California redwood	Woodworkers, carpenters
African boxwood	Woodworkers
Natural resins	Woodworkers, carpenters
Soap bark	Drug processors
Cedar of Lebanon	Woodworkers
Oak, mahogany	Woodworkers
Bacteria and Enzymes	
Bacillus subtilis	Detergent developers
Trypsin	Lab workers

Seeking the Primordial "Asthmagen"

Which agent among the hundreds that can precipitate asthma today was the primordial provocateur? One clue is to examine the most florid provocative agents that are known to precipitate an asthma attack. At first glance Table 5 appears to provide little guidance as to asthma's origins since a multitude of chemicals and natural substances can provoke asthma.

But a closer look at the list provides a tantalizing clue. The first thing to note is that although the list is limited to naturally occurring substances, certain types of substances recur throughout. Insects and their droppings, baking and contact with grains or seed products, and fungi and molds account for the majority of entries. The second thing is that the sensitizing agents found in these occupations are not so much toxic as they are antigenic. This observation suggests that the body is defending itself from a secondary consequence of exposure.

The Agrarian Connection

The assertion that one of these antigenic materials or some associated substance is the *agent provocateur* of asthma hinges on two requirements: (1) it must provoke a strong asthmatic response and (2) it must produce a widespread reaction in the populace as a whole. (An agent that only affected a handful of hypersusceptible persons would have less selective force than one that affected a wider population.)

1. "Powerful" Asthma-Provoking Allergens

Ironically, the most powerful asthmatic agents discovered in recent times are not the excretions of cockroaches or other common household contaminants such as dust mites as some researchers have alleged. While the dust mite is a proven allergen for many asthmatics, close examination of cross-reacting antigens suggests that another culprit lurks within. In fact, the house dust mite is an evolutionary cousin of particularly allergenic mites associated with the storage of grains and other seed crops.[19] In one study that examined a broad cross section of known allergens, the greatest release of histamine in asthma sufferers was provoked by *Dermatophagoides farinae*, the grain mite.[20]

Is there a grain connection? Some conditions, such as "humidifier" or "farmer's lung," are caused by fungi (*Micropolyspora faeni*) that grow on moldy grain. Chest tightness, usually a reflection of lung hyperreactivity, also occurs commonly among grain-dust-exposed workers.[21] But the primary allergen is probably not grain dust so much as an antigenic concomitant of grainery work. Grain workers have, in fact, been found to react strongly to certain previously unidentified antigens.[22] And one case study confirms that one of the potent sensitizers in the grainery is found in a group of grain mites. After handling stored grain, a worker developed immediate nasal and eye symptoms, and when examined in the laboratory, demonstrated hyperreactivity to storage mites known as *Lepidoglyphus destructor*.[23]

2. *Population-wide Impact*

Many of the agents responsible for the most widespread asthma episodes of recent times include some by-products of protein sources that have made up a significant part of the human diet since the agrarian revolution–grain and soybean dusts, *and* their accompanying insect pests.

Further indirect support for an agrarian connection to asthma comes from the origins of the most severe and widespread asthmatic epidemic that occurred in recent times. From 1982 through 1988, a massive and long-lasting asthma outbreak occurred in Spain. In Cartegna, Spain, more than 90 percent of the thousands of people who experienced attacks during the asthma outbreak in 1987 and 1988 proved highly allergic to the coat of the soybean. All had been exposed to soybean dust.[24] An even more extensive series of attacks in Barcelona was also attributable to soybean dust.[25] Asthma outbreaks following exposure to soybean dusts have now been documented across a broader front, showing up in locations distant from Spain.[26]

But why would soybeans, and in particular the hulls of soybeans, provoke such a powerful immunologic reaction? Could the reaction to soybeans be merely fortuitous, a chance occurrence caused solely by the inadvertently high antigenicity of soybeans? While this is certainly a possibility, the evolutionary model would ask a different question: What possible health hazard could such materials have posed in our past?

The Mold Connection

For one thing, all of the substances in the agricultural list of sensitizers are capable of carrying toxins into the body. Specifically, moist or wet soybeans or grains of any kind readily support the growth of many different fungal species, especially *Aspergillus*, which are themselves common allergens. This group of molds is also highly pathogenic and/or toxic to the human body. Aspergillosis (caused by species of *Aspergillus*) is an often life-threatening fungal lung infection, especially in immunodepressed hosts. And related molds produce special toxins as a byproduct of their metabolism.

Aspergillus species include a broad range of fungi that occur in two forms—active growing molds and spores. Their presence in nature is ubiquitous since they thrive in any environment where there is decaying matter. Low-level contamination by *Aspergillus* in all sorts of human habitations is common, particularly where humidity is high. Patients who are hospitalized because of disease, malignancy, or transplantation medications; AIDS patients; or the very young or old are at particular risk of contracting aspergillosis.[27] The common factor in their enhanced risk status is an impaired immune system. Epidemics among such susceptible patients have proven devastating in various hospital settings, particularly where construction has disturbed *Aspergillus* spores and allowed them to become airborne.[28] The nature of the resulting disease is particularly deadly where patients have depressed white cell counts, such as in lymphoma or leukemia during chemotherapy.

When *Aspergillus* spores enter the lungs or nasal tract in an immunocompromised patient, they literally take root, growing hyphae (microtubules) which invade the surrounding tissues and blood vessels. This growth, normally checked by the front-line defense system of macrophages and granulocytes can then progress to block the blood supply to an organ or tissue or cause massive bleeding and further metastatic spread into vital organs. The primary site of invasion and growth is the organ that would be most heavily "defended" by the asthmatic response—the lungs. More than 90 percent of the cases of invasive aspergillosis initially affect the lungs.[29] It stands to reason (but remains to be proven) that the bronchospasms produced in asthmatic attacks were originally protective against aspergillosis and other mold-related threats to health.

Other molds, such as the one responsible for "farmer's lung," can also produce disease, and some fungi, such as the *Trichothecene* group, produce highly toxic chemicals that have been implicated as biological warfare agents.

In public health, it is well recognized that the storage of grains and legumes can be hazardous to health when the stored materials became contaminated with fungi in general or molds in particular. To become moldy, storage crops require humidity, and humidity encourages infestation with contaminating insects, especially the arachnids known as storage mites. One would then predict that a physiological response against such mites evolved sometime after the agrarian revolution as a tocsin or warning that a person is in an environment conducive to mold-related illness. An "asthma attack" could then be seen as a front-line defense against aspergillosis and related conditions associated with mold toxicity.

Predictions

If asthma evolved in direct response to such mold-supporting conditions, one would predict that populations that are only recently agrarian or are nonagrarian would have lower rates of asthma than would postagrarian societies. Such a pattern holds up since asthma is mainly a disease of industrialized nations with a long period of agrarian prehistory. And those few societies that have limited or no agricultural practices altogether, such as the Papua New Guineans, have low asthma rates, even though they are exposed chronically to wood dust, smoke particulates, and insect and animal danders.

A second prediction arising from asthma's protection against molds is that asthma attacks would be more prevalent in any damp environment in which molds thrive. Indirect evidence for this association comes from the observation that living in damp homes or using humidifiers was associated with wheezing; while, in the same homes, exposure to cooking gas was not.[31] Dampness and moldy homes were also associated with reactive lower lung diseases among Canadians.[32]

A third prediction is that a generalized reactivity to a broad constellation of agriculture-associated molds should be the rule and not the exception among reactive, asthmatic populations. In fact, reactivity to a wide cross section of outdoor fungal species, including members of the species *Alternaria* and *Cladosporia* and members of the class Basidomycetes, has generally been reported. Most notable is the fact that these molds are the types most often found around graineries.[33] Molds more closely associated with dwellings, such as those associated with damp basements, bedding, or any damp interior area, are also known to provoke asthma.

Synopsis

These observations suggest an evolutionary answer to the asthma dilemma: Since the domestication of grain some 14,000 years ago, the risks of inhaling moist, contaminated grain by-products–notably fungal spores and molds such as the *Aspergillus* species so commonly associated with modern asthma–must have been substantial. Not only can molds themselves cause serious diseases such as aspergillosis, but moldy wheat, corn, and peanuts almost always contain varying amounts of the most potent human carcinogen known, the aflatoxin B group, as well as certain toxins such as the tricothecenes.

Hence, an immediate reactive response to molds or fungal spores that closed off the lower airways could readily prevent the inhalation of spores into those regions where fungal infections would be most likely. By developing a concomitant allergic sensitivity to those mites that flourish in the damp confines of grainage bins, high-risk individuals could also reduce the likelihood of inhaling the dangerous, mold-infested grains themselves.

In this way, the legacy of a previously adaptive response to the genuine threat of molds and spoiled grain created a generalized hyperreactivity in the lung. And as a result of nonspecific spread in speceficities what was at first a defensive measure to genuine threats to health has become an asthmatic reaction with little or no contemporary adaptive value. How then do we explain the greatly expanded list of allergens in Table 5?

In industrialized countries, much of this reaction occurs to surrogates of past inciting agents. Old reactions to grain mites have given way to newer ones to house mites. The special sensitivity to house dust mites noted in most developed countries can be explained by noting that these insects are distant, cross-reacting cousins of the storage mite.[33] Even persons from immigrant populations where the dust mite is inconspicuous commonly develop an allergy to it soon after reaching the shores of major industrial centers,[34] suggesting preexisting immunity to the more rural grain mite cousin.

The damp climes commonly associated with asthma attacks can now be understood as reflecting the likelihood of conditions that favor the growth of molds in general. Support for this portion of the hypothesis comes from low-income housing areas of Bucharest, Romania, where reactivity to fungal spores was commonly found, especially to *Aspergillus niger.* Coincidentally, the greatest spore prevalence and highest allergenic reactivities were found in those flats with the greatest humidity and the poorest ventilation.[35]

Explaining an Epidemic

It remains to explain why asthma has increased so dramatically in the last 10 to 15 years. One idea is that concentrations of allergens from molds, fungi, and dust mite infestations have increased with the advent of greater energy-saving consciousness and "tight" homes. This association was suggested by a study done in Sweden that charted the emergence of allergic asthma, especially from dust mite infestations, in the decade since greater energy consciousness emerged in Sweden.[36] Further support for this model comes from U.S. studies that show that workers in environmentally "tight" offices have developed a hypersensitive lung disorder following exposure to indoor air contaminated with actinomycete fungal spores.[37]

Why asthma deaths occur so disproportionately in inner cities (New York and Chicago alone account for 21 percent of all U.S. deaths)[38] is only partially explained by this model. Certainly dust mites and cockroaches are common instigators and chemical pollutants are potent irritants. Social factors that limit access to medical care for these populations must also play a role.[39]

So what began in agrarian societies as a critical adaptive response to assure that we were not poisoned by the major biochemical toxins associated with molds on food crops has led to a hypercharged immune system geared to molds and those elements that accompany their production: damp storage bins and cellars, mites and their excretions, and antigens from grains and legumes like soy. A heightened reactivity to any "marker" of cereal or legume molds, including reaction to the crops themselves, begins to make sense according to this model. The fact that the most severe asthma outbreaks recorded in modern times, notably those we reviewed in Spain, were precipitated by reactions to seed crop antigens (soybean dusts) is in keeping with this prediction.[40] Thus, most asthma-provoking agents indicate the presence of dangerous fungal or mold-fostering conditions. Asthma itself can be seen as limiting the deep inhalation of the offending toxic chemicals associated with molds generally and reducing exposure to the spores of the molds themselves.

Evidence for the Gatekeeper Hypothesis

Strong inference supports this model. Since patients with intact immune systems–and possibly effective asthmalike defenses–do not commonly get sick from such spores, some element of the immune system serves as a first line of defense against lung infection with aspergillosis. In fact, when examined carefully, from *6 to 20 percent* of all asthmatics have been found to harbor an allergy to *Aspergillus*.[41]

The generalization of a defensive reactive system that included an IgE, histamine-mediated constriction of the bronchial tubes leading to the lungs would conceivably limit the dissemination of disease-causing spores. Once established as an immunological reaction, the resulting capability to respond to *Aspergillus* and related antigens would allow the immune system to respond to an ever expanding array of real or imagined potential threats. While initially confined to antigens that cross react with *Aspergillus*, the asthmatic response would have expanded to other markers of the presence of pathogenic fungi, notably their spores, dust mites, and ultimately markers of the environments that typically harbor *Aspergillus* species, notably graineries and other mold-generating storage facilities.

Such an evolving reactive system could then explain the broad constellation of antigens that today can trigger an asthmatic attack. Our immune system cannot discriminate dust mites from grain mites, *Aspergillus* antigens from those arising in nonpathogenic fungal sources, seed crop coat antigens from those of grains, or fresh grass pollen from pollens potentially contaminated with tricothecene or other mold-contributed toxins. To the extent that some defensive response was critical for protecting our agrarian forebearers from potentially catastrophic aspergillosis or mold-generated toxicity secondary to pastoral activities, the immune system cannot be blamed for occasionally giving some of their descendants asthma. The fact that this disorder is presently at epidemic proportions cannot be so readily explained. But that is a topic for another book.

Conclusions

In asthma, we are seeing the vestiges of a system that limits the access of potentially offending substances into the anatomical regions of the body where they might do the most damage. The apparent "epidemic" of asthma is an indirect consequence of an overreaction of this primitive system to contemporary exacerbating forces. Among these are industrial pollution and the concentration of allergens produced by encouraging "tight" homes with little or no external ventilation to dilute the offending substances.

In an ironic twist of fate, it appears that the novel environments of human invention are the culprit in exacerbating what was once an adaptive reaction to natural causes that threatened survival. Asthma then is an evolutionary vestige of powerful Darwinian forces of selection.

12 Conclusion

When Darwin first proposed a mechanism for the origin of species, he could hardly have known how intensely his theory would be applied to medical theory. Darwin shared his cousin, Francis Galton's (1822–1911) view that human improvement was ultimately an evolutionary problem. To perfect man, Charles Darwin once wrote, warranted the same attention to judicious breeding as animal breeders lavished on the barnyard species of the English countryside. As he once said, "Excepting in the case of man himself, hardly anyone is so ignorant as to allow his worst animals to breed."[1]

The aberant experiment in forced eugenics during the Nazi era hopefully taught us how draconian are the methods needed to reform the image of man through "applied evolution." And we now recognize the very slow evolutionary mechanisms that directly "reshape" human destiny.

Many in the burgeoning environmental movement warn us daily of the evolutionary limits of human dominion of the biosphere. As more and more species become extinct, we are reminded that we are destroying the tenuous ecological balance of the planet. And well we may. But we are also exerting powerful yet not nearly so visible impacts on the microscopic level. Whole genera of bacteria, fungi, and insects have been given massive selective advantages by our well-intentioned but nonetheless misapplied mission to subdue microbial and insect pests with chemicals. These misguided programs have led to massive outbreaks of multidrug-resistant diseases, the emergence of pesticide-resistant insects, and the development of chemically resistant cancer cells.

We may also be focusing our attention at the wrong end of the evolutionary spectrum. Instead of bringing our evolutionary acumen to bear on the rarest and least successful species—the endangered few—we might do well to recognize that our worst dilemmas are generated by the *most* successful species.

We could well start with *Homo sapiens.* By virtue of our own adaptive success, we have become the most prolific, large species on the planet. In addition to the obvious depradations on the environment that our seemingly limitless "needs" have produced, we might also recognize a basic law of ecology—those species that carry the largest biomass and maintain the highest population densities are the most attractive hosts for parasites and infectious organisms. By being so successful, we have put ourselves not so much at the apex of evolution as fair game for many of the most opportunistic species on the planet. As a people, we are at risk for parasitic and infectious diseases precisely because we have proven so prolific as a species. We are present in sufficient numbers to pose an ideal intermediate and primary host for dozens of arthropods, helminths, and spirochetes. And as we disrupt ecosystems and displace previously successful species, we put ourselves in harm's way of aquiring the bacteria, viruses, and parasites we have supplanted from previous hosts. Is it any surprise that infectious diseases such as AIDS and malaria had their likely origins in primate or monkey species that we killed or dispersed in disturbed jungle habitats? What other new diseases will abound as we push further into the wildernesses of the rain forests of South America?

In the wild, only limited numbers of animals generally prove vulnerable to invasion by opportunistic infections because most animals rarely form social networks or herds sufficiently large to jeopardize the entire species should infection occur. For other large primates, the distance between troops and the limited social interactions even among the most promiscuous of their kind puts an uppermost limit on the access that any infectious organisms can get to the species as a whole.

But this may not be true in the case of *Homo sapiens.* We may have long since eclipsed our "safety margin" for population density in terms of the social isolation, maximum population density, and resistance to transmissibility that normally buffers the global distribution of disease. Indeed, one could trace this escape point to the first global pandemic of plague in the thirteenth century.

Even as we recall the migration along caravan routes taken by these first mass epidemics, we may reconsider the epidemiological implications of our own global reach and interchange. As the new global pandemics of cholera, AIDS, and malaria show, the species as a whole is not only exchanging germ plasm but is freely exchanging pathogens, putting itself at risk of horrific epidemics because of the span of human outreach and expanded social contacts.

It is a truism that the social upheaval generated by war, poverty, and political unrest has historically put the most vulnerable populations at risk of disease. What is new today is the vastly increased population densities of the major metropolitan regions of the world: Mexico City, Lima, Rio de Janero, and Bankgkok to name just four. Each has enormous subcultures of poverty and conditions in which epidemic disease is waiting to break out. And as the AIDS epidemic shows, the normal bounds of poverty pose no limit for sexually transmitted diseases.

Southeast Asia and India represent the newest breeding grounds for AIDS. And variants of HIV are being subjected to selection pressures that lead to viruses even more fit to survive in human populations. Unless we learn to anticipate epidemics through improved surveillance and intervene in their genesis early enough, we will have still more pain and suffering beyond that produced by AIDS.

Synthesis

A crucial message of the evolutionary perspective is that we remain at risk for disease in spite of our medical advances. The interconnectedness of all of the living things on earth, so poetically embraced by the environmental movement, is also the basis for our continuing peril. It is precisely this interconnectedness that allows microorganisms to move from their prior hosts to prey on us so effectively. Even as we recognize the traditional bounds of host specificity, it is humbling to recognize that probably *both* the HIV and plasmodium organisms responsible for AIDS and malaria–the greatest pandemics currently sweeping the earth today–had their modest origins in champanzees or other primates that we displaced in the African rain forests. Ecosystem biology has taught us about interdependence and exploitation—we cannot abruptly move into entirely new environments without peril. The history of malaria, plague, Lyme disease, and exotic viral diseases such as Lassa fever and hemorrhagic fever have shown us that when we disturb the environment, we often imperil ourselves.

Coevolution Reconsidered

Even our most vigorous defense against one disease often sets the stage for another. As we have seen, the rapid activation and proliferation of the immune system in response to the malarial parasite increases the vulnerability of infected persons to the HIV organism that thrives selectively in activated T cells. Similarly, the Epstein-Barr virus grows preferentially in the activated immune system of such patients, paving the way for the development of Burkitt's lymphoma.

The same fungal diseases that decimate AIDS patients may incite asthma in otherwise healthy persons, revealing an ancient defense system. As shown by the rising epidemic of asthma, lung hyperresponsiveness today is no longer a very effective mechanism to limit access of fungal spores to our deeper lung tissues nor a useful device to control inhalation of chemical or agricultural toxins.

This last example highlights the contemporary dilemma of the human condition. We arrive in the twenty-first century with some 4 million years or so of primate evolutionary baggage. In many industrialized nations, we have nutritional deficiencies unmet by current diets, unless judiciously supplemented; vulnerability to viruses such as the HIV organism; and susceptibility to chemical hypersensitivity, parasitic infections, and autoimmune diseases brought about by an immune system more properly tuned to past than to contemporary stimuli. And modern medicine continues to reinforce these vulnerabilities by using chemical controls such as antibiotics when it could be strengthening our innate resistance mechanisms. Our failures in controlling new diseases such as AIDS challenge our approaches to treating infectious diseases as a whole. New vaccines are intrinsically sounder approaches for controlling the risks of infection from malaria or HIV than are chemical assaults with antibiotics after the fact. Yet, our research in these areas has lagged behind our quick-fix chemical therapeutic approaches.

Nature has generated dramatic and sometimes awesome examples of adaptations in the face of often extreme forms of environmental pollution and stress. From the melanic moths that evolved in the first years of the Industrial Revolution in England to the recently recognized resistance of plants to otherwise highly toxic metals, nature has met our incursions. Insecticide resistance is now so rampant as to challenge the chemical approach to the treatment of pest problems. And so it is on the medical front.

Microorganisms have rebounded dramatically from many of our chemical assaults. The same general features of resistance couple bacteria, viruses, parasites, and even cancer cells together–all have proven to be capable of usurping new genes from less virulent forms and of permitting radical rearrangements of their genetic makeup in response to our therapeutic attempts. Such adaptations are so abundant as to force us to reconsider our strategies for controlling diseases through blunt force, since chemical controls are almost always intrinsically limited in the rapidly evolving species that typify most infectious organisms. But when given the opportunity to reinforce prevention programs for worldwide scourges such as TB or to limit the spread of antibiotic-resistant forms, we as a country have balked. The World Health Organization recently requested a paltry $3 million from the United States to fight the reemergence of TB as a global killer, and was turned down.[2]

The Consequences of Evolutionary Neglect

Why has modern medicine chosen to "control" so many diseases in ways that appear to be antithetical to an enlightened evolutionary perspective? Part of the reason may be the traditional reliance of medical practice on allegiance to the individual patient and to the immediate relief of suffering. Sometimes this dual allegience places medical choices that are beneficial for the patient above those that may be inimical to the community. A prime example is antibiotic use. What physician has not used a prophylactic antibiotic or preemptive treatment (say, for a suspected middle-ear infection) without considering the future consequences to the community?

In a sense, it is understandable that physicians ignore evolutionary consequences of their behavior. After all, they are treating the patient before them, not society. Nor can they be faulted for their apparent disregard for the causes of a disease process, especially when the patient needs urgent ministrations to control a fulminant infection or other life-threatening disease process. But while attention has been lavished on individual therapeutics and individualized patient ethics, disproportionately little effort has gone into population-wide medicine and public health ethics.

A notable exception is the World Health Organization's Expanded Program on Immunization. This worldwide program affords protection to 80 percent of the children in developing nations for such diseases as diptheria, whooping cough, tetanus, polio, and measles. Still lacking, unfortunately, are widespread use of other effective vaccines, notably the one against meningitis. Existing vaccines for typhoid, pneumonia, cholera, TB, and influenza generate imperfect immunity, but could still be more widely available. Other diseases, such as venereal warts, cervical cancer associated with human papilloma virus, and glandular fever, remain strong prospects for vaccine development.

Obviously, a malaria vaccine should long ago have been made a top priority. (Others disagree, of course. Even assuming the scientific hurdles are cleared, massive economic, political, and distributional issues are associated with the manufacture of a successful vaccine.) While I have shown where progress has been made in dealing with malaria, scant evidence exists for optimism that the widespread protection needed to control this major scourge is imminent.

The evolutionary paradigm has also only belatedly been applied to health policy. Its neglect has contributed to a slow response to the rapid emergence and spread of modern-day killers such as cholera, AIDS, malaria, and tuberculosis. (The last disease alone affects one-third of the world's population.) The gross misperception that infectious disease was under control and modern medicine could dominate any pathogen was allowed to persist for too many years—as late as 1970, many members of the medical community were heralding the end of infectious diseases.[3] And it was not until 1992 that a committee at the National Institute of Medicine concluded that dramatic steps were needed to control further erosion of an already serious public health situation posed by the recrudescence of infectious disease. Under the leadership of Nobel Laureate Josua Lederberg, president of Rockefeller University in New York, this multidisciplinary committee identified a number of institutional, environmental, and medical factors that have encouraged the evolution of new diseases.[4]

Among these factors are the rapid movement and dispersion of human populations; new patterns of economic development and land use (which put persons into novel ecological relationships with pathogens); the breakdown of public health control measures (which permits rapid disease evolution); and the failure to recognize the capacity of microorganisms to adapt and change under intense selective pressures from both the internal and external environments. To regain control over emergent and epidemic disease, the Lederberg group recommends a dramatic strengthening of vaccination and surveillance programs, better control of the vectors of disease, and, perhaps most saliently, the undertaking of a special education program by the National Institutes of Health. This program would focus on identifying the individual, community, and medical activities that encourage the transmission and selection of resistant pathogens, precisely the type of recommendation that I endorse in this book.

Breaking the Therapeutic Barrier

These steps, while well intentioned, lack the teeth and the focus needed to limit existing epidemics or to ensure that present errors do not recur. To achieve these ends will require policies that require prescreening of antibiotics to assure, as in the case of the 4-quinolones, that only those drugs with limited selection potential against our normal intestinal flora will be used prophylactically. It is also incumbent on hospital administrators, and on infection control and surveillance committees, that antibiotics routinely used in treating infections be carefully monitored and controlled to minimize inappropriate dosages. Further steps to control ecologic disruption on a macroscale must go hand in glove with these and related efforts to limit microenvironmental disruptions.

When we ask ourselves where an evolutionary perspective might have made a difference, the resulting list is provocative:

- Could we have anticipated the emergence of AIDS, as many medical anthropologists once posited?
- Would we have let multidrug-resistant TB get out of hand?

- Would we have generated so many antibiotic-resistant strains—or relied so exclusively on antibiotics in the first place?
- Would we have failed to recognize the origins and genetic predispositions of autoimmune diseases?
- Would diabetes now be so widespread?
- Would cancer treatments so often be futile?
- Would drug-resistant malaria now be out of control?
- Would new diseases like Lyme disease have spread so quickly?

Some tentative answers to these questions are provided by this book. While categorical responses are clearly inappropriate, each of these queries suggests that there might be different health outcomes had we adopted an evolutionary approach. Though simplistic, one way to achieve this end is to encourage evolutionary awareness throughout medical education. Such an awareness would take the form of greater recognition of the role that evolutionary forces have and will play in shaping human disease and our resistance to it.

As but one example, consider the Human Genome Program. As this project to decipher the major genes of the human species goes forward, it will undoubtedly provide greater and greater knowledge about our constitutional vulnerabilities. In turn, we will uncover some of the adaptive features that led to the evolution of the responsible genes. With that knowledge, it will behoove us to pay closer attention to the conditions under which we put our most genetically susceptible populations. We may learn that even trace contaminants pose hazards for some persons. But we might well ask as this massive dissection exercise of our evolutionary origins proceeds—Do we have the wisdom to use this data wisely?

Denial of evolutionary realities has been the bane of modern medicine. As I have sketched in this book, so many contemporary medical failures can be traced to the neglect of the evolutionary consequences of our actions that a new approach is almost obligatory. To do so requires a recrudescence of the awareness that the human condition is an integral part of the biological universe. What happens to us will impinge on virtually all other species. Thus, when we believed (properly so) that malaria posed a dire threat to entire populations, we did not hesitate to spray whole territories and countries with what turned out to be ecological disaster – DDT. As we learn more about the genetic underpinnings of resistance to malaria, would we not do better to consider the evolutionary approaches suggested in this book? Even if we were to use our newfound genetic powers to engineer certain cell lines to carry the resistance factors for disease and transplant them back into the at-risk populations, we would be acting consistently with the evolutionary ethic. This approach is a far cry from the eugenics of the late nineteenth century. With sufficient genetic acumen concerning the evolutionary advantages and disadvantages of certain genotypes, we may strive to duplicate them in miniature within each body by cellular transplants (somatic cell engineering), rather than to select new lineages of humans through the brute force of eugenics.

I have shown that resistance factors to particular parasitic and to a lesser extent viral and bacterial diseases already exist in many subgroups of humans as a result of natural selection. By isolating those factors and making them available through somatic cell engineering of a person's own blood cell lines, we stand to benefit a whole new generation. We already have the example of the researchers who utilized the existence of humans who had been subjected to natural selection for malaria resistance to fashion a vaccine for such resistance. By using the plasmodium antigens captured by the MHC locus HLA B53, this vaccine should be able to provide otherwise genetically at-risk persons with the precise evolutionarily tested antigens needed for effective immunity.

A simple extension of this approach is to use genetic engineering to bring resistance genes into otherwise healthy but vulnerable persons. By conferring resistance genes on certain cell lines and transplanting the cells into new, genetically unrelated but appropriately tolerized hosts, we could successfully bring to bear the legacy of eons of evolutionary advances. To do so, of course, means expanding the definition of "illness" to embrace vulnerability, itself a major ethical hurdle.

Evolutionary medicine can also benefit from the knowledge gleaned from nature that internecine battles between species in the wild often provide clues for modern therapeutics. This is indeed the approach of several fledgling biotechnology companies that are exploring coral reefs and tropical rain forests for species that have developed toxins or other biologically active compounds for self-defense. Many small peptides have been isolated that serve these functions, including cecropins, defensins, and maganins. These peptides have been isolated from the skin and mucous membranes of amphibia and elasmobranchs (frogs and sharks), where they serve as a primary line of defense against bacteria.

In a sense, this approach is a return to the old system used by the antibiotic hunters. Selman Waksman and René Dubos, as well as Sir Alexander Fleming, each achieved mastery over bacterial disease by looking for naturally occurring substances that were already being used by microorganisms to control more invasive or competing species. The actinomycetes were a particularly rich source of antibiotics primarily because they were so successful in dominating the bacterial species that threatened their own survival.

The lesson of evolutionary biology is that we may make *judicious* use of chemotherapeutic and preventive agents that have proven valuable in nature's own battles. We will be successful in moving those agents into our own armamentarium if and only if we recognize the inherent limitations of any therapeutic strategy—unless annihilation is achieved early and without imperiling the immunologic strength of the host, most viral, bacterial, and cancer cells will live to propagate their resistant kind all over again. And with time they will prove even more intractable to control than did the first generation.

The Apotheosis of Evolution

Evolution can be our ally or our enemy. Recognizing that we are part of nature and not above it requires a new form of therapeutic humility and judgment. We need to be aware that as we have evolved to have certain defenses against disease, so have our adversaries; that these defenses are not fail-safe; that many targeted organisms have devised their own strategies to escape control and in so doing may trigger still other diseases like the organ damage in juvenile diabetes or other forms of autoimmunity. These few examples point up why successful therapeutic strategies must recognize evolutionary potential.

Recognizing the evolutionary paradigm also means forswearing the continued synthesis and unbridled use of genotoxic chemicals that select for resistant organisms, particularly since many of the most potent antibacterials in and of themselves can damage the human germ line. Evolution will not stand idly by if we disturb our genetic legacy. If we increase the frequency of mutations or related genetic changes of our own or neighboring species' gene pools, we are courting disaster.

The ends of medicine cannot be limited to ministrations to the ever-changing panoply of human ills and disorders. Medicine must recognize the critical importance of a simultaneous concern about the environment and the evolutionary forces that have shaped our ongoing interaction with the natural world. Without a new coevolutionary ethic, medicine will be trapped in its present reactive mode, with little or no chance for the dramatic reintegration of human and nonhuman biology that a safe world demands. It is time to put humankind back into the evolutionary picture. We have done so in part through recognition of the need to protect endangered species and to preserve ecosystems of particular value. Now it is time for modern medicine to reintegrate an evolutionary perspective into its practices, to recognize our part in evolution.

We shape the diseases that afflict us as much as they have shaped us. Taking responsibility for modern diseases such as AIDS, TB, and Lyme disease requires that we once again step back and recognize the role we have played in their emergence. While it may not be possible to turn back the clock, we can nonetheless restore the balanced relationships that kept these diseases in check over the millennia. This means incorporating evolutionary strategies into their control. But, above all, it means acknowledging that we have evolved to be an integral part of their continuing presence.

Living with modern diseases will mean respecting their evolutionary adaptations—and our own. Their containment will require the most creative application of our hard-won knowledge of molecular immunology and genetics to ferret out disease strengths and weaknesses. But if the history of multidrug resistance in bacteria, viruses, parasites, and cancer provides us with any lesson, it is that these strategies must be applied with great wisdom if we are to avoid becoming victims of our own evolutionary neglect.

Notes

Chapter 1: Introduction

1. See J. B. McKinlay, S. M. McKinlay, and R. Beaglehole, "A review of the evidence concerning the impact of medical measures on recent mortality and morbidity in the United States," *International Journal of Health Services* 19 (1989): 181–208.
2. Quoted in "How to fight AIDS," editorial in the *San Francisco Examiner and Chronicle*, 20 June 1993.
3. Barton Childs, "Genetics in medical education," *American Journal of Human Genetics* 52 (1993): 225–27, 1993.
4. G. C. Williams and R. M. Neese, "The dawn of Darwinian medicine," *Quarterly Review of Biology* 66 (1991): 1–22.
5. M. Lappé, *Germs that will not die* (New York: Simon & Schuster, 1982).
6. S. B. Levy, "Tuberculosis: detecting multidrug resistant tuberculosis early," *Lancet* 341 (1993): 664–65.
7. S. B. Levy, *The Antibiotic paradox: How miracle drugs are destroying the miracle* (New York: Plenum, 1992).
8. I. Illich, *Medical nemesis* (London: Penguin, 1972).

Chapter 2: Ecosystem Disruption and Disease

1. According to G. Cowley, "By encroaching on rain forests and wilderness areas, humanity is placing itself in ever-closer contact with other species and their previously rare but deadly parasites," in "The future of AIDS," *Newsweek*, 22 March 1993, p. 52.
2. See A. Gibbons, "Where are 'new' diseases born?" *Science* 261 (1993): 680–81.
3. Ibid.
4. J. Lederberg, R. E. Shope, and C. Oaks, Jr., eds., *Emerging infections: Microbial threats to health in the United States* (Washington, DC: National Academy Press, 1992).
5. S. S. Morse, "Global microbial traffic and the interchange of disease," *American Journal of Public Health* 82 (1992): 1326–27.

6. See H. R. Bhat, "A brief history of Kyasanur Forest disease," *National Institute of Virology Quarterly Bulletin, New Series* I (1983): 4–5.
7. J. D. Marshall, D. V. Ouy et al., "Ecology of plague in Vietnam: Commensal rodents and their fleas," *Military Medicine* 132 (1967): 896–903.
8. A. D. Alexander et al., "Zoonotic infections in military scout and tracker dogs in Vietnam," *Infection and Immunology* 5 (1972): 745–49.
9. B. Velimirovic, "Plague in South-East Asia. A brief historical summary and present geographical distribution," *Transactions of the Royal Society of Tropical Medicine and Hygiene* 22 (1973): 642–53.
10. J. D. Marshall, R. J. Hoy et al., "Plague in Vietnam, 1965–66," *American Journal of Epidemiology* 86 (1967): 603–16.
11. "Epidemic plague," *Journal of the American Medical Association* 205 (1968): 596–97; F. G. Conrad, F. R. LeCocqu, and R. Krain, "A recent epidemic of plague in Vietnam," *Archives of Internal Medicine* 122 (1968): 193–98.
12. T. Butler, "A clinical study of bubonic plague. Observations of the 1970 Vietnam epidemic with emphasis on coagulation studies, skin histology and electrocardiograms," *American Journal of Medicine* 53 (1972): 268–76.
13. T. Butler et al., "*Yersinia pestis* infection in Vietnam: I. Clinical and hematologic aspects," *Journal of Infectious Disease* 129 (Suppl. 1974): 578–84.
14. P. Trong, T. Q. Nhu, and J. D. Marshall, Jr., "A mixed pneumonic–bubonic plague outbreak in Vietnam," *Military Medicine* 132 (1967): 93–97.
15. A. Vennema, "Morbidity and mortality in children under 16 at the provinicial hospital in Quang Ngai, South Vietnam, 1965–68," *Public Health* 84 (1970): 291–98.
16. F. M. Burkle, Jr., "Plague as seen in South Vietnamese children. A chronicle of observations and treatment under adverse conditions," *Clinical Pediatrics* 12 (1973): 291–98.
17. J. D. Marshall, D. V. Quy, and F. L. Gibson, "Asymptomatic pharyngeal plague infection in Vietnam," *American Journal of Tropical Medicine* 16 (1967): 175–77.
18. J. E. Williams et al., "Atypical plague bacillus isolated from rodents, fleas and man," *American Journal of Public Health* 68 (1978): 262–64.
19. Detailed bacteriologic studies can be found in B. W. Hudson, T. J. Quan, V. R. Sites, and J. D. Marshall, "An electrophoretic and bacteriologic study of *Yersinia pestis* isolates from central Java, Asia and the Western Hemisphere," *American Journal of Tropical Medicine and Hygiene* 22 (1973): 642–53.
20. See H. Hoogstraal, "Argasid and nuttellid ticks as parasites and vectors," *Advances in Parasitology* 24 (1985): 136–235.
21. Ibid., pp. 174–76.
22. Hoogstraal states that "Ticks are apparently the unequivocal original source of borreliae. Alteration between tick and vertebrate hosts may be necessary for the long-term viability and survival of borreliae. . . . vertebrates can amplify the infection in nature by supplying the borreliae "clean" feeding ticks, but only after having been primarily infected by infected ticks . . ." Ibid., p. 214.
23. Ibid., p. 178.

24. Ibid., p. 181.
25. A. G. Barbour and D. Fish, "The biological and social phenomenon of Lyme disease," *Science* 260 (1993): 1610–15.
26. P. Ewald, "The evolution of virulence," *Scientific American,* April 1993, 86–93.
27. Hoogstraal, note 20, p. 214.
28. See S. J. Brown, F. M. Graziano, and P. W. Askenase, "Immune serum transfer of cutaneous basophil-associated resistance to ticks," *Journal of Immunology* 129 (1982): 2407–12.
29. P. Banks, "Sounding the alarm on dengue fever," *The Journal of NIH Research* I (November-December 1989): 40–42.
30. R. Streatfield, G. Bielby, and D. Sinclar, "A primary dengue 2 epidemic with spontaneous hemorrhagic manifestations," *Lancet* 342 (1993): 560–61.
31. Ibid.
32. Ibid.
33. Banks, note 29, p. 42.
34. C. J. Mitchell et al., "Isolation of eastern equine encephalitis virus from *Aedes albopictus* in Florida," *Science* 257 (1992): 526–27.
35. M. E. Loevinsohn, "Climactic warming and increased malaria incidence in Rwanda," *Lancet* 343 (1994): 1714–18.
36. See the series by D. Sarokin and J. Schulkin, "The role of pollution in large-scale population disturbances," *Environmental Science and Technology* 26 (1992): 1476–84.

Chapter 3: Understanding Selection

1. C. Darwin, *On the origin of species,* (New York: Macmillan, 1962; 1st ed., 1859).
2. See, for example, G. C. Williams and R. M. Nesse, "The dawn of Darwinian medicine," *Quarterly Review of Biology* 66 (1991): 1–22, especially p. 3.
3. T. B. Smith, "Disruptive selection and the genetic basis of bill size polymorphism in the African finch *Pyrenestes,*" *Nature* 363 (1993): 618–20.
4. E. Mayr, *Population, species and evolution* (Cambridge, MA: Harvard University Press, 1970), 20.
5. See N. Eldredge and S. J. Gould, "Punctuated equilibria: An alternative to phyletic gradualism," in T. J. M. Schopf, ed., *Models in paleobiology* (San Francisco: Freeman Cooper, 1972), 305–32; and S. J. Gould and N. Eldredge, "Punctuated equilibria: The tempo and mode of evolution reconsidered," *Paleobiology* 3 (1977): 115–51.
6. Mayr points out that only a certain amount of diversity can be accommodated in a single gene pool without producing too high a proportion of inviable recombinants: "Organizing genetic diversity into protected gene pools, that is, a species, guarantees that these limits are not overstepped. This is the biological meaning of species," Mayr, note 4, p. 20.
7. See R. A. Fisher, *The genetical theory of natural selection,* 2nd ed. (New York: Academic Press, 1958; 1st ed., 1930).
8. For a more complete and elaborate definition of selection, see E. F. Keller and E. A. Lloyd, *Keywords in evolutionary biology* (Cambridge, MA: Harvard University Press, 1992).

9. This essential feature of evolution has been discussed at length by one of the pioneers of modern-day evolutionary theory, Ernst Mayr, in *Toward a new philosophy of biology: Observations of an evolutionist* (Cambridge, MA: Harvard University Press, 1990). See especially pp. 457–60.
10. See M. Lappé, *When antibiotics fail* (Berkeley, CA: North Atlantic Press, 1986).
11. Much of this evolution occurs in intemediate hosts, often waterfowl, which serve as both the primordial and recurrent sources of all influenza viruses: see R. G. Webster et al., "Evolution and ecology of influenza A viruses," *Microbiology Reviews* 56 (1992): 152–79.
12. For a full discussion of influenza evolution, see C. M. Pease, "An evolutionary epidemiological mechanism, with application to type A influenza," *Theoretical Population Biology* 31 (1987): 422–52.
13. A notable exception to the general rule of high mutation rates in RNA viruses exists: see G. D. K. Baldridge, B. J. Beaty, and M. J. Hewlett, "Genomic stability of La Crosse virus during vertical and horizontal transmission," *Archives of Virology* 108 (1989): 89–99.
14. See J. J. Holland, J. C. De La Torre, and D. A. Steinhauer, "RNA virus populations as quasi-species," *Current Topics in Microbiology and Immunology* 176 (1992): 1–20.
15. This phenomenon is known as "Muller's ratchet" after H. J. Muller who first described the ratchetlike way by which most mutated individuals are irreversibly lost in asexually reproducing populations through random drift and nonreplacement. See L. Chao, "Fitness of RNA virus decreased by Muller's ratchet," *Nature* 348 (1990): 454–55.
16. See S. F. Elena, F. Gonzalez Candelas, and A. Moya, "Does the VP1 gene of the foot and mouth disease virus behave as a molecular clock?" *Journal of Molecular Evolution* 35 (1992): 223–29.
17. E. Domingo, "RNA virus evolution and the control of viral disease," *Progress in Drug Research* 33 (1989): 93–133.
18. A. T. Burness et al., "Genetic stability of Ross River virus during epidemic spread in nonimmune humans," *Virology* 167 (1988): 639–43.
19. This remarkable discovery was made by C. S. Hahn, S. Lustig, E. G. Strauss, and J. H. Strauss, "Western equine encephalitis virus is a recombinant virus," *Proceedings of the National Academy of Science* 85 (1988): 5997–6001.
20. See V. Moenning, "Changes in the dynamics of viral infectious diseases," *Deutsche Tierarztlichte Wochenschrift* 99 (1992): 290–92. (English abstract.)
21. A. Mitchison, "Will we survive?" *Scientific American*, September 1993, 135–43 (quote from p. 143).

Chapter 4: Life, Death, and Cancer

1. R. T. Prehn, "A clonical selection theory of chemical carcinogenesis," *Journal of the National Cancer Institute* 32 (1964): 1–17.
2. L. A. Gavrilov and N. S. Gavrilov, *The biology of the life span: A quantitative approach* (Chur, Switzerland: Harwood Academic Press, 1991).

3. See G. M. Martin, "Genetic and evolutionary aspects of aging," *Federation Proceedings* 38 (1979): 1962–67.
4. M. Peacoke and J. Campisi, "Cellular senescence: A reflection of normal growth control, differentiation or aging?" *Journal of Biological Chemistry* 45 (1991): 147–55.
5. G. A. Sacher, "Life table modification and life prolongation," in C. E. Finch and L. Hayflick, eds., *Handbook of the biology of aging* (New York: Van Nostrand Reinhold, 1977), 588.
6. See T. Dobzhansky, *Mankind evolving* (New Haven and London: Yale University Press, 1962).
7. This view is capsulized in the statement by three leading gerontologists that organisms are not "programmed to survive much beyond the ages required to ensure reproductive success." See S. J. Olshansky, B. A. Carnes, and C. K. Cassel, "Fruit fly aging and mortality," *Science* 260 (1993): 1565–66 (letter).
8. See Martin, note 3.
9. J. E. Riggs, "Aging and mortality: Manifestations of natural non-selection," *Mechanisms of Aging and Development* 62 (1992): 127–35.
10. According to Williams and Neese, "An intuitively useful if not entirely accurate restatement is that selection maximizes the abilities of organisms to gain genetic representation in future generations." "The dawn of Darwinian medicine," *Quarterly Review of Biology* 66 (1991): 1–22.
11. J. R. Carey, J. W. Curtsinger, and J. W. Vaupel, "Fruit flies, aging and mortality," *Science* 260 (1993): 1566–69.
12. L. Hayflick, "The longevity of cultured human cells," *Journal of the American Geriatric Society* 22 (1974): 1–12.
13. Olshansky et al., note 7.
14. J. F. Kerr, A. H. Wyllie, and A. R. Currie, "Apoptosis: A basic biological phenomenon with ride-ranging implications in tissue kinetics," *British Journal of Cancer* 26 (1972): 239–57.
15. C. Franceschi, "Cell proliferation, cell death and aging," *Aging* (Milano) 1 (1989): 3–15.
16. D. P. Lane, "A death in the life of p53," *Nature* 362 (1993): 786–87.
17. For a review, see J. G. Sinkovics, "Retroviral and human cellular oncogenes," *Annals of Clinical and Laboratory Science* 14 (1984): 343–54.
18. Ibid.
19. F. P. Li, P. Correra, and J. F. Fraumeni, Jr., "Testing for germ line p53 mutations in cancer families," *Cancer Epidemiology, Biomarkers and Prevention* 1 (1991): 91–94.
20. See W. N. Hittelman et al., "Early genetic changes during upper aerodigestive tract tumorigenesis," *Journal of Cellular Biochemistry* 17 (Fall 1993): 233–36; and V. P. Collins and C. D. James, "Gene and chromosomal alterations associated with the development of human gliomas," *FASEB Journal* 7 (1993): 926–30.
21. S. Ohno, "Cellular oncogenes as the ancestors of endocrine and paracrine growth factors and their evolutionary relic status in vertebrates," *Modern Trends in Human Leukemia* 6 (1985): 224–27.
22. A. Jacobs, "Gene mutations in myelodysplasia," *Leukemia Research* 16 (1992): 47–50.

23. O. Brison, "Gene amplification and tumor progression," *Biochimica et Biophysica Acta* 1155 (1993): 24–25.
24. These proto-oncogenes include the *erbβ, ras,* and *myc* genes. See Brison, note 24.
25. J. C. Bergh, "Gene ampliflication in human lung cancer. The *myc* family genes and other proto-oncogens and growth factor genes," *American Review of Respiratory Diseases* 142 (1990): 520–26.
26. W. S. Kendal, "A perspective on tumor progression," *Canadian Journal of Surgery* 36 (1993): 133–36.
27. R. Clarke et al., "Hormone resistance, invasiveness, and metastatic potential in breast cancer," *Breast Cancer Research and Treatment* 24 (1993): 227–39.
28. R. Sager, I. K. Gadi, L. Stephens, and C. T. Grabowy, "Gene amplification: An example of accelerated evolution in tumorigenic cells," *Proceedings of the National Academy of Science* 82 (1985): 7015–19.
29. Ibid.
30. J. G. Klign, M. Bontenbal, J. Alexieva-Figusch, and J. A. Foekens, "Clinical breast cancer, new developments in selection and endocrine treatment of patients," *Journal of Steroid Biochemistry and Molecular Biology* 43 (1992): 211–21.
31. See Bergh, note 26.
32. M. Schwab, "Enhanced expression of the cellular oncogene c-*myc* and progression in human neuroblastoma," *Advances in Enzyme Regulation* 31 (1991): 329–38.
33. G. Palka et al., "Leukemic evolution in three patients with myelodysplastic syndrome and unusual chromosome changes," *Cancer Genetics and Cytogenetics* 61 (1992): 162–64.
34. D. W. Hammond et al., "Cytogenetic analysis of a United Kingdom series of non-Hodgkin's lymphomas," *Cancer Genetics and Cytogenetics* 61 (1992): 31–38.
35. U. Trautman et al., "Multiple chromosomal changes and karyotypic evolution in a patient with myelofibrosis," *Cancer Genetics and Cytogenetics* 61 (1992): 6–10.
36. L. C. Peterson, L. L. Lindquist, S. Church, and N. E. Kay, "Frequent clonal abnormalities of chromosome band 13014 in B-cell chronic lymphocytic leukemia," *Genes, Chromosomes and Cancer* 4 (1992): 273–80.
37. K. F. Wong, J. K. Chang, Y. C. Chu, and Y. H. L. Kwong, "Clonal evolution in primary 5q-syndrome," *Cancer* 70 (1992): 100–3.
38. This multidrug transporter is termed P-glycoprotein or P170 and is discussed at length in S. E. Kane, I. Pastan, and M. M. Gottesman, "Genetic basis of multidrug resistance of tumor cells," *Journal of Bioenergetics and Biomembranes* 22 (1990): 593–618.
39. H. Enright et al., "Inversion of chromosome 16 and dysplastic eosinophils in accelerated phase of chromic myeloid leukemia," *Leukemia* 6 (1992): 381–84.
40. See, for instance, the discussion in H. E. Kaiser, "Cancer growth and progression in the framework of comparative oncology: A new approach to cancer therapy," *Anticancer Research* II (1991): 1453–67.
41. See Klijn et al., note 31.
42. Ibid.
43. D. L. Hill and C. J. Grubbs, "Retinoids and cancer prevention," *Annual Reviews of Nutrition* 12 (1992): 161–81.

44. M. Huang et al., "Use of all *trans*-retinoic acid in the treatment of acute promyelocytic leukemia," *Blood* 72 (1988): 567–72.
45. T. Koike et al., "Brief report: Severe symptoms of hyperhistaminemia after the treatment of acute promyelocytic leukemia with tretinoin," *New England Journal of Medicine* 327 (1992): 385–87.
46. B. D. Cheson, "The maturation of differentiation therapy," *New England Journal of Medicine* 327 (1992): 422–23.
47. K. J. Scanlon, W. Z. Wang, and H. Han, "Cycolsporin A suppresses cisplatin-induced oncogene expression in human cancer cells," *Cancer Treatment Reviews* 17 (1990: Suppl. A): 27–35.
48. S. Ikuyama and H. Mishina, "Fanconi's anemia as nature's evolutionary experiment on carcinogenesis," *Tohoku Journal of Experimental Medicine* 153 (1987): 87–102.
49. M. A. Lappé, "Tumor specific antigens: Possible origin in premalignant lesions," *Nature* 223 (1969): 82–84; and M. A. Lappé, "Failure of long-term control of 3-methylcholanthrene-induced skin tumors in the autochtonous host," *Journal of the Reticuloendothelial Society* 10 (1971): 120–30.
50. See R. T. Prehn, "The immune reaction as a stimulator of tumor development," *Science* 176 (1972): 170–71.
51. Discussed in M. A. Lappé and J. Schalk, "Necessity of the spleen for balanced sex ratios following maternal immunization with male antigen," *Transplantation* 11 (1971): 491–95.

Chapter 5: Infectious Diseases

1. C. T. Walsh, "Vancomycin resistance: Decoding the molecular logic," *Science* (1993): 308–9.
2. See the July 29, 1993, issue of the *New England Journal of Medicine.*
3. M. Lappé, *Germs that will not die: Medical consequences of the misuse of antibiotics* (New York: Doubleday/Anchor Press, 1982) and *When antibiotics fail* (Berkeley, CA: North Atlantic Press, 1986).
4. Among the most serious events was a mass outbreak of antibiotic-resistant salmonella infections among Californians, linked to contaminated hamburgers and the veterinary misuse of chloramphenicol on dairy farms. See J. S. Spika et al., "Chloramphenicol-resistant *Salmonella newport* traced through hamburger to dairy farms—A major persisting source of human salmonellosis in California," *New England Journal of Medicine* 316 (1987): 565–70.
5. A. Gibbons, "Exploring new strategies to fight drug-resistant microbes," *Science* 257 (1992): 1036–37.
6. R. A. Malt, "Tetracycline resistant *Neisseria*," *New England Journal of Medicine* 315 (1986): 1548–49.
7. See K. R. Mansford and B. Slocombe, "The evolution of antibiotic production and public health problems," *Chemioterapia* 6 (1987): 234–40.
8. M. Barber, "Naturally occurring methicillin-resistant staphylococci," *Journal of General Microbiology* 35 (1964): 183–90.

9. K. Crossley, B. Landesman, and D. Zaske, "An outbreak of infections caused by strains of *Staphylococcus aureus* resistant to methicillin and aminoglycosides. II. Epidemiologic studies," *Journal of Infectious Diseases* 139 (1979): 280–87.
10. J. M. Boyce and W. A. Causey, "Increasing occurrence of methicillin resistant *S. aureus* in the United States," *Infection Control* 3 (1982): 337–83.
11. M. A. Pfaller et al., "Variation from standards in *Staphylococcus aureus* susceptibility testing," *American Journal of Clinical Pathology* 88 (1987): 231–35.
12. N. Rao, S. Jaccobs, and L. Joyce, "Cost-effective eradication of an outbreak of methicillin-resistant *S. aureus* in a community teaching hospital," *Infection Control and Hospital Epidemiology* 9 (1988): 255–60.
13. L. L. Livornese, Jr. et al., "Hospital acquired infection with vancomycin resistant *Enterococcus faecium* transmitted by electronic thermometers," *Annals of Internal Medicine* 117 (1992): 112–17.
14. M. Y. Stoeckle and R. G. Douglas, Jr., "Infectious diseases," *Journal of the American Medical Association* 270 (1993): 223–24.
15. Ibid.
16. J. Weisser and B. Wiedemann, "Brief report: Effects of ciprofloxacin on plasmids," *American Journal of Medicine* 82 (1987: Suppl. 4A): 21–22.
17. D. C. Hooper, J. S. Wolfson, E. Y. Ng, and M. N. Swartz, "Mechanisms of action of and resistance to ciprofloxacin," *American Journal of Medicine* 82 (1987: Suppl. 4A): 12–20; and G. C. Crumplin, "Plasmid-mediated resistance to nalidixic acid and new 4-quinolones," *Lancet* 11 (1987): 854–55.
18. C. Edlund and C. E. Nord, "A review on the impact of 4-quinolones on the normal oropharyngeal and intestinal human microflora," *Infection* 16 (1988): 8–16.
19. L. Dubreuil et al., *Journale Pharmaceutique de Belge* 45 (1990): 311–18.
20. D. R. Chaberg, D. H. Culver, and R. P. Gaynes, "Major trends in the microbial etiology of nosocomial infection," *American Journal of Medicine* 91 (1992: Suppl. 3B): 72S–75S.
21. T. R. Frieden et al., "Emergence of vancomycin-resistant enterococci in New York City," *Lancet* 342 (1993): 76–79.
22. See Stoeckle and Douglas, note 14.
23. R. S. Schwalbe, J. T. Stapelton, and P. H. Gilligan, "Emergence of vancomycin resistance in coagulase-negative staphylocci," *New England Journal of Medicine* 316 (1987): 927–30.
24. Walsh, note 1.
25. M. H. Wilcox, R. C. Spencer, and G. R. Weeks, "Vancomycin resistant enterococci," *Lancet* 342 (1993): 615–16.
26. See Frieden et al., note 21.
27. L. O. Gentry, "Bacterial resistance," *Orthopedic Clinics of North America* 22 (1991): 379–88.
28. K. H. Shaw, P. N. Rather, R. S. Hare, and G. H. Miller, "Molecular genetics of aminoglycoside resistance genes and familial relationships of the aminoglycoside modifying enzymes," *Microbiology Reviews* 57 (1993): 138–63.

29. F. W. Goldstein et al., "Plasmid mediated resistance to multiple antibiotics in *Salmonella typhi*," *Journal of Infectious Diseases* 153 (1986): 261–66.
30. C. C. Sanders and C. Watanakunakorn, "Emergence of resistance to beta-lactams, aminoglycosides, and quinolones during combination therapy for infection due to *Serratia marcescens*," *Journal of Infectious Diseases* 153 (1986): 617–20.
31. Cited in M. L. Cohen, "Epidemiology of drug resistance: Implications for a post-antimicrobial era," *Science* 257 (1992): 1050–55.
32. B. Aronsson, R. Molby, and C. E. Nord, "Antimicrobial agents and *Clostridium dificile* in acute enteric disease: Epidemiological data from Sweden, 1980–1982," *Journal of Infectious Diseases* 151 (1985): 476–81.
33. Ibid.
34. Ibid.
35. Cohen, note 31.
36. G. Urbina, M. E. Cavazza, and I. Perez-Schael, "Heterogeneous plasmid population from enterotoxigenic *Escherichia coli* strains isolated in Venezuelan children with acute diarrhea," *G-E-N* 43 (1989): 194–201.
37. A. M. Cassel-Beraud, P. Coulages, and C. Richard, "Evolution des résistances aux antibiotiques des souches de Shigella dysenteriae typhe I (bacilles de Shiga) 'isolées' à Tanarive et sur la Côte est de Madagascar," *Archives de l'Institute Pasteur de Madagascar* 56 (1989): 71–76.
38. T. Butler, M. R. Islam, M. A. K. Azad, and P. K. Jones, "Risk factors for the development of hemolytic uremic syndrome during shigellosis," *Journal of Pediatrics* 110 (1987): 894–97.
39. R. B. Sack, "Enterohemorrhagic *Escherichia coli*," *New England Journal of Medicine* 317 (1987): 1535–57.
40. P. I. Tarr et al., "*Escherichia coli* 157: H7 hemorrhagic colitis," *New England Journal of Medicine* 328 (1988): 1697.
41. For an exception where a cautionary note *was* sounded, see the editorial section of the July 16, 1988, issue of *Lancet*.
42. C. O. Tacket et al., "Protection by milk immunoglobulin concentrate against oral challenge with enterotoxigenic *E. coli*," *New England Journal of Medicine* 318 (1988): 1240–43.
43. C. E. Nord, L. Kager, and A. Heimdahl, "Impact of antimicrobial agents on the gastrointestinal microflora and the risk of infections," *American Journal of Medicine* 76 (1984): 99–106.
44. J. M. Hammond, P. D. Potgieter, G. L. Saunders, and A. A. Forder, "Double-blind study of selective decontamination of the digestive tract in intensive care," *Lancet* 340 (1992): 5–9.
45. E. Manso et al., "Vancomycin-resistant enterococci," *Lancet* 342 (1993): 615–16 (letter).
46. B. S. Block, L. J. Mercer, M. A. Ismail, and A. H. Moawad, "*Clostridium dificile* associated diarrhea follows perioperative prophylaxis with cefotoxitin," *American Journal of Obstetrics and Gynecology* 153 (1985): 835–38.

47. E. L. Arsurea, R. A. Fazio, and P. C. Wickremesinghe, "Pseudomembranous colitis following prophylactic antibiotic use in primary cesarean section," *American Journal of Obstetrics and Gynecology* 151 (1985): 87–89.
48. D. N. Gerdin et al., "*Clostridum dificile* associated diarrhea and colitis in adults," *Archives of Internal Medicine* 146 (1986): 95–100.
49. See, especially, H. C. Neu, "The crisis in antibiotic resistance," *Science* 257 (1992): 1064–73.
50. M. L. Grayson and G. M. Eiopoulos, "Antimicrobial resistance in the intensive care unit," *Seminars in Respiratory Infection* 5 (1990): 204–14.
51. P. W. Ewald, "The evolution of virulence," *Scientific American,* April 1993, 86–93.
52. M. F. Parry, "Epidemiology and mechanisms of antimicrobial resistance," *American Journal of Infection Control* 17 (1989): 286–94.
53. A. J. Morrison, Jr., and R. P. Wenzel, "Nosocomial urinary tract infections due to enterococcus. Ten years' experience at a university hospital," *Archives of Internal Medicine* 146 (1986): 1549–51.
54. See Parry, note 52.
55. D. M. Jaffe et al., "Antibiotic administration to treat possible occult bacteremia in febrile children," *New England Journal of Medicine* 317 (1987): 1175–80.
56. D. A. Goldmann and J. D. Klinger, "*Pseudomonas cepacia:* Biology, mechanisms of virulence, epidemiology," *Journal of Pediatrics* 108 (1986): 806–12.
57. For a detailed comparison of the effectiveness (and lack thereof) of ten different prophylactic regimens for post-caesarean endometritis, see S. Faro et al., "Antibiotic prophylaxis: Is there a difference?" *American Journal of Obstetrics and Gynecology* 162 (1990): 900–9.
58. Grayson and Eiopoulos, note 50; E. Beregogne-Berezin, "Evolution de l'antibiotherapie et nouvelles perspectives," *Presse Medicale* 19 (1990): 373–77; H. C. Neu, "General concepts on the chemotherapy of infectious diseases," *Medical Clinics of North America* 71 (1987): 1051–65.
59. D. S. Fedson, "Penicillin-resistant pneumococci," *Lancet* 11 (1988): 1451–52.
60. Ibid. Even after the United Kingdom permitted pneumococcal vaccine use in 1978, fewer than 10,000 doses were distributed in the first 6 years of use.
61. V. J. Gururaj, J. K. Patrick, and P. F. Rogers, "*Hemophilus influenzae* type B vaccine: Use in the pediatric population," *Pediatrics* 80 (1987): 731–35.
62. A. B. Kaiser, "Drug therapy: Antimicrobial prophylaxis in surgery," *New England Journal of Medicine* 315 (1986): 1129–38.
63. Correspondence section of "Antimicrobial prophylaxis in surgery," *New England Journal of Medicine* 316 (1987): 1089–90.
64. See J. O. Klein, "The febrile child and occult bacteremia," *New England Journal of Medicine* 317 (1987): 1219–20. Klein's exact words were: "Despite the lack of convincing evidence to show that antimicrobial therapy is beneficial for children with occult bacteremia, physicians are justified in choosing an antibiotic regimen . . . for selected children with clinical features suggestive of bacteremia."
65. See Stoeckle and Douglas, note 14.

66. C. M. Kunin and H. Y. Efron, "Audits of antimicrobial usage, Veterans Administration Ad Hoc Interdisciplinary Committee on Antimicrobial Drug Usage," *Journal of the American Medical Association* 237 (1977): 1001–7, 1134–37, 1241–45, 1366–69, 1481–84, 1605–8, 1723–25, 1859–60, 1969–70.
67. I discuss some of these options in my books, *When antibiotics fail* and *Germs that will not die* (note 3). See also, K. Sehnert, *Health World*, September/October 1990, 43–46.
68. J. A. Shapiro, "Natural genetic engineering in evolution," *Genetica* 86 (1992): 99–111.
69. R. M. Krause, "The origin of plagues: Old and new," *Science* 257 (1992): 1073–77.
70. See especially, M. Douglas Baker, L. M. Bell, and J. R. Avner, "Outpatient management without antibiotics of fever in selected patients," *New England Journal of Medicine* 329 (1993): 1437–41.

Chapter 6: Lethal Germs

1. An update on therapeutic modalities and differential diagnosis of sepsis has recently been published: see W. A. Knaus et al., "The clinical evaluation of new drugs for sepsis," *Journal of the American Medical Association* 270 (1993): 1233–41.
2. S. P. Fisher-Hock et al., "Pathogenic potential of filoviruses," *Journal of Infectious Diseases* 166 (1992): 753–63.
3. C. J. Peters et al., "Filovirus contamination of cell cultures," *Development of Biological Standards* 76 (1992): 267–74.
4. S. S. Kalter and R. L. Heberling, "Primate viral diseases in perspective," *Journal of Medical Primatology* 19 (1990): 519–35.
5. P. W. Ewald, "The evolution of virulence," *Scientific American*, April 1993: 86–93.
6. Ibid.
7. E. A. Herre, "Population structure and the evolution of virulence in nematode parasites of fig wasps," *Science* 259 (1993): 1442–45.
8. See Ewald, note 5.
9. R. Lopez-Linares, "Policies that sustain poverty," *Health Action*, September 1992, 6–7.
10. R. I. Glass et al., "Cholera in Africa: Lessons on transmission and control for Latin America," *Lancet* 338 (1991): 791–94.
11. Cholera Working Group, "Large epidemic of cholera-like disease in Bangladesh caused by *Vibrio cholerae* O 139 synonym Bengal," *Lancet* 342 (1993): 387–90.
12. Centers for Disease Control, "Imported cholera associated with a newly described toxigenic *Vibrio cholerae* O 139 strain—California, 1993," *Morbidity and Mortality Weekly Report* 42 (1993): 501–3.
13. See Ewald, note 5.
14. A. Kochi, "The global tuberculosis situation and the new control strategy of the World Health Organization," *Tubercle* 72 (1990): 1–6.
15. M. Y. Stoeckle and R. G. Douglas, Jr., "Infectious diseases," *Journal of the American Medical Association* 270 (1993): 223–24.
16. Centers for Disease Control, "Transmission of multidrug-resistant tuberculosis among immunocompromised persons in a correctional system: New York, 1991," *Morbidity and Mortality Weekly Reports* 41 (1992): 507–9.

17. Centers for Disease Control, "National action plan to combat multidrug-resistant tuberculosis," *Morbidity and Mortality Weekly Report* 41 (1992): 1–48. In the healthy adult population in the United States, the *lifetime* risk of acquiring TB is about 1 percent. And most of the infections that do occur pass without notice and leave only a telltale positive tuberculin test.
18. P. Hastier et al., "Tuberculose disseminée et multirésistante chez un patient seropositif pour le virus de l'immunodeficience humaine," *Annals de Medicine Internelle* 142 (1991): 67–68.
19. M. Hawken et al., "Increased recurrence of tuberculosis in HIV-1 infected patients in Kenya," *Lancet* 342 (1993): 332–36.
20. High recurrence rates after apparent recovery have been reported out of Kinshasa, Zaire: See J. H. Perriens et al., "Increased mortality and tuberculosis treatment failure rate among HIV seropositive compared with HIV seronegative patients with pulmonary tuberculosis treated with 'standard' chemotherapy in Kinshasa, Zaire," *American Review of Respiratory Disease* 144 (1991): 750–55.
21. Centers for Disease Control, "Interstate outbreak of drug resistant tuberculosis involving children–California, Montana, Nevada, Utah," *Morbidity and Mortality Weekly Report* 32 (1983): 516–18.
22. J. R. Livengood et al., "Isoniazid-resistant tuberculosis," *Journal of the American Medical Association* 253 (1985): 2847–49.
23. Ibid.
24. See A. Mahmoudi and M. D. Iseman, "Pitfalls in the care of patients with tuberculosis," *Journal of the American Medical Association* 270 (1993): 65–68.
25. L. T. Ratcliffe, C. R. Mackenzie, P. T. Lukey, and S. R. Ress, "Reduced natural killer cell activity in multi-drug resistant pulmonary tuberculosis," *Scandinavian Journal of Immunology* 11 (Suppl. 1992): 167–70.
26. M. Earnest and J. A. Sbarbaro, "A plague returns," *The Sciences*, September/October 1993, 14–18. They describe the critical role this therapeutic approach now plays in controlling the TB epidemic in Denver.
27. Resistance genes for the major antibiotics used for TB occur spontaneously at a rate between 1×10^5 for isoniazid to 1×10^6 for rifampin. That is, resistance is found in 1 in every 100,000 or 1 in every 1 million bacilli. If we assume that the average rate of mutation for each of the four antibiotics being used is 1 in 100,000, the likelihood of all four mutations occurring at random in a single TB organism is the product of the probability of occurrence of each of the four mutation rates, or about 1×10^{20}. This likelihood is so infinitesimally small, given the existence of only about 2×10^9 TB organisms in any one infected patient, as to make the likelihood of finding a germ with quadruple resistance almost a mathematical impossibility–unless preexistent mutations exist in a fresh infection and multiple-resistance genes can be transmitted in groups to the TB organism the way they are in other bacteria. Both of these events are highly likely.
28. E. A. Filley and G. A. Rook, "Effect of mycobacteria on sensitivity to the cytotoxic effects of tumor necrosis factor," *Infection and Immunity* 59 (1991): 2567–72.

29. See Earnest and Sbarbaro, note 26.
30. See Mahmoudi and Iseman, note 24.

Chapter 7: AIDS

1. J. T. Flynn, "AIDS and the origin of species," *New York State Journal of Medicine* 88 (1988): 53–54.
2. See the essay by C. Frutchey, education director of the San Francisco AIDS Foundation, in the *San Francisco Chronicle,* June 28, 1993.
3. P. Donovan, "A prescription for sexually transmitted diseases," *Issues in Science and Technology,* Summer 1993, 40–46.
4. Ibid.
5. P. B. Blair et al., "Immunologic deficiency associated with mammary tumor virus infection," *Journal of Immunology* 106 (1971): 364–70.
6. J. Weber and M. McClure, "HIV quiet but not silent," *Nature* 364 (1993): 110.
7. T.R.E. Southwood, "The natural environment and disease: An evolutionary perspective," *British Medical Journal* 294 (1987): 1086–89.
8. V. Courgnaud et al., "Genetic differences accounting for evolution and pathogenicity of simian immunodeficiency virus from a sooty mangabey monkey after cross-species transmission to a pig-tailed macaque," *Journal of Virology* 66 (1992): 414–19.
9. See, in particular, the general article by G. Cowley, "The future of AIDS," *Newsweek,* March 22, 1993, 47.
10. Although other diseases affect a large number of persons worldwide (for example, parasitic diseases such as malaria will have infected upward of 200 million persons in any current year), the fact that such diseases cause chronic illness and not early death permits some of their carriers to reproduce before they die. The uniformly high mortality rate of AIDS ensures that virtually all vulnerable persons will die.
11. P. W. Ewald, "Evolution of HIV in Africa," *Science* 257 (1992): 10.
12. A. Larson, "Social context of human immunodeficiency virus transmission in Africa: Historical and cultural bases of east and central Africa sexual relations," *Reviews of Infectious Diseases* 2 (1989): 716–31.
13. See, for example, K. Neal, "Origins of HIV," *Lancet* 340 (1992): 58 (letter).
14. P. Ewald, "The evolution of virulence," *Scientific American,* April 1993, 90.
15. Ibid., p. 91.
16. T. Zhu et al., "Genotypic and phenotypic characterization of HIV-1 in patients with primary infection," *Science* 261 (1993): 1179–81.
17. A. R. McLean, V. C. Emergy, A. Webster, and P. D. Griffiths, "Population dynamics of HIV within an individual after treatment with Zidovudine," *AIDS* 5 (1991): 485–90.
18. In a typical study, the genetic variance of an HIV strain in an AZT-treated patient was examined at 10, 18, and 27 months after treatment was initiated. After 18 months, one key base residue in the DNA coding for an important viral enzyme already indicated the presence of two viral types. By 27 months, the shift had progressed further, and at least three different subtypes were present, with the total replacement of the original strain of HIV by one with the new base component in its DNA.

All of these changes were associated with increasing resistance to AZT as treatment progressed and ultimately failed. See J. Wahlberg et al., "Dynamic changes in HIV-1 quasi-species from AZT-treated patients," *FASEB Journal* 6 (1992): 1002; and C. A. Boucher et al., "Ordered appearance of Zidovudine resistance mutations during treatment of 18 human immunodeficiency virus-positive subjects," *Journal of Infectious Disease* 165 (1992): 105–10.

19. B. R. Edli et al., "In vitro resistance to Zidovudine and alpha-interferon in HIV-1 isolates from patients: Correlations with treatment duration and response," *Annals of Internal Medicine* 117 (1992): 457–60.
20. D. A. Steinhauer and J. J. Holland, "Rapid evolution of RNA viruses," *Annual Reviews of Microbiology* 4 (1987): 409–33.
21. Data available in G. Myers et al., eds, *Human retroviruses and AIDS* (Los Alamos, NM: Los Alamos National Laboratories, 1990).
22. M. A. Nowak, R. M. May, and R. M. Anderson, "The evolutionary dynamics of HIV-1 quasi-species and the development of immunodeficiency disease," *AIDS* 4 (1990): 1095–1103.
23. Ibid., p. 1103.
24. A. R. McLean and M. A. Nowak, "Competition between Zidovudine-sensitive and Zidovudine-resistant strains of HIV," *AIDS* 6 (1992): 71–79.
25. H. Burger et al., "Evolution of human immunodeficiency virus type 1 nucleotide sequence diversity among close contacts," *Proceedings of the National Academy of Science* 88 (1991): 11,236–40.
26. See, for example, S. J. Sperber and C. J. Schleupner, "Salmonellosis during infection with human immunodeficiency virus," *Reviews of Infectious Diseases* 9 (1987): 925–34.
27. These case studies are summarized in F. J. Leavitt, "Opportunistic infection," *Nature* 263 (1993): 577.
28. A. Gateley et al., "Herpes simplex virus type 2 meningocephalitis resistant to acyclovir in a patient with AIDS," *Journal of Infectious Disease* 161 (1990): 711–15.
29. F. Bevilacqua et al., "Acyclovir resistance/susceptibility in herpes simplex virus type 2 sequential isolates from an AIDS patient," *Journal of Acquired Immune Deficiency Syndrome* 4 (1991): 967–69.
30. S. Safrin et al., "A controlled trial comparing foscarnet with vidarabine for acyclovir-resistant mucocutaneous herpes simplex in the acquired immunodeficiency syndrome," *New England Journal of Medicine* 325 (1991): 551–55.
31. For an exception, see H. J. Stellbrilnk, H. Albrecht, T. Loning, and H. Geteen, "Herpes simplex virus type 2 ulcers resistant to acyclovir in an AIDS patient–Successful treatment with foscarnet," *Klinische Wochenschrift* 69 (1991): 274–78.
32. Yung-Kang Chow et al., "Use of evolutionary limitations of HIV-1 multidrug resistance to optimize therapy," *Nature* 361 (1993): 360–63. The chemicals used were AZT, ddI, and pridinone.
33. J. Cohen, "Harvard group makes a splash–Twice," *Science* 261 (1993): 678.
34. See, in particular, the advocacy statement of M. S. Hirsch, "Chemotherapy of human immunodeficiency virus infections: Current practice and future prospects," *Journal of Infectious Disease* 161 (1990): 845–57.

35. B. A. Larder, P. Kellam, and S. D. Kemp, "Zidovudine resistance predicted by direct detection of mutations in DNA from HIV-infected lymphocytes," *AIDS* 5 (1991): 137–44.
36. T. C. Meng, M. A. Fischl, and D. D. Richman, "AIDS clinical trails group: Phase I/II study of combination ddI and ddC in patients with AIDS," *American Journal of Medicine* 88 (1990): 27S–30S.
37. J. E. Groopman, "Treatment of AIDS with combinations of antiretroviral agents: A summary," *American Journal of Medicine* 90 (1991): 27S–30S.
38. M. A. Wainberg and R. G. Margolese, "Strategies in the treatment of AIDS and related diseases: The lessons of cancer chemotherapy," *Cancer Investigation* 10 (1992): 143–53.
39. D. D. Richman, "Playing chess with reverse transcriptase," *Nature* 361 (1993): 588.
40. O. E. Odeleye and R. R. Watson, "The potential role of vitamin E in the treatment of immunologic abnormalities during acute immune deficiency syndrome," *Progress in Food and Nutrition Science* 15 (1991): 1–19.
41. F. Tihole, "Possible treatment of AIDS patients with live lactobacteria," *Medical Hypotheses* 26 (1988): 85–88.
42. J. Y. Kim, D. R. Germolec, and M. I. Luster, "Panax ginseng as a potential immunomodulator: Studies in mice," *Immunopharmacology and Immunotoxicology* 12 (1990): 257–76.
43. See B. A. Larder, G. Darby, and D. D. Richman, "HIV with reduced sensitivity to AZT isolated during prolonged therapy," *Science* 243 (1989): 1731–34.
44. A. J. Orfuss et al., "General discussion," in: "Symposium on nonchemotherapeutic approaches to control of staphylococcal infection," *Bulletin of the New York Academy of Medicine* 44 (1968): 1227–36.
45. On the cells that line the vagina, the mucosal defense system includes a protective coat that contains a special mucin secretion. This protective material commonly includes secretory IgA antibodies, lysozomes, lactoferrin, and certain proteinase inhibitors, all present in a special matrix. See H. Nagura, "Mucosal defense mechanism in health and disease," *Acta Pathologica Japonica* 42 (1992): 387–400.
46. J. C. Sanford, "Applying the PDR principle to AIDS," *Journal of Theoretical Biology* 130 (1988): 469–80.
47. See the review by R. M. Baum, "AIDS: Scientific progress, but no cure in sight," *Chemical and Engineering News,* July 5, 1993, 20–27.
48. Ibid.
49. Quoted by L. Garrett, "AIDS studies open right doors," *The Press Democrat* (Santa Rosa, CA), September 7, 1993.

Chapter 8: Attacks Against the Self

1. D. J. Allison, "Christopher Columbus: First case of Reiter's disease in the Old World?" *Lancet* 11 (1980): 1309 (letter).
2. G. Reiter, "Uber eine bisher unerkannte Spirchateninfktiern," *Deutsches Medisches Wochenschrift* 42 (1914): 1535–37.
3. P. Doury et al., "Le rheumatisme de l'anguillulose," *Nouvelle Presse Medicale* 4 (1975): 805–7.

4. P. Ehrlich, "On immunity with special reference to cell life. Croonian Lecture," *Proceedings of the Royal Society, Series B* 66 (1900): 424–28.
5. F. M. Burnet and N. K. Jerne's work are cited in W. E. Paul (ed.), *Fundamental immunology* (New York: Raven Press, 1984). See also F. M. Burnet, *The clonal selection theory of acquired immunity* (Nashville, TN: Vanderbilt University Press, 1959).
6. These genes include over 100 V or variable genes; 12 D or diversity genes; 4 J or joining genes; and a set of C or constant genes. As an antibody-producing cell goes through development, it "picks through" this set of genes to make a V-D-J-C gene unique for its own makeup. Since there are two different types of chains that make up the antibody molecule itself (heavy, using V-D-J-C; and light, using only V-J and C), the total number of combinations possible is 4,800×400 or 1,920,000 different gene combinations. See G. J. V. Nossal, "Life, death and the immune system," *Scientific American*, September 1993, 53–62.
7. F. Lozano, C. Rada, J. M. Jarvis, and C. Milstein, "Affinity maturation leads to differential expression of multiple copies of kappa light-chain trans gene," *Nature* 363 (1993): 271–73.
8. See K. Rajewsky, "The power of clonal selection," *Nature* 363 (1993): 208.
9. The more complex details of this process are described elegantly in a recent article by I. L. Weissman and M. D. Cooper, "How the immune system develops," *Scientific American*, September 1993, 65–71.
10. Q. Ge, M. B. Frank, C. O'Brien, and I. N. Targoff, "Cloning of a complementary DNA coding for the 100-kD antigenic protein of the PM-Scl autoantigen," *Journal of Clinical Investigation* 90 (1992): 559–70.
11. H. Saitoh et al., "CENP-C, an autoantigen in scleroderma, is a component of the inner kinetochore plate," *Cell* 70 (1992): 115–24.
12. S. Paillard and F. Strauss, "Analysis of the mechanism of interaction of simian Ku protein with DNA," *Nucleic Acids Research* 19 (1991): 5619–24.
13. A. Douvas, "Does Scl-70 modulate collagen production in systemic sclerosis," *Lancet* 2 (1988): 475–77.
14. M. B. Frank et al., "The mapping of the human 52kD Ro/SSA autoantigen gene to human chromosome 11 and its polymorphisms," *American Journal of Human Genetics* 52 (1993): 183–91.
15. U. Utz et al., "Skewed T-cell receptor in genetically identical twins correlates with multiple sclerosis," *Nature* 364 (1993): 243–47.
16. B. L. Kotzin, "Twins and T-cell responses," *Nature* 364 (1993): 187–88.
17. See J. G. P. Sissons, "Superantigens and infectious disease," *Lancet* 341 (1993): 1627–28.
18. See, in particular B. C. Cole, "The immunobiology of *Mycoplasma arthritides* and its superantigen MAM," *Current Topics in Microbiology and Immunology* 174 (1991): 107–19.
19. K. E. Ellerman and A. A. Like, "Staphylococcal enterotoxin-activated spleen cells passively transfer diabetes in BB/Wor rat," *Diabetes* 41 (1992): 527–32.
20. Ibid.

21. M. Lappé, "Silicone reactive disorder: A new autoimmune disease caused by immunostimulation and superantigens," *Medical Hypotheses* 41 (1993): 348–52.
22. G. Solomon, "A clinical and laboratory profile of symptomatic women with silicone breast implants: Evidence in support of a unique disease with rheumatic features," *Seminars in Arthritis and Rheumatism* (in press).
23. See L. G. Veasy et al., "Resurgence of acute rheumatic fever in the intermountain area of the United States," *New England Journal of Medicine* 316 (1987): 421–27.
24. From a paper presented at the Symposium on Autoimmunity, held at Queen Mary and Westfield College, in Great Britain, in the spring of 1992, and cited by R. Hortoin, "Autoimmunity: Towards the year 2001," *Lancet* 339 (1992): 922–23.
25. B. Tadmore, C. Putterman, and Y. Naparstek, "Embryonal germ-layer antigens: Target for autoimmunity," *Lancet* 339 (1992): 975–78.
26. R. D. Inman et al., "HLA class-1 related impairment of IL-2 production and lymphocyte response to microbial antigens in reactive arthritis," *Journal of Immunology* 142 (1989): 4256–60.
27. B. A. Torres, N. D. Griggs, and H. M. Johnson, "Bacterial and retroviral superantigens share a common binding region on class II MHC antigens," *Nature* 364 (1993): 152–54.
28. B. Fleischer et al., "An evolutionary conserved mechanism of T cell activation by microbial toxins," *Journal of Immunology* 146 (1991): 11–17.
29. R. D. Innan et al., "Post-dysenteric reactive arthritis: A clinical and immunogenetic study following an outbreak of salmonellosis," *Arthritis and Rheumatism* 31 (1988): 377–85.
30. See, especially, J. Sierper et al., "Aetiological role of bacteria associated with reactive arthritis in particular juvenile chronic arthritis," *Annals of Rheumatic Disease* 51 (1992): 1208–14.
31. Ibid.
32. A. Keat, "Reiter's syndrome and reactive arthritis in perspective," *New England Journal of Medicine* 309 (1983): 1606–15.
33. R. Burgos-Vargas, A. Howard, and B. M. Ansell, "Antibodies to peptidoglycan in juvenile onset ankylosing spondylitis and pauciarticular onset juvenile arthritis associated with chronic iridocyclitis," *Journal of Rheumatology* 13 (1986): 760–62.
34. C. M. Higgins et al., "Ankylosing spondylitis and HLA-B27," *Annals of the Rheumatic Diseases* 51 (1992): 855–62.
35. These properties include the release of a pathogenic peptide related to B27 antigens; the occurrence of a common receptor; and an alteration in self-antigens: see L. MacLean, "HLA-B27 subtypes: Implications for the spondyloarthropathies," *Annals of the Rheumatic Diseases* 51 (1992): 929–31.
36. The major histocompatibilty complex (MHC) codes for proteins that carry polypeptide fragments of foreign antigens processed by certain cells of the immune system to the cell's surface, where they are "displayed." These antigen-processing cells use one group of MHC proteins known as class I to pick up and hold for presentation peptides from proteins made *inside* the cell; and another, class II, to collect and

process peptides taken into the cell from *outside* substances or, in the case of bacteria, whole organisms or their membranes.

37. A full description of the mechanisms associated with HLA includes their role in abnormalities in antigen presentation; in control of the T cells selected in the thymus for "duty"; in control of immune responsiveness; and so on. For a full discussion, see the review by J. A. Hansen and J. L. Nelson, "Autoimmune diseases and HLA," *Critical Reviews in Immunology* 10 (1990): 307–328.
38. P. Hedrick, cited in J. Clatyon and H. Gee, "The evolutionary angle," *Nature* 365 (1993): 111–12.
39. A. Abringer et al., "Sequence similarity between HLA-DR1 and DR4 subtypes associated with rheumatoid arthritis and proteus/serratia membrance haemolysins," *Annals of the Rheumatic Diseases* 51 (1992): 1245–46.
40. J. Roudier et al., "The Epstein-Barr virus glycoprotein gp110, a molecular link between HLA DR4, HLA DR1 and rheumatoid arthritis," *Scandinavian Journal of Immunology* 27 (1988): 367–72.
41. See, for example, K. P. Morrison, K. Yng, and H. D. Caldwell, "Chlamydial disease pathogenesis: Ocular hypersensitivity elicited by a genus-specific 57-KD protein," *Journal of Experimental Medicine* 169 (1989): 246–50.
42. R. I. Morimoto, "Cells in stress: Transcriptional activation of heat-shock genes," *Science* 259 (1993): 1409–10.
43. See, for example, J. S. Gaston, "Are heat shock proteins involved in autoimmunity?" *International Journal of Clinical and Laboratory Research* 22 (1992): 90–94.
44. W. Van Eden et al., "Cloning of the mycobacterial epitope recognized by T lymphocytes in adjuvant arthritis," *Nature* 331 (1988): 171–73.
45. E. J. Hogervorst et al., "Modulation of experimental autoimmunity: Treatment of adjuvant arthritis by immunization with a recombinant vaccinia virus," *Infection and Immunology* 59 (1991): 2029–35.
46. J. R. Lamb et al., "Stress proteins may provide a link between the immune response to infection and autoimmunity," *International Journal of Immunology* 1 (1989): 191–96. See also, P. Res, J. Thle, and R. de Vries, "Heat-shock proteins and autoimmunity in humans," *Springer Seminars in Immunopathology* 13 (1991): 81–98.
47. A. Haregewoin, B. Singh, R. S. Gupta, and R. W. Finberg, "A mycobacterial heat shock protein responsive delta T cell clone also responds to the homologous human heat shock protein: A possible link between infection and autoimmunity," *Journal of Infectious Diseases* 163 (1991): 156–60.
48. For a complete elaboration of this hypothesis, see S. M. Friedman et al., "A potential role for microbial superantigens in the pathogenesis of systemic autoimmune disease," *Arthritis and Rheumatism* 34 (1991): 468–78.
49. J. B. Winfield and W. N. Jarfour, "Stress proteins, autoimmunity and autoimmune disease," *Current Topics in Microbiology and Immunology* 167 (1991): 161–89.
50. See B. Fleischer, "T cell stimulation by microbial toxins," *Journal of Immunology* 146 (1991): 11–17.
51. See E. K. Legrand, "An evolutionary perspective of endotoxin: A signal for a well-

adapted defense system," *Medical Hyptheses* 33 (1990): 49–56. Endotoxin-related shock may actually be indirectly induced by antibiotics. It does occur preferentially in patients with gram-negative infections who are subjected to massive antibiotic treatment. Indeed, one of the cardinal signs of massive antibiotic use is the conversion of microbes to so-called L forms–organisms that lack cell walls.

52. Cited in R. Horton, "Autoimmunity: Toward the year 2001," *Lancet* 339 (1992): 922–23.
53. P. N. Fultz, "Replication of an acutely lethal simian immunodeficiency virus activates and induces proliferation of lymphocytes," *Journal of Virology* 65 (1991): 4902–9.
54. L. Imberti et al., "Selective depletion in HIV infection of T cells that bear specific T cell receptor V beta sequences," *Science* 254 (1991): 860–62. This idea was originally suggested by studies that showed that HIV selectively stimulates and replicates in $CD4^+$ cells that express a particular V beta element on their surface: see J. Laurence, A. S. Hodtsev, and D. N. Posnett, "Superantigen implication in dependence of HIV-1 replication in T cells on TCE V beta expression," *Nature 358 (1992): 255–59.*
55. Y. Kawabe and A. Ochi, "Selective anergy of V beta 8^+ $CD4^+$ T cells in staphylococcus enterotoxin B-primed mice," *Journal of Experimental Medicine* 172 (1990): 1065–70.
56. M-L. Gougeon et al., "Is a dominant superantigen involved in AIDS pathogenesis?" *Lancet* 342 (1993): 50–51.

Chapter 9: Vulnerability to Disease

1. E. J. Calabrese, "Environmental quality indices predicted by evolutionary theory," *Medical Hypotheses* 3 (1977): 1, pp. 241–44.
2. See A. G. Motulsky, "Nutrition and genetic susceptibility to common diseases," *American Journal of Clinical Nutrition* 55 (1992): 1244S-1245S.
3. M. Rath and L. Pauling, "Hypothesis: Lipoprotein (a) is a surrogate for ascorbate," *Proceeedings of the National Academy of Science* 87 (1990): 6204–7.
4. See C. Thompson, D. Stinson, and A. Smith, "Seasonal affective disorder and season-dependent abnormalities of melatonin suppression by light," *Lancet* 336 (1990): 703–6.
5. J. C. Nossent, "Systemic lupus erythematosis on the Caribbean island of Curacao: An epidemiological investigation," *Annals of Rheumatology* 51 (1992): 1197–1201.
6. H. J. Muller, "Mutations and human health," paper presented at Food and Drug Administration symposium on radiation and health, Washington, DC, 1963.
7. See W. J. Meggs, "Neurogenic inflammation and sensitivity to environmental chemicals," *Environmental Health Perspectives* 101 (1993): 24–37, for an explanatory hypothesis that links these four conditions.
8. These possibilities were explored in my last book, *Chemical Deception* (San Francisco: Sierra Club Books, 1991).
9. H. Emerson and L. D. Latimore, "Diabetes mellitus. A contribution to its epidemiology based chiefly on mortality statistics," *Archives of Internal Medicine* 34 (1924): 585–630.

10. Adapted from S. B. Eater, M. Konner, and M. Shostak, "Stone agers in the fast lane: Chronic degenerative diseases in evolutionary perspective," *The American Journal of Medicine* 84 (1988): 739–49.
11. G. A. Spinas and U. Keller, "Insulin autoimmune syndrome and HLA-DR4," *Lancet* 339 (1992): 1549.
12. This convenient partitioning is used throughout the text; however, some researchers have challenged the accuracy of these distinctions since the causes and pathogenesis of diabetic forms often overlap and are undoubtedly more complex than this simple bifurcation implies. See A. A. Rossini, J. P. Mordes, and E. S. Handler, "Speculations on etiology of diabetes mellitus. Number hypothesis," *Diabetes* 37 (1988): 257–61.
13. W. C. Knowler, D. J. Pettitti, K. M. F. Saad, and P. H. Bennett, "Diabetes mellitus in the Pima Indians: Incidence, risk factors and pathogenesis," *Diabetes and Metabolism Review* 6 (1990): 1–27.
14. W. C. Knowler, D. J. Pettiti, P. H. Bennett, and R. C. Williams, "Diabetes mellitus in the Pima Indians: Genetic and evolutionary considerations," *American Journal of Physical Anthropology* 62 (1983): 107–14.
15. B. V. Howard et al., "Evidence for marked sensitivity to the antilipolyitc action of insulin in obese maturity onset diabetics," *Metabolism* 28 (1979): 744–50.
16. W. P. Newman and R. G. Brodows, "Insulin action during acute starvation: Evidence for selective insulin resistance in normal man," *Metabolism* 32 (1983): 590–96.
17. J. N. Neel, "Diabetes mellitus: A 'thrifty genotype' rendered detrimental by 'progress'?" *Human Genetics* 14 (1962): 353–62.
18. D. J. Pettiti et al., "Congenital susceptibility to NIDDM. Role of intrauterine environment," *Diabetes* 37 (1988): 622–28.
19. M. E. Mohs, T. K. Leonard, and R. R. Watson, "Interrelationships among alcohol abuse, obesity and type II diabetes mellitus: Focus on Native Americans," *World Review of Nutrition and Diet* 56 (1988): 93–172.
20. See M. Wendorf, "Diabetes, the ice free corridor, and the Paleo-Indian settlement of North America," *American Journal of Physical Anthropology* 79 (1989): 503–20.
21. L. MacLean, "HLA-B27 subtypes: Implications for the sponyloarthropathies," *Annals of the Rheumatic Diseases* 51 (1992): 929–31.
22. Indeed, Neel has modified his hypothesis. See J. V. Neel, "The thrifty genotype revisited," in J. Koberling and R. B. Tattersall, eds., *The genetics of diabetes mellitus, Serona Symposium No. 47* (London/New York: Academic Press, 1982).
23. R. P. Donahue et al., "Central obesity and coronary heart disease in men," *Lancet* 1 (1987): 821–24.
24. R. E. Eckel, "Insulin resistance: An adaptation for weight maintenance," *Lancet* 340 (1992): 1452–53.
25. See A. Lernmark et al., "Autoimmunity of diabetes," *Endocrinology and Metabolism Clinics of North America* 20 (1991): 589–617.
26. For a comprehensive review, see A. Gree, E.A.M. Gale, and C. C. Patterson, "Incidence of childhood onset insulin dependent diabetes mellitus: The Eurodiabetes Study," *Lancet* 339 (1992): 905–8.

27. M. P. Stern et al., "Genetic and environmental determinants of type II diabetes in Mexican Americans," *Diabetes Care* 14 (1991): 649–54.
28. J. A. Todd, "Genetic control of autoimmunity in type 1 diabetes," *Immunology Today* 11 (1990): 122–29.
29. Y. Uchigata et al., "HLA-DR4 genotype and insulin-processing in insulin autoimmune syndrome," *Lancet* 340 (1992): 1467.
30. A. I. Drash, "What do epidemiologic observations tell us about the etiology of insulin dependent diabetes mellitus?" *Schweize Medische Wochenschrift* 120 (1990): 39–45.
31. C. M. Vadheim et al., "Preferential transmission of diabetic alleles within the HLA gene complex," *New England Journal of Medicine* 315 (1986): 1314–18.
32. V. A. Thomas et al., "Altered expression of diabetes in BB/Wor rats by exposure to viral pathogens," *Diabetes* 40 (1991): 255–58.
33. J. Karjalainen et al., "A bovine albumin peptide as a possible trigger of insulin dependent diabetes mellitus," *New England Journal of Medicine* 327 (1992): 302–7.
34. N. Maclaren and M. Atkinson, "Is insulin dependent diabetes environmentally induced?" *New England Journal of Medicine* 327 (1992): 348–49.

Chapter 10: Malaria

1. F. B. Livingstone, "Sickling and malaria," *British Medical Journal* 1 (1957): 762–63.
2. D. R. Brooks and D. A. McLennan, "The evolutionary origin of *Plasmodium falciparum*," *Journal of Parasitology* 78 (1992): 564–66; and A. A. Lal and I. F. Goldman, "Circumsporozoite protein gene from *Plasmodium reichenowi*, a chimpanzee malaria parasite evolutionarily related to the human malaria parasite *Plasmodium falciparum*," *Journal of Biological Chemistry* 266 (1991): 6686–89.
3. C. Laderman, "Malaria and progress: Some historical and ecological considerations," *Proceedings of the Society of Science and Medicine* 9 (1975): 587–94.
4. R. Horuk et al., "Receptor for the malarial parasite *Plasmodium vivax:* The erythrocyte chemokine receptor," *Science* 261 (1993): 1182–84.
5. F. B. Livingstone, "Anthropological implications of sickle-cell distribution in West Africa," *American Anthropologist* 60 (1958): 533–62.
6. See the comprehensive review in F. L. Dunn, "Malaria in the Western Hemisphere," *Human Biology* 37 (1965): 385–401.
7. World Health Organization, *Resistance of vectors of diseases to pesticides* (Technical Report No. 655). Geneva: WHO, 1980.
8. L. J. Bruce-Chwatt, "Recent trends of chemotherapy and vaccination against malaria: New lamps for old," *British Medical Journal* 291 (1985): 1072–76.
9. W. Peters, "Recent developments in chemotherapy and drug resistance," in M. Ristic, T. P. Abroise, and J. P. Kreier, eds., *Malaria and babesiosis* (Dordrecht, Netherlands: Martinus Nihoff, 1984), pp. 141–50.
10. T. H. Van, C. V. Thanh, and A. T. Kim, "Severe malaria in a provincial hospital in Vietnam," *Lancet* 336 (1990): 1316.
11. For sickle-cell trait prevalences of, say, 10 percent, the percent of malaria-susceptible individuals with normal hemoglobin is about 89.75 percent and those with sickle-cell hemoglobin (also malaria resistant, but with a limited life span because of sickling

crises) is about 0.25 percent. The formula is $p_2+2pq+q_2=1$. In this instance, the gene frequency of *p* (or normal hemoglobin) is approximately 0.947, that for sickle cell homoglobin, 0.053.

12. P. W. Ewald, "Evolution of virulence," *Scientific American,* April, 1993, 86–93.
13. W. H. Durham, *Coevolution: Genes, culture, and human diversity* (Stanford, CA: Stanford University Press, 1991), p. 151.
14. Laderman, note 3.
15. Durham, note 12.
16. O. C. Stine, G. J. Dover, D. Zhu, and K. D. Smith, "The evolution of two West African populations," *Journal of Molecular Evolution* 34 (1992): 336–44.
17. T. Vulliamy, P. Mason, and L. Luzzatto, "The molecular basis of glucose-6-phosphate dehydrogenase deficiency," *Trends in Genetics* 8 (1992): 138–43.
18. A. V. Hill et al., "Common West African HLA antigens are associated with protection from severe malaria," *Nature* 352 (1991): 595–600. Comments appear in *Nature* 352 (1991): 565–67.
19. A. V. S. Hill et al., "Molecular analysis of the association of HLA-B53 and resistance to severe malaria," *Nature* 360 (1992): 434–39.
20. J. P. Lepers et al., "Transmission and epidemiology of newly transmitted falciparum malaria in the central highland plateau of Madagascar," *Annals of Tropical Medicine and Parasitology* 85 (1991): 297–304.
21. G. Modiano et al., "Protection against malaria morbidity: Near-fixation of the alpha thalassemia gene in a Nepalese population," *American Journal of Human Genetics* 48 (1991): 390–97.
22. J. Le Bras and P. Ringwald, "Situation de la chimiorésistance du *Plasmodium falciparum* en Afrique en 1989," *Médicine Tropique* (Marseilles) 50 (1990): 11–16.
23. J. P. Chippaux et al., "Evolution de la chimiosensibilité de *Plasmodium falciparum* a la chloroquine et à la mefloquine au Benin entre 1980 et 1989," *Bullétin de la Societé de Pathologie Exotique Filiales* 83 (1990): 320–29; see also, C. C. Draper, M. Hills, V. A. Kilimali, and G. Brubaker, "Serial studies on the evolution of drug resistance in malaria in an area of East Africa: Findings from 1979 up to 1986," *Journal of Tropical Medicine and Hygiene* 91 (1988): 265–73.
24. See C. C. Draper et al., note 23.
25. D. Richard Lenoble et al., "Evolution de la résistance de *Plasmodium falciparum* a la chloroquine au Gabon entre 1984 et 1987–88," *Annals de Societé de Belge: Médicine Tropique* 69 (1989): 113–19.
26. M. Danis et al., "Evolution de la chimioresistance des cas de paludisme a *Pl. falciparum* d'oringeafricaine dans un hopital parisien," *Bullétin de la Societé de Pathologie Exotique Filiales* 80 (1987): 490–96.
27. See, in particular, J. Garcia et al., "Evolution of resistance of *Plasmodium falciparum* to antimalarial drugs in Rwanda, 1985–1987," *Transactions of the Royal Society of Tropical Medicine and Hygiene* 83 (1989): 490.
28. Specific resistance patterns are reported in J. Gascon, M. Soldevila, A. Merlos, and J. L. Bada, "Pharmacoresistance de *Plasmodium falciparum* au Rwanda: Une étude in vivo," *Biomedicine and Pharmacotherapeutics* 41 (1987): 250–53.

29. See discussion by F. O. ter Kuile, F. Nosen, C. Luxemburger, and N. J. White, "Mefloquine prophylaxis," *Lancet* 342 (1993): 551.
30. D. J. Wyler, "Malaria chemoprophylaxis for the traveler," *New England Journal of Medicine* 329 (1993): 31–37.
31. Two new candidate drugs, mefloquine and halofantrine, have not to date (1993–1994) been studied in large enough populations to measure their true effectiveness.
32. G. S. Murphy et al., "Vivax malaria resistant to treatment and prophylaxis with chloroquine," *Lancet* 341 (1993): 976–1000.
33. M. P. Mulumba et al., "Le paludisme de l'enfant à Kinshasa (Zaire)," *Médicine Tropique* (Marseilles) 50 (1990): 53–64.
34. P. Bastien, P. Saliou, and M. Genilini, "Etude de la chlorquine-résistance de *Plasmodium falciparum* à Vanuatu (1980–1984): Apparition, évolution, distribution," *Bullétin de la Societé de Pathologie Exotique Filiales* 81 (1988): 226–37.
35. See "Development of recommendations for the protection of short-stay travellers to malaria endemic areas: Memorandum from two WHO meetings," *Bulletin of the World Health Organization* 55 (1988): 177–96; and T. E. A. Peto and C. F. Gilks, "Strategies for the prevention of malaria in travellers: Comparison of drug regimens by means of risk-benefit analysis," *Lancet* 1 (1986): 256–61.
36. See Wyler, note 30.
37. For a critical review, see C. Brosset et al., "HTLV1 et coinfections," *Médicine Tropique* (Marseilles) 51 (1991): 399–406.
38. K. M. Lam, N. Syed, H. Whittle, and D. H. Crawford, "Circulating Epstein-Barr virus carrying B cells in acute malaria," *Lancet* 337 (1991): 876–88.
39. See the review by R. F. Ambinder, "Human lymphotropic viruses associated with lymphoid malignancy: Epstein-Barr and HTLV 1," *Hematology and Oncology Clinics of North America* 4 (1990): 821–33.
40. See Bruce-Chwatt, note 8, for details of this campaign.
41. Ibid.
42. J. Juvez et al., "Epidémiologie du paludisme et lutte antipaludique à Mayotte," *Bullétin de la Societé de Pathologie Exotique Filiales* 80 (1987): 505–19.
43. See the discussion in A. D. Harries, "Malaria: Keeping the mosquitos at bay," *Lancet* 342 (1993): 506–7.
44. See L. J. Bruce-Chwatt, "The challenge of malaria vaccine: Trials and tribulations," *Lancet* 11 (1983): 371–73.
45. Ibid. See also F. E. G. Cox, "Another route to a vaccine?" *Nature* 360 (1992): 417–18.
46. A. V. S. Hill, note 19.

Chapter 11: Evolution and Asthma

1. M. Kaliner and R. Lemanske, "Rhinitis and asthma," *Journal of the American Medical Association* 268 (1992): 2807–29.
2. L. M. Lichtenstein, "Allergy and the immune system," *Scientific American,* September 1993, 117–21.
3. W. J. Meggs, "Neurogenic inflammation and sensitivity to environmental chemicals," *Environmental Health Perspectives* 101 (1993): 234–37.

4. Other chemical mediators of asthma include leukotrienes, prostaglandins, chemotactic factors, substance P, neurokinen A, and calcitonin.
5. See P. Cotton, "Asthma consensus is unconvincing to many," *Journal of the American Medical Association* 270 (1993): 297.
6. J. A. Price, "Non-pharmacologic means of preventing asthma," *Lung* 168 (1991: Supple.): 86–91.
7. D. J. Hendrick, "Asthma: Epidemics and epidemiology," *Thorax* 44 (1989): 609–13.
8. M. A. Kaliner, "Asthma deaths: A social or medical problem?" *Journal of the American Medical Association* 269 (1993): 1994–95.
9. M. R. Seart, "Epidemiological trends in bronchial asthma," in M. A. Laniner et al., eds., *Asthma: Its pathology and treatment* (New York: Marcel Decker, 1991), pp. 1–49.
10. R. T. Taylor and P. W. Newacheck, "Impact of childhood asthma on health," *Pediatrics* 90 (1992): 657–62; see also, H. R. Anderson, "Is the prevalence of asthma changing?" *Archives of Diseases in Childhood* 64 (1989): 172–75.
11. See Cotton, note 5.
12. K. B. Weiss and D. K. Wagener, "Changing patterns of asthma mortality: Identifying target populations at high risk," *Journal of American Medical Association* 264 (1990): 1683–87.
13. S. T. Holgate, "Recent advances in understanding the pathogenesis of asthma and its clinical implications," *Quarterly Journal of Medicine* 66 (1988): 5–19.
14. M. Profet, "The function of allergy: Immunological defense against toxins," *Quarterly Review of Biology* 66 (1991): 23–62.
15. J. L. Huang, S. Y. Wang, and K. H. Hsieh, "Effect of short-term exposure to low levels of SO_2 and N_2O on pulmonary function and metacholine and allergen bronchial sensitivities in asthmatic children," *Archives of Environmental Health* 46 (1991): 296–99. Similar negative findings were found for sulfuric acid aerosols, see R. Aris, D. Christian, D. Sheppard, and J. R. Balmes, "Lack of bronchoconstrictor response to sulfuric acid aerosols and fogs," *American Review of Respiratory Disease* 143 (1991): 744–50.
16. See, for example, studies from Mexico: F. A. Berciano, J. Dominguez, and F. V. Alvarez, "Influence of air pollution on extrinsic asthma," *Annals of Allergy* 62 (1989): 135–41; South Africa: S. Zwi et al., "Respiratory health status of children in the eastern Transvaal highveld," *South African Medical Journal* 78 (1990): 647–53; Israel: A. I. Goren, J. R. Goldsmith, S. Hellmann, and S. Brenner, "Follow-up of schoolchildren in the vicinity of a coal-fired power plant in Israel," *Environmental Health Perspectives* 94 (1991): 101–6; Finland: A. Ponka, "Asthma and low-level air pollution in Helsinki," *Archives of Environmental Health* 46 (1991): 262–70; France: F. Krainik et al., "Influence sur la santé publique de la pollution atmospherique," *Seminars de l'Hospital* 57 (1981): 884–90; and, the United States: D. E. Abbey, P. K. Mills, F. F. Pteresen, and W. L. Beeson, "Long-term ambient concentrations of total suspended particulates and oxidants as related to incidence of chronic disease in California Seventh Day Adventists," *Environmental Health Perspectives* 94 (1991): 43–50.
17. C. E. O'Neil, "Mechanisms of occupational airways diseases induced by exposure to organic and inorganic chemicals," *American Journal of Medical Sciences* 299 (1990): 265–75.

18. The table was compiled from the following sources: W. R. Parkes, *Occupational lung disorders,* 2nd ed. (London: Butterworths, 1986); J. A. Merchant, *Occupational respiratory diseases* (Washington, D.C.: U.S. Department of Health Services, September 1986); W. N. Rom, *Environmental and occupational medicine* (Boston: Little, Brown, 1985); W. K. C. Morgan and A. Seaton, *Occupational lung diseases,* 2nd ed. (Philadelphia: Saunders, 1984); J. E. Cotes and J. Steel, *Work-related lung disorders* (Boston: Blackwell Scientific, 1984); and J. F. Murray and J. A. Nadel, *Textbook of respiratory medicine* (Philadelphia: Saunders, 1988), courtesy of Dr. Margaret Green.
19. A. Sanchez Palacios et al., "Skin cross reactivity between *D. pteronyssinus* and storage mites in atopic children," *Journal of Investigative Allergy and Clinical Immunology* 1 (1991): 179–84.
20. M. J. Mercer and C. H. Van Nieker, "Clinical characteristics of childhood asthma," *South African Medical Journal* 79 (1991): 77–79.
21. M. Chan-Yeung, D. Enarson, and S. Grzybowski, "Grain dust and respiratory health," *Canadian Medical Association Journal* 15 (1985): 969–73.
22. D. A. Enarson et al., "Predictors of bronchial hyperexcitability in grainhandlers," *Chest* 87 (1985): 452–55.
23. M. Del Mar Garces Sotillos et al., "Late asthma caused by inhalation of *L. destructor,*" *Annals of Allergy* 67 (1991): 126–28.
24. R. Gonzalez, L. Zapatero, F. Caravaca, and J. Carreira, "Identification of soybean proteins responsible for respiratory allergies," *International Archives of Allergy and Applied Immunology* 95 (1991): 53–57.
25. M. Aceves et al., "Identification of soybean dust as an epidemic asthma agent in urban areas by molecular marker and RAST analysis of aerosols," *Journal of Allergy and Clinical Immunology* 88 (1991): 124–34.
26. J. M. Anto, "Community outbreaks of asthma associated with inhalation of soybean dust," *New England Journal of Medicine* 320 (1989): 1109–12.
27. See the important editorial by R. H. Rubin, "The compromised host as sentinel chicken," *New England Journal of Medicine* 317 (1987): 1151–53.
28. F. S. Rhame et al., "Extrinsic risk factors for pneumonia in the patient at high risk of infection," *American Journal of Medicine* 76 (1984): 42–53; and S. M. Opal et al., "Efficacy of infection control measures during a nosocomial outbreak of disseminated aspergillosis associated with hospital construction," *Journal of Infectious Disease* 153 (1986): 634–37.
29. R. C. Yhoung et al., "Aspergillosis: The spectrum of disease in 98 patients," *Medicine* 49 (1970) 147–73.
30. C. Dekker et al., "Childhood asthma and the indoor environment," *Chest* 100 (1991): 922–26.
31. R. E. Dales, R. Burnett, and H. Zwanenburg, "Adverse health effects among adults exposed to home dampness and molds," *American Review of Respiratory Disease* 143 (1991): 505–9.
32. See Kaliner and Lemanske, note 1, p. 2808.
33. See, especially, M. J. Colloff, G. A. Stewart, and P. J. Thompson, "House dust acarofauna and Der p 1 equivalents in Australia: The relative importance of *Dermatophagoides*

pteronyssinus and *Euroglyphus mayneia*," *Clinical and Experimental Allergy* 21 (1991): 225–30.

34. J. A. Price, "Non-pharmacologic means of preventing asthma," *Lung* 168 (1991: Suppl.): 286–91.
35. M. Chilira, C. Nicolau, and L. Florescu, "Houses and allergic respiratory syndromes," *Reviews of Roumanian Medicine and Internal Medicine* 28 (1990): 341–46.
36. M. Wickman et al., "House dust mite sensitization in children and residential characteristics in a temperate region," *Journal of Allergy and Clinical Immunology* 88 (1991): 89–95.
37. See M. J. Utell and J. M. Samet, "Environmentally mediated disorders of the respiratory tract," *Medical Clinics of North America* 74 (1990): 291–306; and L. di Berardino et al., "An indoor mycoaerological investigation at homes of allergic patients," *Folia Allergoloica and Immunologica Clinica* 36 (1990): 431–36.
38. See Weiss and Wagener, note 12.
39. See Kaliner, note 8.
40. See, in particular, the following article for a detailed analysis of this outbreak: J. Sunyer, J. M. Anto, M.-J. Rorigo, F. Morrell, and the Clinical and Toxicoepidemiological Committee, "Case-control study of serum immunoglobin E antibodies reactive with soybean in epidemic asthma," *Lancet* 1 (1989): 179–82.
41. H. J. Schwartz and P. A. Greenberger, "The prevalence of allergic bronchopulmonary aspergillosis in patients with asthma," *Journal of Laboratory and Clinical Medicine* 117 (1991): 138–42.

Chapter 12: Conclusion

1. C. Darwin, *The descent of man and selection in relation to sex* (1871; New York: Random House, Modern Library Edition, 1970), p. 501.
2. "U.S. denies request for $3 million to fight TB," *The New York Times*, International section, 26 December 1993.
3. See "Combating emerging infections in the USA," *Lancet* 340 (1992): 1031–32.
4. J. Lederberg et al., *Emerging infections: Microbial threats to health in the USA* (Washington, DC: National Institute of Medicine, 1992).

Index

Page numbers in **boldface** refer to tables in the text